IVAN NEDELKO

THE SMELL OF THE CASH

CONTENTS

INTRODUCTION 2
CHAPTER 1. Defining accumulation zones. 13
    Chapter. 1.1. Buyer's Accumulation zones (BAZ) 16
    Chapter 1.2. Seller's accumulation zone.(SAZ) 17
    Chapter 1.3. Pattern 1-2-3 18
    Chapter 1.4. The principle of constructing the AZ. 19
    Chapter 1.5. Determining 50% of the Accumulation Zone. 24
    Chapter 1.6. The Accumulation Zone inside the Accumulation Zone. ... 27
    Chapter 1.7. AZ at the support or resistance level 31
    Chapter 1.8. Entry points used with AZ. 33
        1.8.1. The first touch rule. 33
        1.8.2. Multiple touches rule. 34
        1.8.3. Buy on the test of the upper boundary of accumulation. 34
        1.8.4. Sale on the test of the lower boundary of the Seller's AZ. 35
        1.8.5. Quick accumulation boundary test. 36
        1.8.6. Early Entry and Right Entry concepts 38
        1.8.7. The principle of reducing accumulation zones. Pull-up of accumulation zones. 39
        1.8.8. Weak Low. Weak High. 40
        1.8.9. Failed auction. 42
CHAPTER 2. Accumulative Flat 44
    Chapter 2.1. Trading from the flat. 47
        2.1.1. Entry at the breakdown of the upper or lower boundary of the flat formed by   resistance or support. 47
        2.1.2. 50% AF height test. 48
        2.1.3. Entry after consolidation. 50
        2.1.4. Trading inside the flat. 51
CHAPTER 3. Reversal levels. 55
    Chapter 3.1. Method of entry using RL. 57
CHAPTER 4. The use of indicators. 59
    Chapter 4.1. VWAP 59
    Chapter 4.2. AVWAP. 63
    Chapter 4.3. Buy on GAP and engulfing. 66
    Chapter 4.4. Guides. 67
    Chapter 4.5. SMA guides. 72
    Chapter 4.6. Volume profiles. 73
    Chapter 4.7. Indicator of the screen visible area volume profile. 78
    Chapter 4.8. Profile in the candle. 80
    Chapter 4.9. Using a fixed range 81
        4.9.1. Vertical volume indicator, MACD, Stochastic 84
        4.9.2 Climax. 85
CHAPTER 5. Unscrambling and putting everything together. 91

ADDITIONAL MATERIALS. TRADING OF REVERSAL PATTERNS USING OPTIONS 122
FUNDAMENTALS WHEN CHOOSING STOCKS 130
NOW LET'S TALK ABOUT RISK MANAGEMENT 135
TRADING ON DIVERGENCES. 146
THE FIRST TOUCH RULE. 151
TRADING ON GAPS. ADVANCED VERSION. 155
BEARISH GAP AND GO 159
BULLISH RETEST GAP UP AND BULLISH GAP AND GO. 163
BASIC OPTION STRATEGIES. 202
BULL CALL SPREAD OPTION STRATEGY 207
BEAR CALL SPREAD OPTION STRATEGY 209
SHORT CALL OPTION STRATEGY 210
LONG PUT OPTION STRATEGY 211
LONG CALL OPTION STRATEGY 212
ADDITIONAL INFORMATION DIRECTLY RELATED TO THE OPERATION OF THE SYSTEM. 214
UNUSUAL OPTIONS ACTIVITY (UOA) 250
Choosing a Broker. 260
EPILOGUE 275

INTRODUCTION

> For all those
> who are fed up with work and
> fruitless going round
> in circles every day.

This book is dedicated to those who have come to make money in the financial markets. Every day, I receive dozens of complaints about lost deposits in my Private Chat. And the anguish from continuous loss of money made me sit down at my desk to set out the basics of a successful trading strategy.

I truly hope that I can give you the opportunity to trade as well as I do with my students at Rich Harbor. The entire necessary material is explained by examples of specific trades and presented in an easy-to-understand order. However, do not consider me an innovator; I'm more of a practitioner who has successfully combined several strategies into one. But, again, do not underestimate my work, because this is a summary of several years of my life, which formed the basis of this book. There are really many interesting and effective ideas in it.

Now you don't need to read books by renowned authors and spend precious time studying their strategies. I have already done all this for you. And set out in a convenient format here.

I would like to note that this course is for those who already understand technical analysis. This is a compilation of the knowledge accumulated over the years of my daily practice. If I had been given a chance to master this material a few years ago, I would not have lost several million rubles, and I would have become a dollar millionaire, because now the strategy described below brings me 5% profit every day, which means 80% per month or 960% per year! 70% of my trades are successful! And this is certainly not the limit....

Introduction

Here are some examples of the recent successful trades:

Yes, for a layman, this example would probably seem like a hoax, a fiction. But it is absolutely real in my actual practice.

Thus, the risk of a trade doesn't exceed 2% or $2000 for a $100,000 deposit. This is the amount I usually start to trade with every day in my Private Chat.

This is the kind of cryptomarathons I initiate.
And then, just a few days later, I get a result of 400%.

The Smell Of The Cash

Introduction

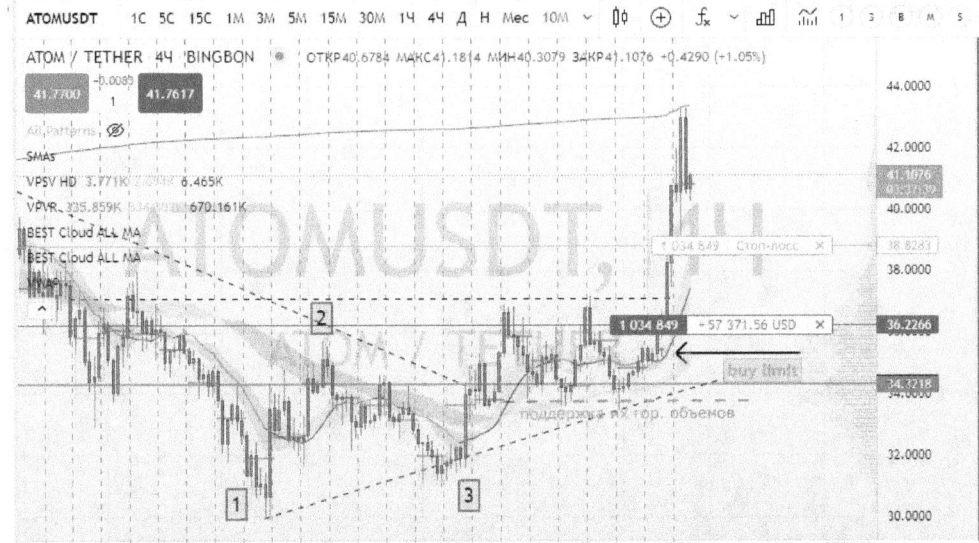

And this, my dear readers, is how you will learn to analyze the market and make similar successful trades.

Yes, yes! This is real! But you have two ways:
- You can just use my signals and earn with me by becoming a client of Rich Harbor.
- Or you can become a professional like me and, after training, trade on your own and maybe even teach other people!

> **Trading is an art that gives unlimited possibilities.**

This is probably the only type of business with such profitability.

It is definitely the only hobby that can make you a millionaire and enable you to leave your regular job.

And then you can spread your wings and fly anywhere you want and with anyone you like.

You will gain financial independence and hence many other freedoms.

You will no longer need bosses; and you will be able to quit your work for hire.

Many of you certainly dream about it. Same-type daily work can drive you crazy. Believe me, I know this feeling.

I am a dentist with 15 years of practice under my belt. And I can tell you honestly that I really enjoyed the first 10 years. I didn't feel tired or stressed. I was young, high-spirited, and capable of conquering any professional peaks. That's why it's fundamentally important to make the right decision as early as the young age of 25 about where you're going to work and live. Make a difference. And if I had been told about investing, trading and compound interest after graduation, today I would have had at least 15 million rubles on my brokerage account, which would have become a reliable safety cushion for me. And that's even without applying my strategy, but simply with the relaxed passive investing that brokers offer.

But our system, even at the higher education level, does not offer such knowledge. In our country, only 10% of the population is involved in this process. And this is one of the reasons of poverty. The mass media should inform the population about the unique opportunities the stock market offers. And maybe even legally oblige citizens to undergo training.

But perhaps there's another reason here - maybe our government doesn't want its people to be rich and happy? After all, if everyone goes to the stock market and successfully earns there, who will work in factories, beauty salons, and dentist's offices?

Yes, there can be a long discussion here. But think about the following fact - in the U.S., the government gave stimulus checks of several thousand dollars to its citizens during the pandemic, so that people would feel supported and cared for from the state. Do you know what Americans did with that money? More than half of them invested it to the brokerage accounts. And this is the official statistic.

I will not further advance this political topic because it is not directly related to the subject of my book. But I would like to finish by saying that our government has only gave us a few thousand rubles for this purpose. In our country, we are the only one who can care about ourselves and we shouldn't expect help from anywhere else.

I just want you to understand what motivated me then, 5 years ago, to study this type of earnings and open a school later:
- **Low salary,**
- **Low standard of living,**
- **Constant chronic fatigue from daily stressful work,**
- **Lack of personal growth and development.**

Believe me, I'm not a crazy man who chases money and wants to become a millionaire to buy a Ferrari and show off with it. It's definitely not worth doing in my city, because, first of all, I will immediately smash it up due to awful roads and, secondly, this type of car is just not suitable for minus 40-degree frosts.

> *My true motivation is freedom and pushing my boundaries! The opportunity to take a flight to wherever you want at any time. To afford myself the food, clothes, car, house I want to have.*
>
> *To live a decent, good life and pay taxes. To be law-abiding citizen and sleep well.*
>
> *To benefit society by learning how to trade and invest. This is a great opportunity for my self-fulfilment. Instead of pulling out teeth from dawn to dusk to feed my family!*

Introduction

I encourage you to wake up from oblivion and open your eyes to everything that is going on!

No one will make you rich unless you want it!

And wealth should really be desired, it should be raved about. And only then everything will work out.

And don't forget that wealth is not just about money. Money is just a part of it. But you can hardly be happy without it when everyone is obsessed with money.

For me, wealth is:

- Money,
- Success,
- Health,
- Sports,
- Family,
- Journeys,
- Self-development,
- Good work team,
- Opportunity to help people,
- Feeling yourself a part of a sound community,
- Doing charity work.

Now take a look at this screenshot:

You see the $24,000 profit there, don't you?

And that's a ratio of 1 to 12!

That is, by entering with a thousand rubles, you could earn 12 thousand in just a few days.

Have you ever seen it in any other place? In the slot machines?

Yes, few people in our country believe in financial markets after the infamous MMM and the recent fraud of Finiko. For the vast majority, it's a scam and fraud.

Introduction

Why study and strive for something, when you can have plain living with a salary of 30 thousand roubles a month?

After all, it's enough to survive. You can eat in dive bars, wear rags, use medicine services of poor quality, and take your children to schools and kindergartens with burnt-out staff.

Why should you strive for more? Be like everyone else! Keep calm and live. That's what I hear most often and what scares me.

And that's why I created this project. It is my protest. It is my desire to show and prove that it is possible to live differently. To enjoy a better and more decent life.

Rich Harbor is not just a thought out of my head. It is a quiet and peaceful place where you can take a break and, by turning on your computer, earn as much as you want in just a couple of hours. And then go anywhere you want on your yacht.

> **And the motto isn't simple.**
> **"Teaching trading for pushing the boundaries."**
>
> **<u>Think about it! First - teaching,</u>**
> **<u>and then - pushing the boundaries.</u>**
>
> **Yes, that's right.**
>
> **I'm not offering people a "Money" or "Happiness" button. You do have to work hard, but not as hard as I had to.**
>
> **I, as an experienced guide who has taken many lumps, can only show you the way to wealth and freedom.**

Now let's talk about the companies that provide money for management.

Not all Russians can invest and trade with their own money. And many are simply afraid of it. And this is understandable.

That's why there are companies in this world that give their money for management.

Yes, you heard it right! Such an opportunity really exists!

The business of such companies is built on such a model.

And they have several ways to make a profit:
- 1. On possible failures of inexperienced players.
- 2. On the principle of receiving steady profits from successful traders.

Visit their websites. They all have an American jurisdiction, and in this country, as you know, fraud is excluded.

www.leellootrading.com

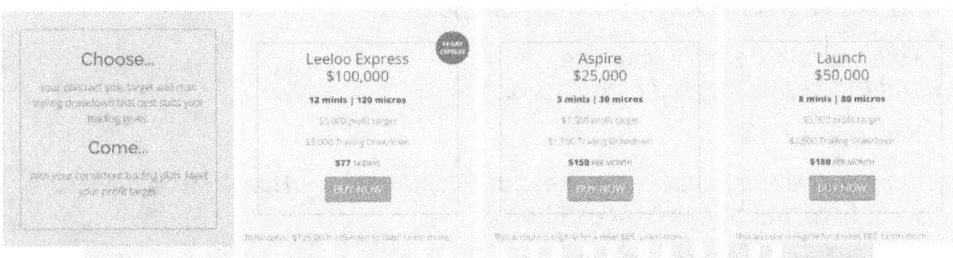

www.topsteptrading.com

Get 20% off your first Trading Combine and news to start your week.

Introduction

www.topstepfx.com

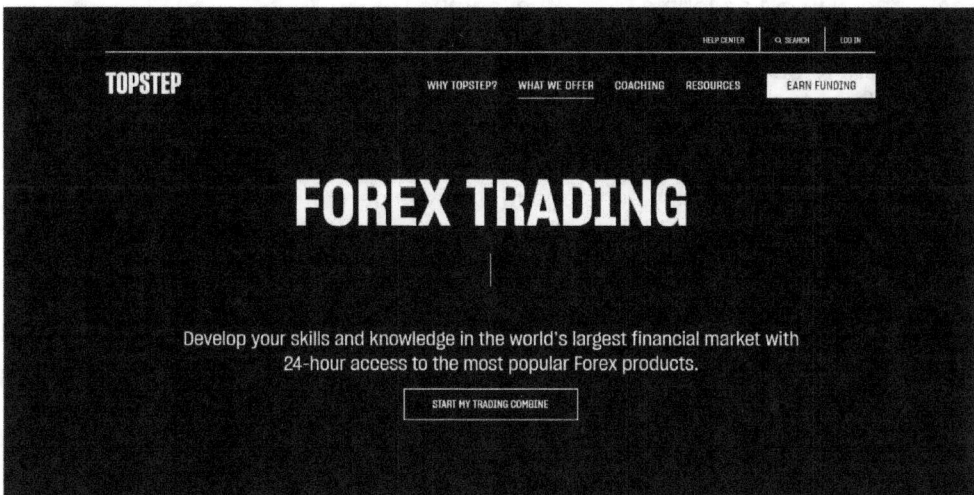

ApexFunding

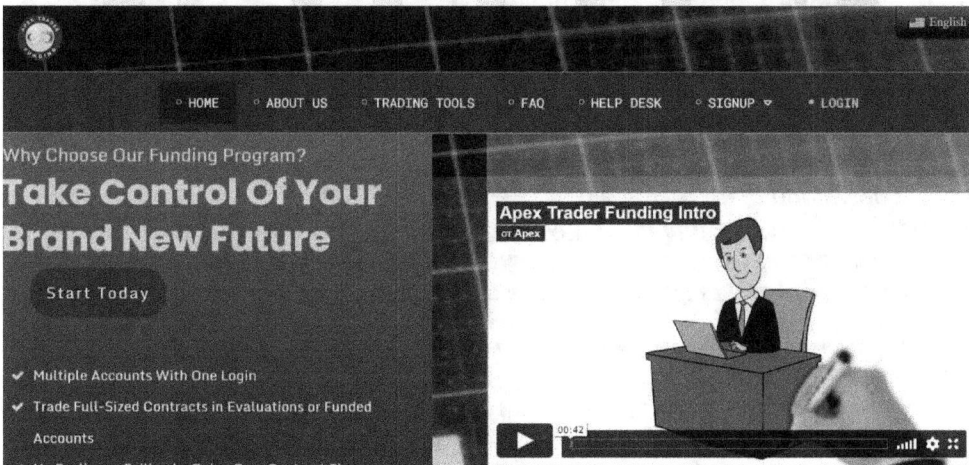

This prop company has probably the easiest test period.
You can trade even on the news and on weekends.
The long-standing reputation and Canadian origin add credibility to the company.
It offers operational support of the highest level.
I can't choose a prop company for you. You have to do it yourself. Fundamentally, they are all very similar. Even personal profiles in them have the same layout.
Only TopStep is different in design and approach. They have 2 levels for checking a trader's qualification and there are a several other conditions that will make it

much more difficult for you to get the cherished account. I would recommend to try them after you get accounts from other companies.

But they do give you a free ATAS for a month. And it's a great opportunity if you can't afford to buy yourself a license for a year.

I don't trade combines without ATAS! It is the only platform that allows you to see what is hidden behind the usual charts!

I help clients get a real trading account to manage and make money on it.

The service is extremely popular and this is understandable.

If you take a look at my Private Chat, you will see us doing it every day.

And my website has all the necessary training materials carefully selected by me.

Many materials are exclusive for the Russian readers and were translated into Russian with my assistance.

So, welcome.

For more information, visit this link.

A few words about the software I use:

In the description of the strategy below I will use charts from different sources:
- Everyone's favorite TradingView,
- And the most powerful analytical platform ATAS. (I plan a dedicated extensive course for it.)
- NinjaTrader. I developed unique indicators that allow determining the flow of orders and levels of horizontal volumes. And if ATAS is still a hard nut to crack for you, then you will definitely like this option. You can always download them on my site.

In this course, my goal is simply to introduce you to how these two platforms can enhance each other. I.e. they give a very powerful synergistic effect.

But using only one platform is quite acceptable in the beginning.

"I am here to tell you that your own ability is far greater than your wildest imagination. I guarantee that you are using only a part of your true potential. This is the fact of life and it is also true for trading. Let me assure you that anyone can excel in stocks if they tune in. It takes the right knowledge, your commitment to the learning process, and your desire to retain. It won't happen overnight, but with the right tools.

In the stock market and in life, we choose to win and we choose to lose. We lose because we want to lose and we win when we decide that we will be winners. While this statement may seem wrong or obviously unfair to you, I know it's true.

In more than three decades as a full-time stock trader, I have witnessed people losing because they want, consciously or unconsciously, to fail. And I have seen those who once and for all decided that they would be successful, and they have gone the way from mediocre to outstanding traders. Winning, without a doubt, is a choice!

If you don't accept it, then, by default, you have to believe that you have no control over your destiny. And if that's true, what's the point of even trying to succeed at anything - just to see if you get lucky?

Everyone has a champion trader inside. It's just a matter of knowledge, desire, and commitment. Most of all, you should believe in your abilities. I assure you that you can achieve much more in trading than you think and with much less risk than the so-called experts. But until you accept that winning is a choice, you will not unlock your full potential. Nor will you control your own destiny because you have not taken full responsibility for the outcome; therefore, you are not fully empowered. Those who want to win look for successful role models, develop a roadmap for success, and accept failure as a valuable teacher. They put the plan into action, learn from their results, and make improvements until they succeed.

Winners are people who can't stand to lose. Some start out that way, while others eventually grow sick and tired of being mediocre and decide that they will no longer put up with failing in their dreams. This attitude probably contradicts to what you heard when you were a child: don't be a miserable loser. Speaking from my experience, you show me a "good" loser and I will show you someone who is likely to lose. If you want to trade like a champion, you should think like a champion. Until you convince yourself that success is a choice, you are a defeated winner. This doesn't mean you're a loser; it just means you haven't yet learned or accepted the truth about winning. Champions don't leave greatness to chance. They decide they are going to be winners and they live every day with this goal in mind.

In 1990, I made the choice to become a champion investor. That was almost seven years after I made my first trade. Seven years! I had been fooling around for almost ten years. Back then, in March 1990, I decided to make a firm commitment to becoming the best stock broker in the world. I've been working on that ever since, and the rest is an old matter.

If you put your heart, soul and mind into something, then why not do everything possible to achieve great success? If you work hard and take a sound approach to trading, you deserve to succeed. But it takes persistence and the right attitude. If you're not ready to take complete control of your financial destiny, you probably shouldn't even read this book. Why? Because this book is about taking charge of your trading and your life and taking full responsibility for your results. How can you develop 100 percent ability to respond effectively without taking 100 percent responsibility?

The success plan in these pages has worked for me and many others who have followed in my footsteps. It can and will work for you, but only if you are open to new ideas and accept the reality that becoming a champion stock trader is not about being talented or having a degree in finance from an Ivy League school. It all starts with the inspiring belief that winning is, without a doubt, a choice."

Mark Minervini.
Champion in investing.

Believe me, everyone can do it!

CHAPTER 1.
Defining accumulation zones.

This is a key concept in my training program. Learning to find the accumulation zones, you will get the key to success, and all other tools will only help you to determine these areas.

> **So, the accumulation zone is an area on the chart in which the position accumulation by a big player takes place.**

All experienced traders have long known that the big player does not want to enter the market with one large position, because it will be obvious at once, and everyone will be able to join and earn, which is not profitable. That's why accumulation zones appear on the chart. Accumulation is followed by redistribution, which is where we make our money.

Chapter 1. Defining accumulation zones

I suggest starting training with a clean spy futures chart. What do you see?

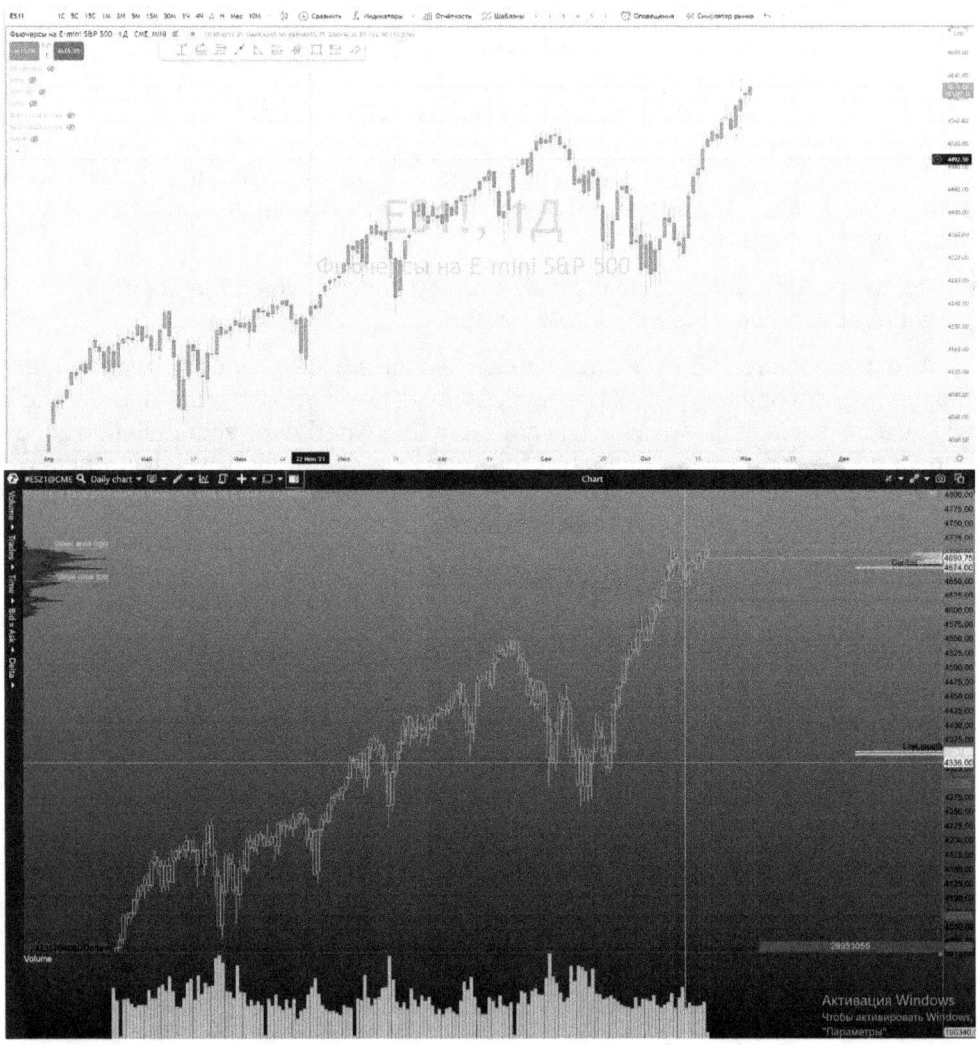

I'm sure there are so many men, so many minds when looking at this picture. Some will just see rectangles of different colors running up and down. And some will see clusters of these rectangles. And so on...
In general, nothing is clear!
"But where should I buy and where should I sell?" - you ask.
The point of learning trading strategies is to show the student certain patterns in the movement of the quote, which are called trading signals, on a blank chart with the help of indicators, patterns, and software. And they enable you to earn.

Chapter 1. Defining accumulation zones

Moreover, it is fundamentally important to start learning from a specialist who has extensive experience and has selected only a few strategies out of several thousand possible by trial and error.

But let's continue learning. So, what do you see now?

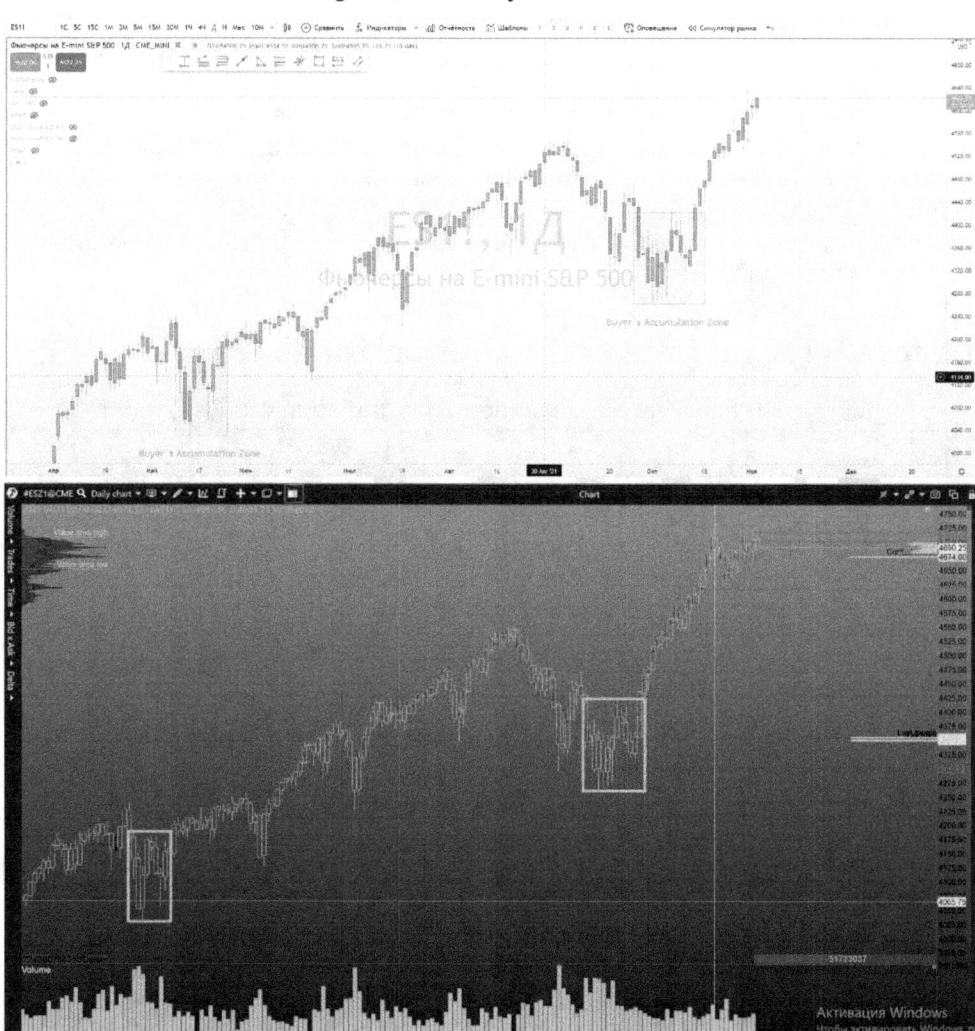

That's right. You see certain areas, not just a uniform movement of the quote. Something was clearly going on in these areas. But what? It was a redistribution of the large buyer's position.

What are the reason and purpose of it?

Chapter 1. Defining accumulation zones

Imagine that you are a large institutional buyer who bought these futures for a billion dollars or more. How will you sell when you take such a huge position into profit? It won't work with just one candlestick and one day! It may work, but you will attract everyone's attention and hungry wolves will tag you along, wanting to join the feast. To share your prey with you. Would you agree?

That's why big players don't drop everything at once, but divide the position over several days, maybe even months.

But thanks to vigilance you'll get in this training, you'll be as easy and effortless as I am to see these cherished areas even through the clutter of indicators. And I started with definition of accumulation zones (AZ) for a reason. Study them carefully in the charts below, and start looking for them yourself.

This is the key to understanding the entire trading strategy, and therefore to success in trading!

Chapter. 1.1 Buyer's Accumulation zones (BAZ)

Everything is simple. The accumulation zone traded into buying is the buyer's AZ.

Chapter 1. Defining accumulation zones

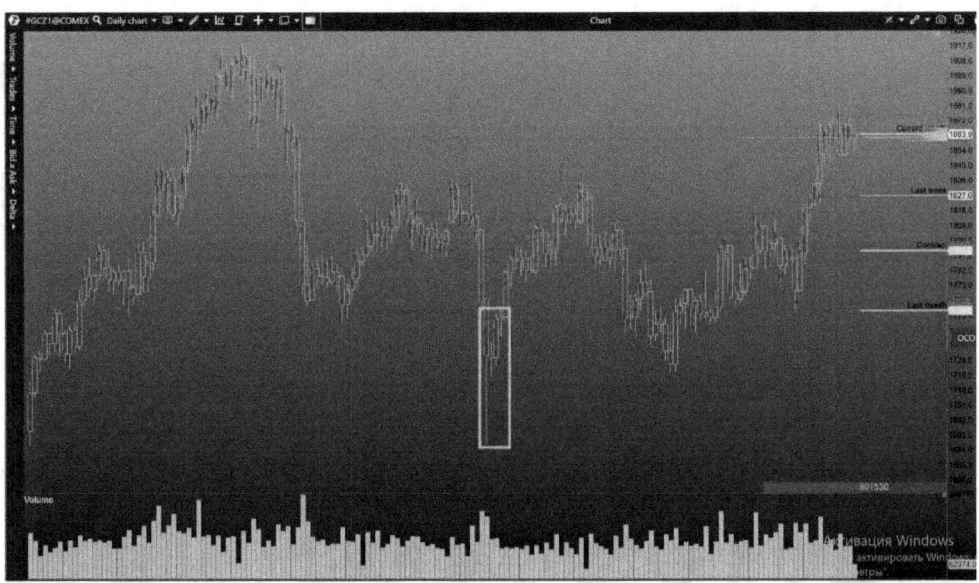

Note that the form and amount of time it took to form BAZ may vary. But fundamentally important thing is that you will find the AZ on any timeframe.

Chapter 1.2 Seller's accumulation zone.(SAZ)

It's also simple! This is the reverse area of the buyer's accumulation zone, i.e. the AZ that was traded into sales.

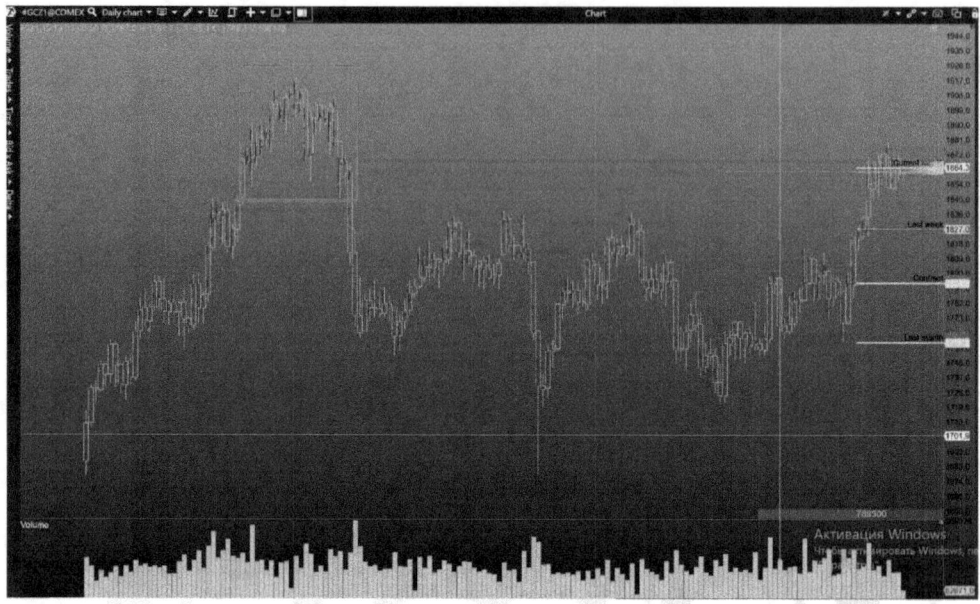

Chapter 1.3. Pattern 1-2-3

AZ is often called the 1-2-3 pattern. And indeed, if you look closely, you can see these numbers.

I use them very often when analyzing charts on my website in a Private Chat. I will explain their purpose a bit later.

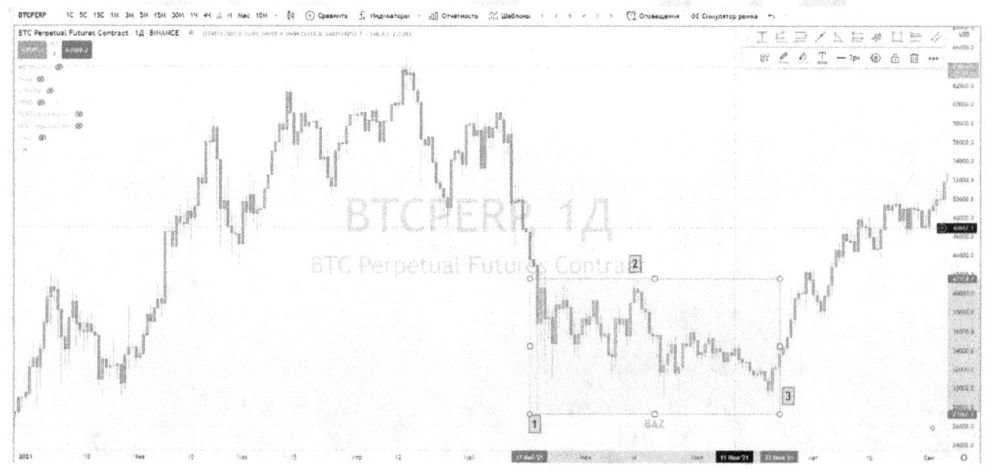

Chapter 1. Defining accumulation zones

It is very important to place the points correctly.

If we have a SAZ, then point 2 should always be on the lower boundary of the AZ. It's a kind of zigzag.

If we see a BAZ, then point 2 should be above points 1 and 3. And they, in turn, can be either at the same level or at different levels.

Chapter 1.4. The principle of constructing the AZ.

So, we have learned how to find the AZ on the chart. Now we have to draw them correctly, because the concept of the AZ boundary is very important in my strategy.

The AZ boundary is a pretty clear level on the chart, which can be approximately estimated by determining the area touched by the candlestick tail or body.

There is no difference in the concept of the AZ boundary for BAZ or SAZ.

The principle of construction is the same.

Another important point! We will be mostly concerned with the lower boundary of SAZ and the upper boundary of BAZ, because this is where we will look for a point to open the deal!

The lower edge of the buyer's accumulation boundary and the upper edge of the seller's boundary will often lie on significant supports and resistances.

You will learn to see this over time.

So, back to our Litecoin chart.

How do you determine the accumulation boundary? I offer you 3 options and you can try to determine at your discretion.

Option 1

Is the lower boundary here at the very top?
Or maybe it's a little lower here?
Option 2.

It is surely at the very bottom of the SAZ?

Chapter 1. Defining accumulation zones

Option 3.

I'm sure you have no idea and are confused!
But you're lucky! You have me).
So, the answer to the question I asked earlier is as follows: the lower boundary of SAZ is the approximate level touched by the one of the tails of the candlestick included in this AZ.
This means that only option 3 is correct!

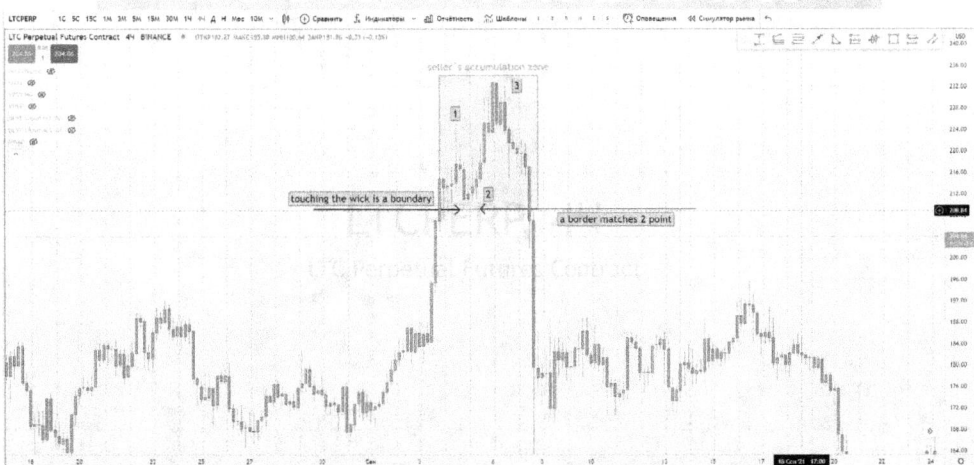

Look carefully. In this case, this boundary coincided with point 2 of the 1-2-3 pattern presented earlier. And this will almost always be the case.
Let's try to find the upper boundary of the buyer's accumulation zone that we need, using the Ripple as an example.

Chapter 1. Defining accumulation zones

What do you think about this price, which coincides with several touches?

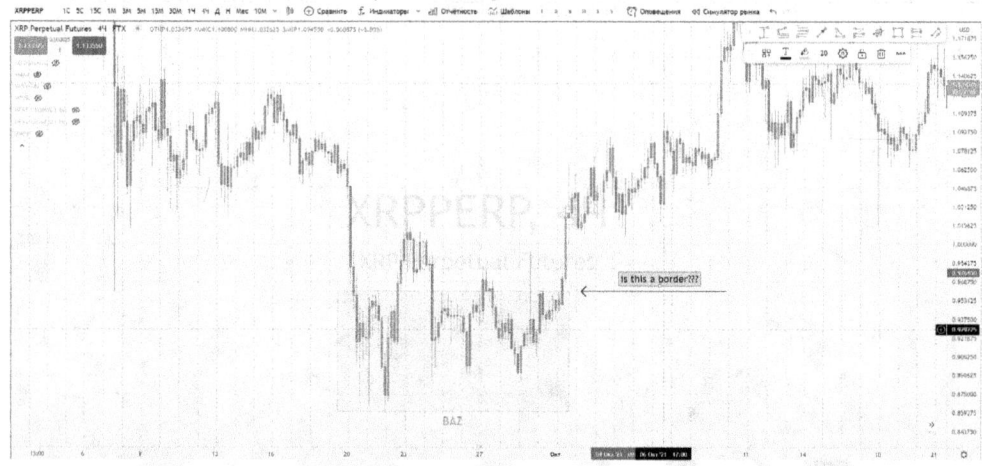

Or this option, where the price also makes several touches?

Chapter 1. Defining accumulation zones

Or maybe this option is correct? What do you think?

The answer is as follows.
The upper boundary of BAZ is approximately the level touched by one or more tails or bodies of candlesticks in the highest point inside the AZ. And it will coincide with point 2 of the 1-2-3 pattern too.
Which means that the last option is correct!
Let's see:

Finding accumulation boundary is also a very important skill.

Chapter 1. Defining accumulation zones

Be sure to practice it!

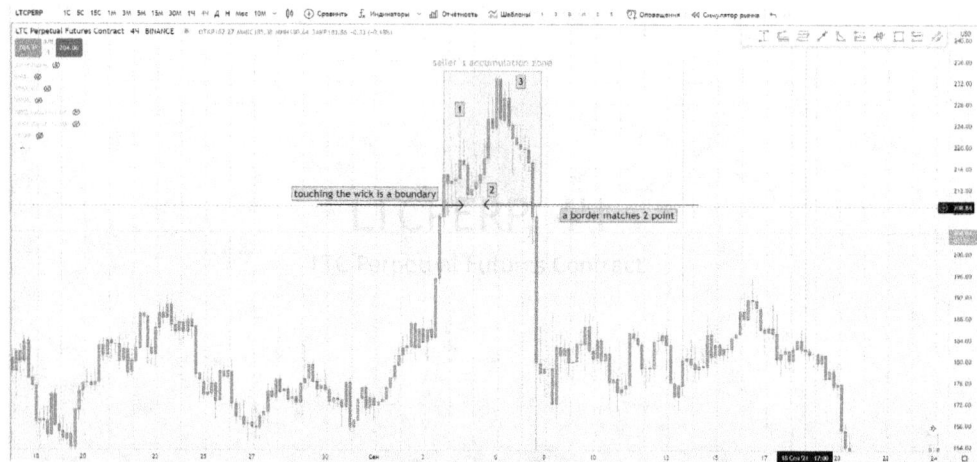

Chapter 1.5.
Determining 50% of the Accumulation Zone.

Another important skill is determining 50% of the height of the AZ. It doesn't matter whose AZ it is. It's just that this level will come in very handy.

As you've probably figured out by now, I'm not chasing complexity in trading. And so, to find that magic level, you just need to divide the height of the AZ by 2. And that's it!

And if you are correct in drawing the AZ boundaries, then you will succeed.

> **Note.**
> Why do I always say and will keep saying "Approximate Levels"?
> Because there is nothing 100% accurate or cent-to-cent in trading. But take my word for it, it is my strategy that allows you to get as close to such high indicators as possible.

Chapter 1. Defining accumulation zones

So, here's an example of 50% of BAZ:

Let's take a look at SAZ.
Everything is identical!
It is inherent in the market to be similar inside.
Here is an example of Litecoin.

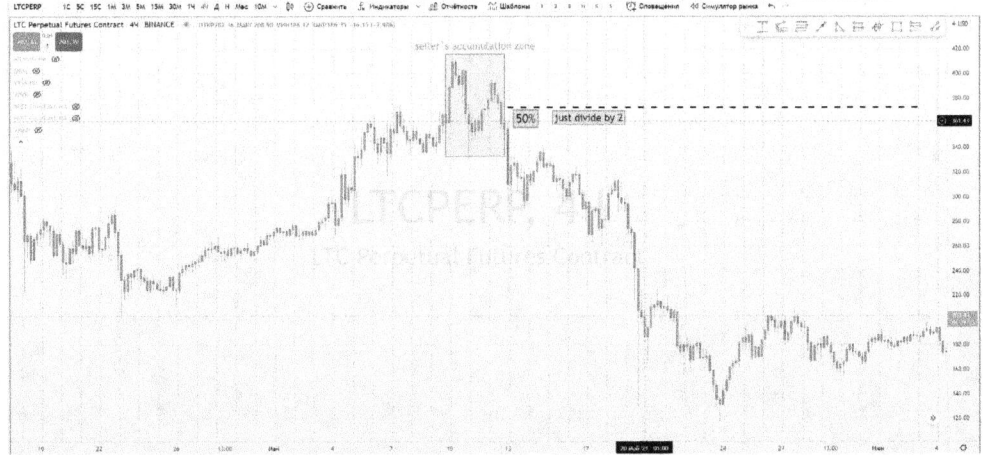

Now it's time for a little secret!
You probably won't see this anywhere else. So get ready!

The trick.
Using the Fixed Volume Profile to find another level that may differ from 50% on the chart.

Chapter 1. Defining accumulation zones

Often you'll see failures to achieve the level or vice versa 50% level. So I decided to find out why it is so.

It turned out to be simple. The 50% level does not always coincide with the POC level of the volume profile inside the AZ.

And this should not confuse you.

You just need to stretch the Fixed Volume Profile to the boundaries of the accumulation and see where the level of maximum volume is. And if it doesn't coincide with the 50% level, then these levels should be combined into one resistance or support area.

Here are two examples below to help you understand:

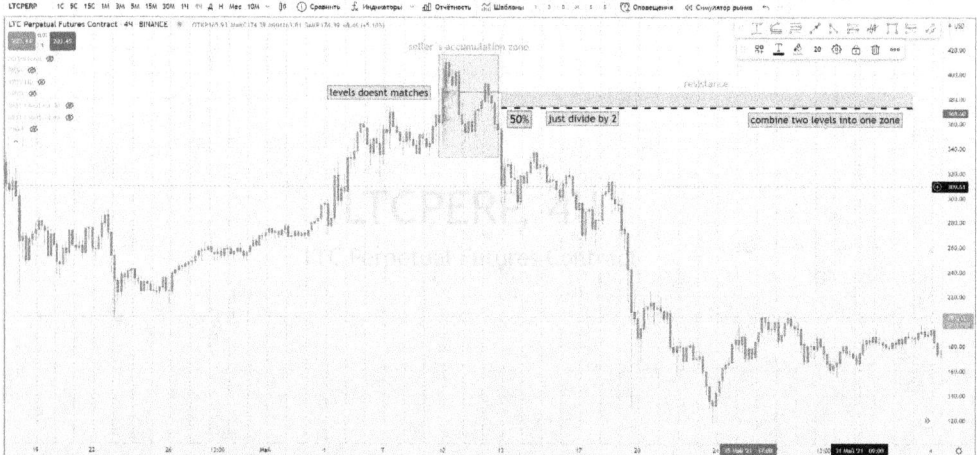

Take a closer look and see how I have skillfully combined these two important levels into one resistance area.

Here's an example of a BAZ:

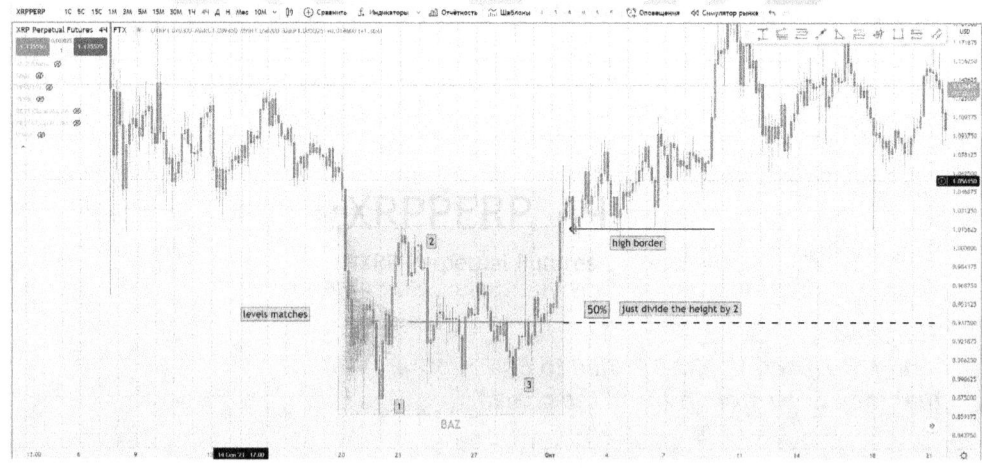

Chapter 1. Defining accumulation zones

And here you can clearly see how the levels coincided. Which means that this level, not the area, is very strong and you should expect a reaction from it in the future.

> **The trick.**
> **Always extend all levels to the right on the chart**
> **as far right as possible so as not to miss the opportunity!**
> **Believe me, it was not just a secret, but a revelation!)) Practice it at home.**

And here's what it looks like in Atas:

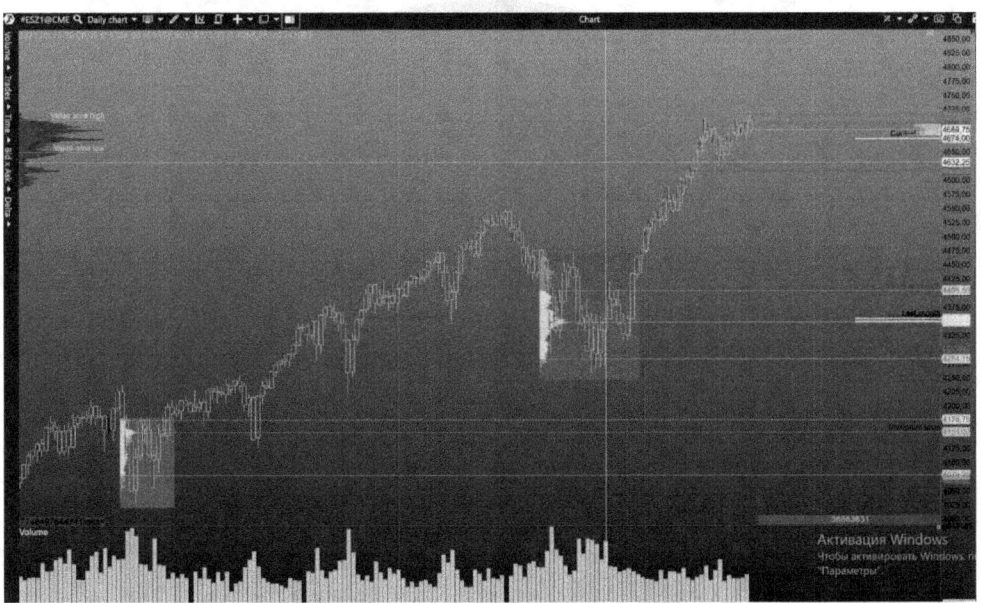

Chapter 1.6.
The Accumulation Zone inside the Accumulation Zone.
The matryoshka doll principle.

It sounds like a wordplay, but this point certainly deserves a separate chapter.

The matryoshka doll principle can be seen in many places in the market. I'll talk more about it later.

But it is important that you learn how to identify the AZ within other larger AZs on a higher timeframe.

It comes only with experience.

Chapter 1. Defining accumulation zones

Here, look at this, but don't wrack your brain.

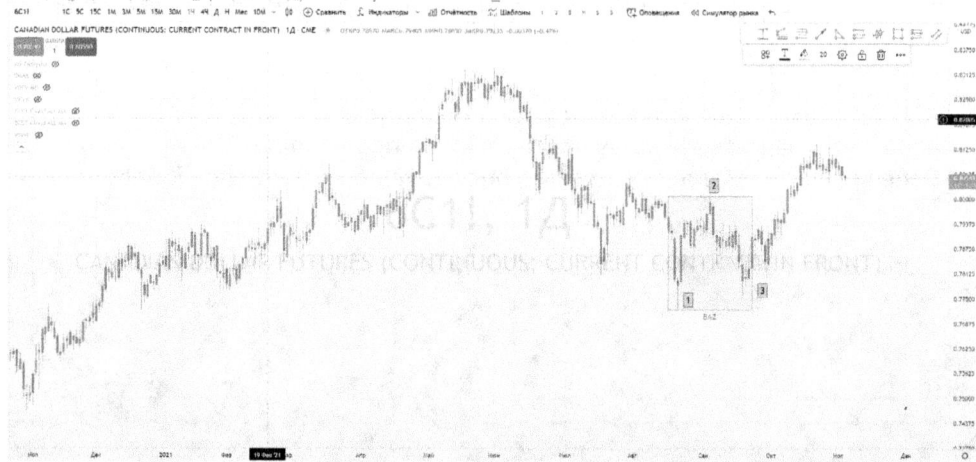

It is a chart with Canadian dollar futures D1. I've successfully found a BAZ and marked a 1-2-3 pattern.

Now I suggest we go down to the hourly timeframe and see what's going on there.

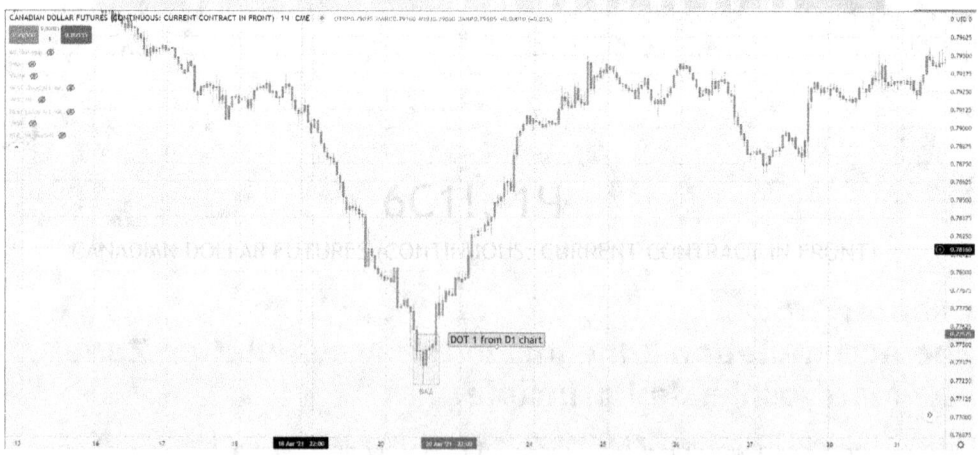

And here we have found and marked the BAZ, which is Point 1 on the D1 chart. You know what I mean? Remember about the matryoshka doll.

Let's move on.

Chapter 1. Defining accumulation zones

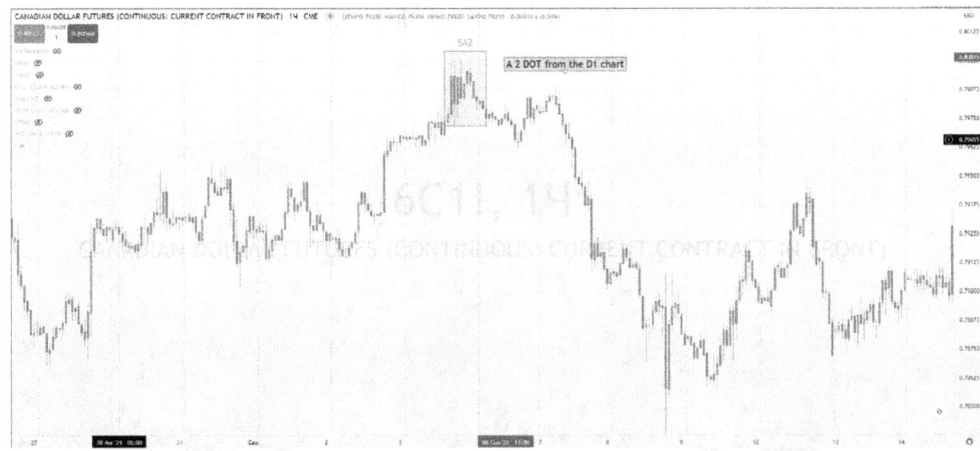

I went to point 2 on D1 and found the SAZ.
And what about point 3?

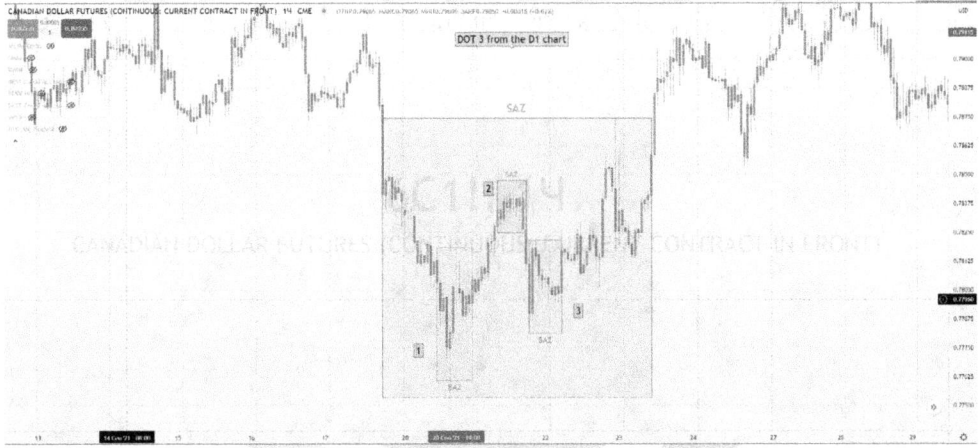

And here I see a BAZ within the hourly timeframe.

Attention!
Now you have to compare and understand that the points 1-2-3
from the older timeframe are nothing more
than BAZ and SAZ on a smaller timeframe.

The Smell Of The Cash

Chapter 1. Defining accumulation zones

And here is a picture that should put everything in its place in your head:

The Point 3, which was analyzed above, consists, if you look closely, of BAZ and SAZ or pattern 1-2-3!!! And all this is just inside the BAZ of the higher timeframe.
Here is the wide version:

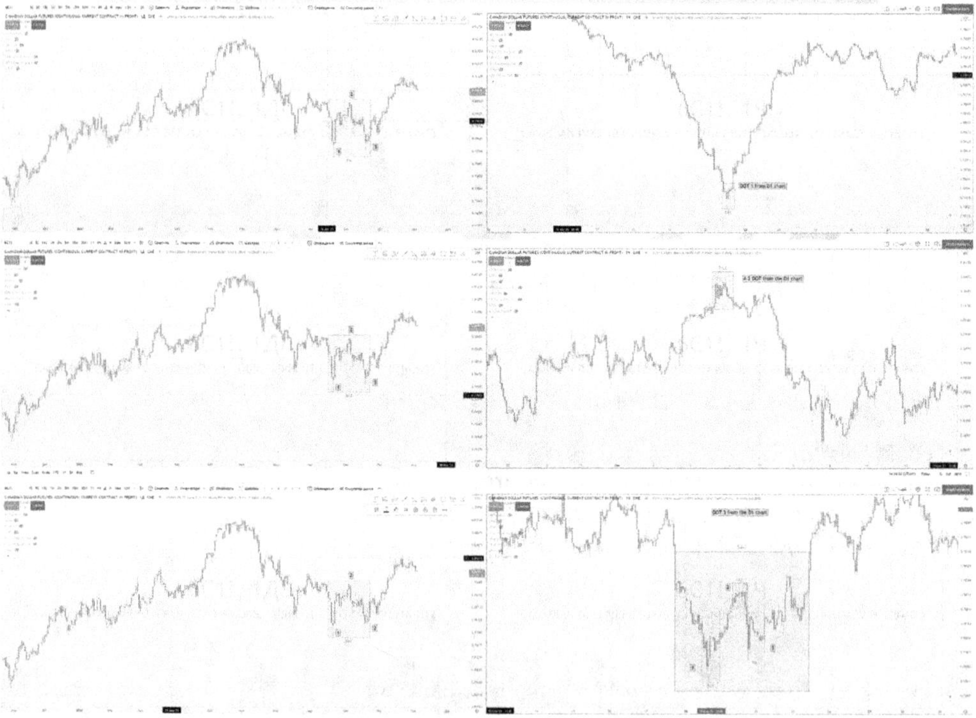

The Smell Of The Cash

Chapter 1.7. AZ at the support or resistance level

Very often you will find an AZ at important support or resistance levels.
And this is very important for successful trading, because such areas, and not the usual ones outside important levels, are our target.
Why?
Because our chances to succeed in such AZs are much higher.
In other words, the AZ formed at an important level confirms its strength.
And it becomes clear to you - the price will move further from the strength level.
Here are the examples:
I suggest going back to the previous Canadian futures chart.

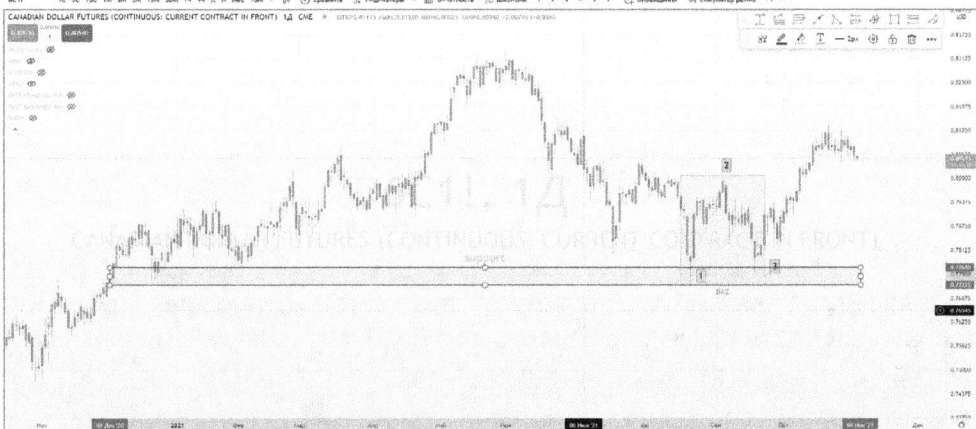

Look at the important support and our BAZ. After having tested it, it fired a powerful profit impulse. This is our money! Soon we will combine everything and you will see how it all works.

Chapter 1. Defining accumulation zones

What a good example. Always mark the AZ on the chart and then the important levels above or below them. Wait for the price to return and continue waiting. Wait until a new AZ is formed. In this example, this is SAZ.

You can already see the profit on the chart, right?

A little later, I will tell you how to open the deal).

And here is the example of Bitcoin. Testing the support and subsequent formation of BAZ would lead to a profit with a good mathematical expectation.

Here's a good example. The price went to test support and, having formed the Buyer's AZ, gave us the opportunity to buy.

But the best time to buy was a little later, at the pull-up.

1.8. Entry points used with AZ.

1.8.1. The first touch rule.

If the price abruptly left the AZ, that means there is a very big player sitting there. And this player is most likely to defend their area.

Look at the example of oil:

You see, we had several great buying opportunities at once.
Here's another example:

It's simple, right?

Chapter 1. Defining accumulation zones

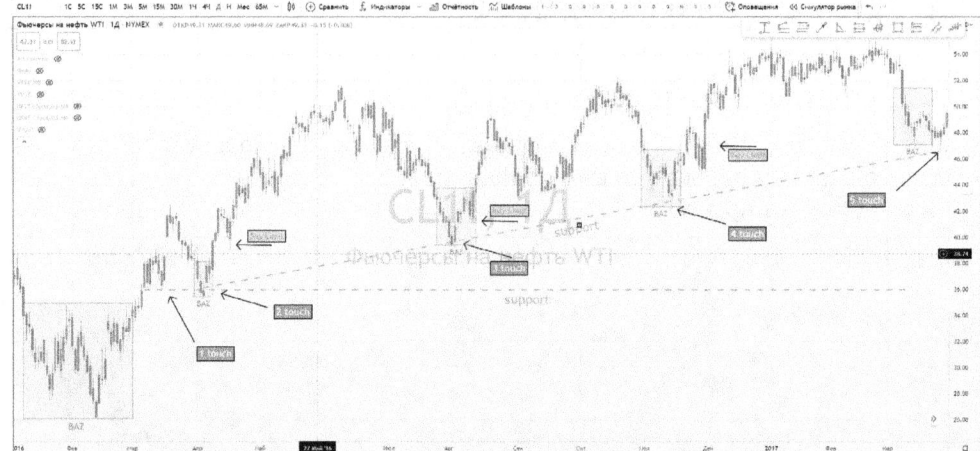

And do not forget that the support will not always be horizontal.

By connecting the two closest lows, you can get excellent support and several more trading opportunities.

1.8.2. Multiple touches rule.

It's simple - if the price has formed a new AZ at an important level, then we can wait for the second and more touches.

Just examine the charts above.

1.8.3. Buy on the test of the upper boundary of accumulation.

Rewind and think of the upper boundary of accumulation. I said that its determination is very important for us.

> **Remember!** The price will always hit either the upper boundary of accumulation, or 50%, and only sometimes the lower or upper one.

So, here's the algorithm:
- We mark the Buyer's AZ. Why the Buyer's AZ? Because there has already been a shot or distribution from it and we can anticipate them again.
- Shift the level to the right from the upper boundary.
- Wait for the test.

Chapter 1. Defining accumulation zones

Look. There were as many as two excellent buys on the test of the upper boundary of accumulation.

Especially risky traders can use the technique of early entry, but I prefer the correct entry after the formation of a new AZ on the level test. But we'll discuss it later.

1.8.4. Sale on the test of the lower boundary of the Seller's AZ.

Here's a good example. It was possible to make great money by placing a sell order after testing the lower boundary to the Sellers' AZ. And then take another profit by performing an Early Entry.

1.8.5. Quick accumulation boundary test

You will see this phenomenon quite often, so you should be able to recognize and not miss it.

So, this phenomenon is characterized by a sharp movement of the price up or down without an AZ test, which indicates the strength of the players in the area. Or we can say that the test took place, but almost at the moment of leaving the area.

We should open a deal by placing the order above or below a small accumulation, which will be a test of the AZ boundary.
Stop should be placed behind the low or high of this area.

Here's a good example. Examine it.
Look at the figure - there is a quick test of the lower boundary of the Seller's AZ in the middle and several failures to reach the level that would prevent you from opening a deal.

Chapter 1. Defining accumulation zones

Failure to reach the level occurs when the test candlestick tail does not touch the accumulation boundaries slightly.

You should not always expect 100% touching of the accumulation boundaries.

> **The rule of stretching the levels to the right from the boundaries and from 50% still applies!**

Yes, most likely, you will wait a very long time for the price to test these levels, but nevertheless, you should definitely extend them and set reminders in the terminal!

Don't forget the strength of these levels, and since price initially took off in a strong momentum, that means we have a powerful player who is sure to defend their AZ.

Let's see:

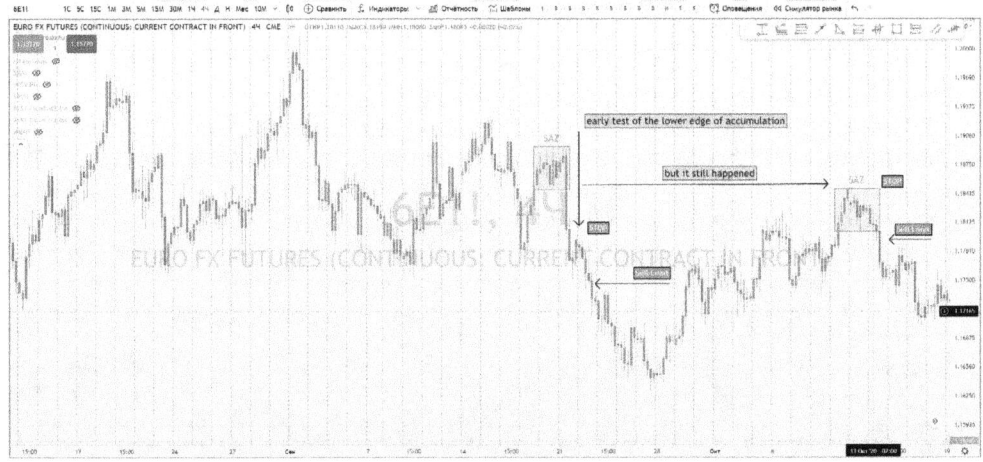

And we see that the price has tested the lower boundary of the Seller's AZ only 5 days later. Which means we could have made a profit if we had an alert!

1.8.6. Early Entry and Right Entry concepts

Early Entry is made directly on the test of the upper or lower AZ boundary level.

It allows you earning more thanks to a greater potential, but it is associated with risks.

First of all, this is the risk of failure of the future setup. We can never be 100% sure that a new AZ will be formed on the test and the price will move in the right direction. Therefore, it is better to wait for the formation of such a new AZ on the test and only then buy it with a stop for its low.

I'll explain it with examples:

Look - in this example, the early entry technique would have brought us success, because the Buyer's AZ was formed in the right direction. And it was possible to top up even after the Right Entry.

But what prevented the price from going lower and breaking our plans? Nothing! **In trading, you should not rely on hope. You should always act based on the facts!**

The Right Entry is made immediately after the Early Entry. Or alone. And after the appearance of the first signs of forming a new AZ on the test of the previous one. The order is placed behind point 2. Stop - behind point 3.

Chapter 1. Defining accumulation zones

In other words, you first need to make sure that the price has moved in the right direction and only then open a deal.

1.8.7. The principle of reducing accumulation zones. Pull-up of accumulation zones.

A true indication for selecting an instrument to your watch list would be to change the size of the accumulation zones downward.

That is, first you have to determine the largest accumulation zone from where a major player started their route and, in the future, while topping up, will form smaller accumulation zones.

And it is desirable that the second and subsequent AZ were higher than the previous ones. This is the so-called pull-up principle.

But sometimes you will encounter the fact that the AZs lie on the same level and form a powerful support.

Chapter 1. Defining accumulation zones

Look at this:

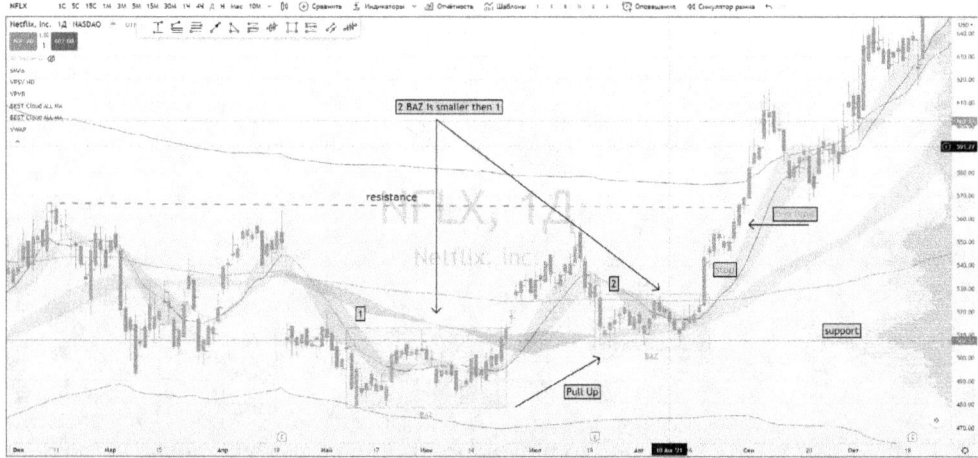

At first, 1 AZ of Buyers was formed on Netflix and then 2 AZ of Buyers, but it was 30% smaller and laid on POC support, which certainly gave us a great point to buy on a resistance breakout.

Here's how it looked like at first:

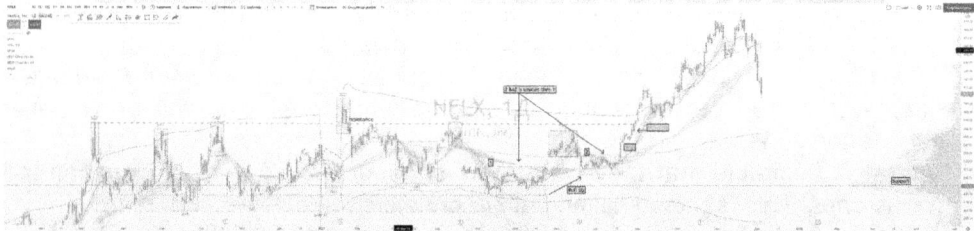

As you can see, a very powerful support was formed from several Buyer's AZs, and pull-up of the last AZ was a signal to buy.

1.8.8. Weak Low. Weak High.

To enhance my trading strategy, I introduce these concepts.

> *A weak low is when there was not a sharp price rejection by the opposite side. The AZ has a low in the form of an arc, not a zigzag.*
>
> *A weak high is the opposite phenomenon.*

Chapter 1. Defining accumulation zones

Let's study them with examples:

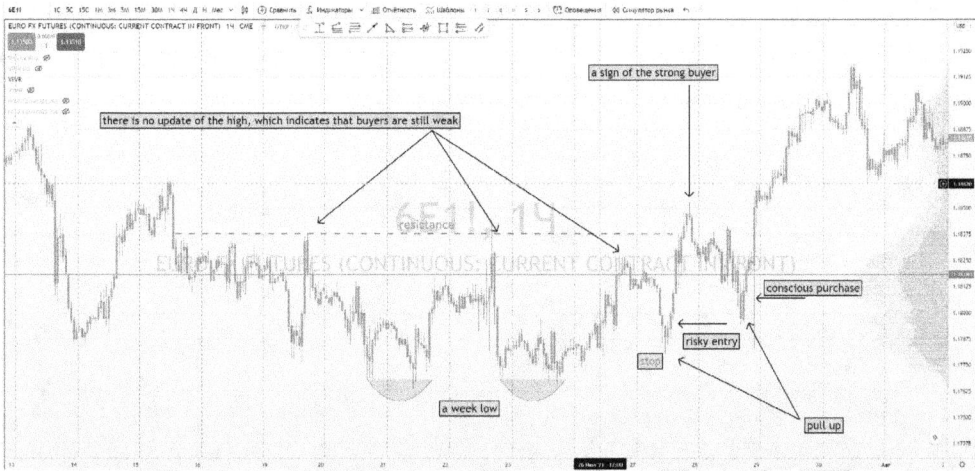

Resistance was formed, which has been tested a number of times. And each time the price went down sharply. But there were no sharp movements there either. Two weak lows formed on the same level. The first buy was for the risk takers, because the resistance was not yet broken and there were no signs of reversal. The pattern could have easily broken and you would have lost your money. But the second entry after breaking resistance was conscious and logical. And it would bring you the desired profit.

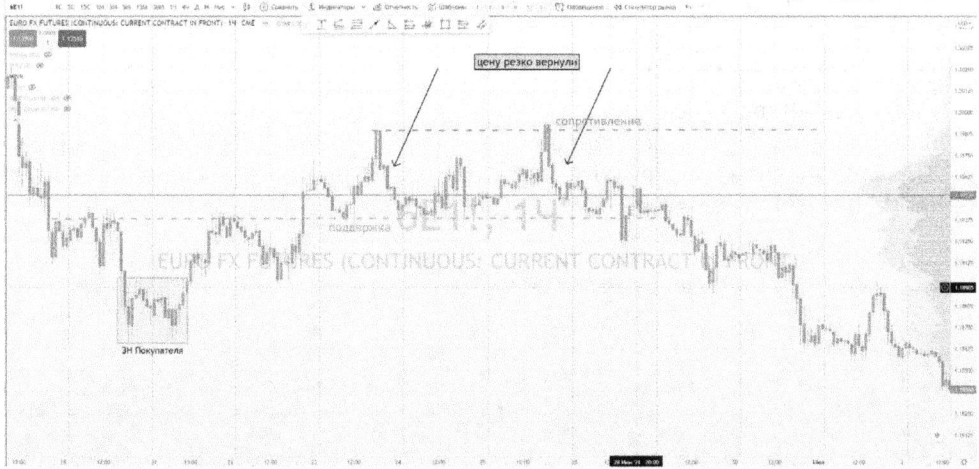

And here is the opposite example of a strong high. See how the price was sharply returned to support twice. There is nothing similar to the AZ in the form of

Chapter 1. Defining accumulation zones

an arc. A very strong resistance was formed. And selling on the break in support was predictable. Engulfing is the key.

Here is another sign of buyer weakness. After the sell pulse, a new Buyer's AZ in the form of a hemisphere was formed and the resistance was not broken and the price went higher on its test. Instead, they reached a new low, which was a confirming signal for the following sales.

The ability to read the chart is a paramount skill that will come to you with experience. As you can see, you can successfully trade even without indicators! But they will increase the percentage of your profitable trades.

1.8.9. Failed auction.

Interesting name, isn't it?

It occurs when two or more candlesticks have the same tails at the same level.

This indicates that this level is weak, and most likely, there will be a breakdown rather than a bounce when you try to test it.

Chapter 1. Defining accumulation zones

Let's look at examples:

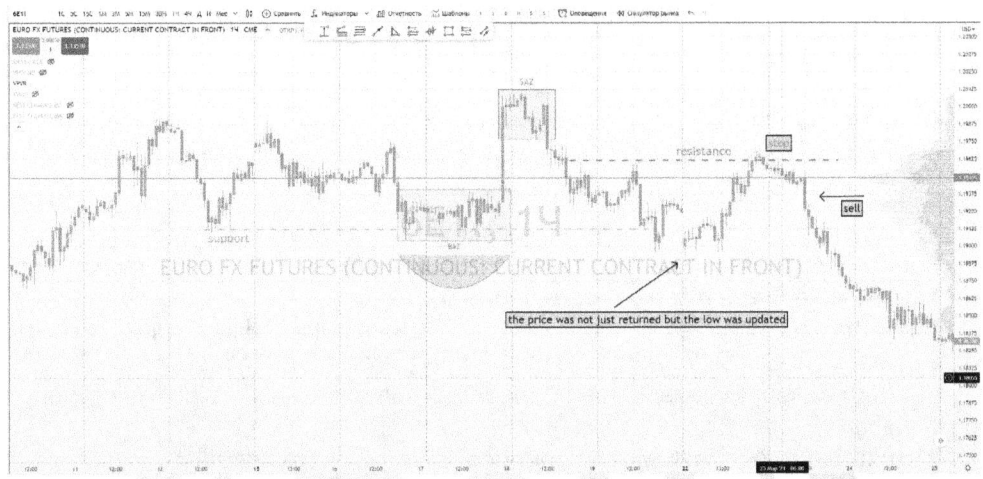

Please look here. A new Buyer's AZ was formed after the decline. We wait for the 50% level test and earn by buying. But, after seeing two candlesticks in the new Buyer's AZ, we get worried and see that the level is weak and probably will be broken in the next test. And that is what happened.

Therefore, always watch for levels inside the Accumulation Zones.

This is where I think I should end my story about the magical phenomenon that came to us from the VSA, the Accumulation Zones.
Be sure to study this chapter several times and practice on your charts.

CHAPTER 2
Accumulative Flat

> *AF is an equally interesting phenomenon in the market. It is characterized by clear boundaries of support and resistance, from which players are "driven" up and down until one of the sides wins.*

You can never be 100% sure where exactly the flat will be traded to.
But more often it is done in the opposite direction from the original movement.
That is, AF is more often a reversal formation!
The difference between AF and AZ is that AF does not look like the 1-2-3 pattern. It has clear boundaries. And its size on the chart is often much bigger.
But both concepts have the same meaning, namely the redistribution of money from players.
It's just that in AF this happens not once as in AZ, but repeatedly!
And the AF structure includes several AZs of both sellers and buyers!
That is, it is a more extensive phenomenon, and therefore it has a greater profit potential.
The longer the accumulation lasted, the greater the redistribution, and hence the profit!
The skill of finding AF on the chart is also very important for working on strategy.
So let's find some of them!

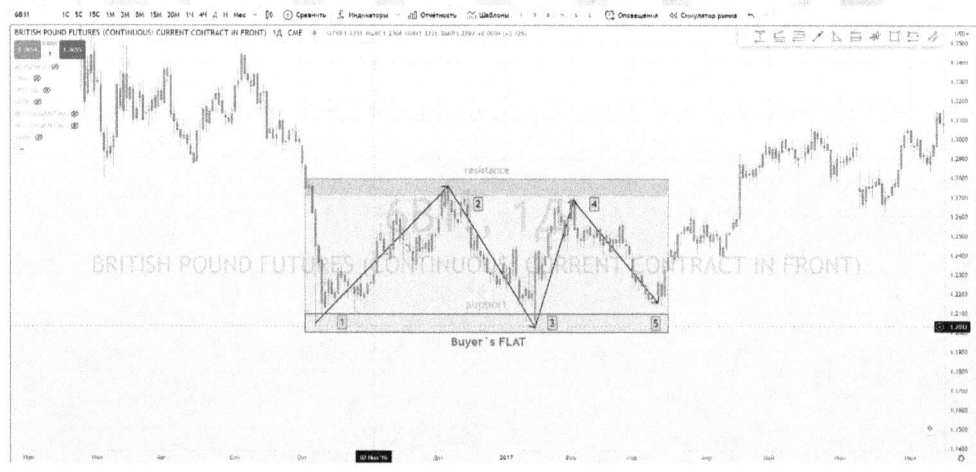

Pound futures.
I'm sure this phenomenon is hard to miss on a chart.
See how the price was "driven" inside. Up and down 5 times!
In order to accumulate a position and skyrocket from this formation.

Chapter 2. Accumulative Flat

Support and resistance have very clear boundaries.
And now it's so:

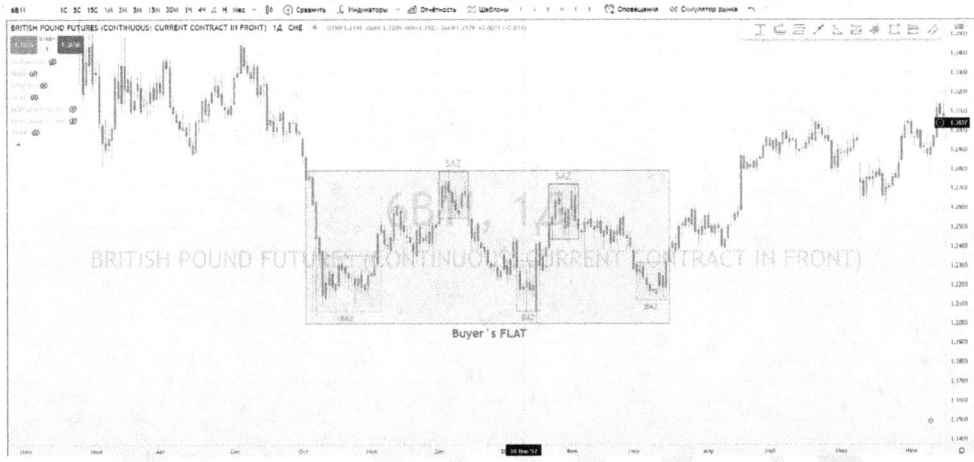

As I said, the AF consists of Sellers' and Buyers' AZs. But now we know how to find them!

It is very important to skillfully determine the AZ inside the flat, because my entry points, which I will give a little later, are based on them.

And, as always, they are very accurate and similar to a sniper shot or a sharp surgeon's knife!

Let me remind you that I developed my trading system on my own. Even before getting acquainted with the works of such renowned authors like Minervini and others. Later, after studying them, I found a lot in common. But I would like to emphasize - my entries are even earlier and even more accurate in a number of cases!

Chapter 2. Accumulative Flat

And here is a flat of sellers on the AUD futures.
As you can see, the initial movement was up, and then it was traded down.
Support and resistance levels are also clearly visible.

And you can see AZ inside the flat.

The trick.

**50% of the mid-height of the flat is the level
of the same importance as the AZ.
Always mark it and apply the volume profile to find it!**

See how perfectly the price bounced from the 50% level.
Moreover, it was possible to make an early entry just on a 50% test, which is risky.

Chapter 2. Accumulative Flat

Or, as I do, wait for the formation of the Buyer's AZ at this level and then buy!
Yes, in this example, we do not see the implementation and upward movement into buying, but this is the exception rather than the rule!
In 90% of cases, such patterns work well!

Chapter 2.1. Trading from the flat.

Look, we already know that a flat is a reversal formation, so if we have sellers in the flat, then we should look for a point to buy.

> **The trick.**
>
> **This rule only works in most cases.**
> **Not 100% of the flats are reversal.**

So, there are several points for trading:

2.1.1 Entry at the breakdown of the upper or lower boundary of the flat formed by resistance or support.

Let's go back to the pound futures.
How would I trade it?

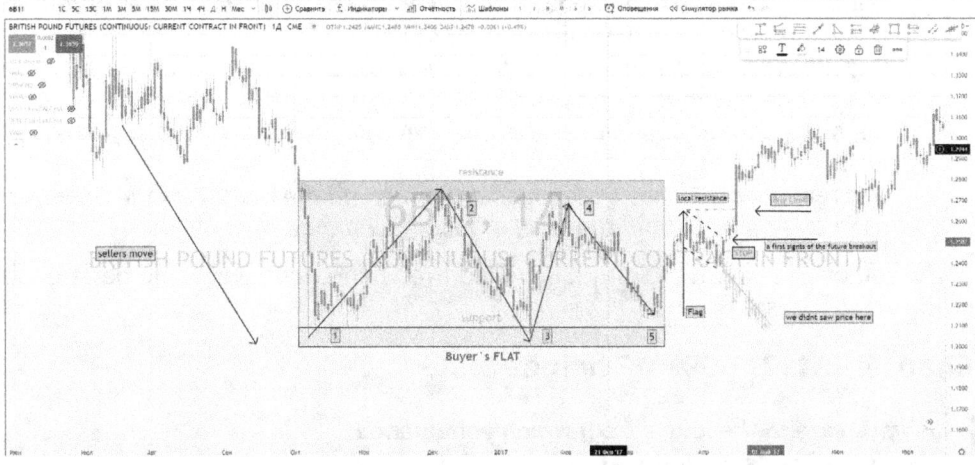

- *I would determine the kind of movement before the formation of the AF.*
- *Seeing that it was from sellers, I would set a buy limit for a breakout of local resistance at one of the peaks, after I made sure that the price did not rush to test the support again.*
- *Pay attention to the figure of TA Flag and the first two days when the price came out of it, making it clear that the movement has begun.*
- *Thus, we got a point with an excellent risk-profile ratio.*

The Smell Of The Cash

Chapter 2. Accumulative Flat

- **Look to the right and see how the price tested this level.**

Now as for the sellers:

Let's return to the sellers' flat on the AUD futures.
We will apply our method of finding a point, but this time for sales:

- **We determined the momentum of buyers before the flat, made sure that these are buys. So we are looking for sales.**
- **Pay attention to the points 5-6-8. Do you see signs of a downtrend? Highs are getting lower. It is important.**
- **Then it's enough just to set the Sell Limit slightly below the support and wait.**
- **It is reasonable to put a stop loss either behind the last AZ of the Seller, or, as in this case, behind the level of local resistance.**

As you can see from the chart, if we did everything right, we would get a good profit!

Chapter 2.1.2. 50% AF height test.

> Always extend the levels from which you opened the deal when leaving the AF.
>
> In the future, you will have more than one opportunity to earn!

Chapter 2. Accumulative Flat

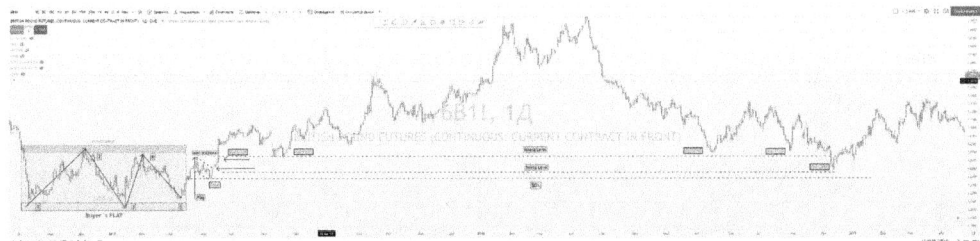

Look at the picture.
Do you remember about 50% on AZ?
The same rule works here!
It is enough just to determine 50% of the flat height and you will get a very strong level, which will hit the price more than once in the future.

The trick.

Well, do not forget to pull the fixed volume profile on the flat, so that you get another strong level!

Chapter 2. Accumulative Flat

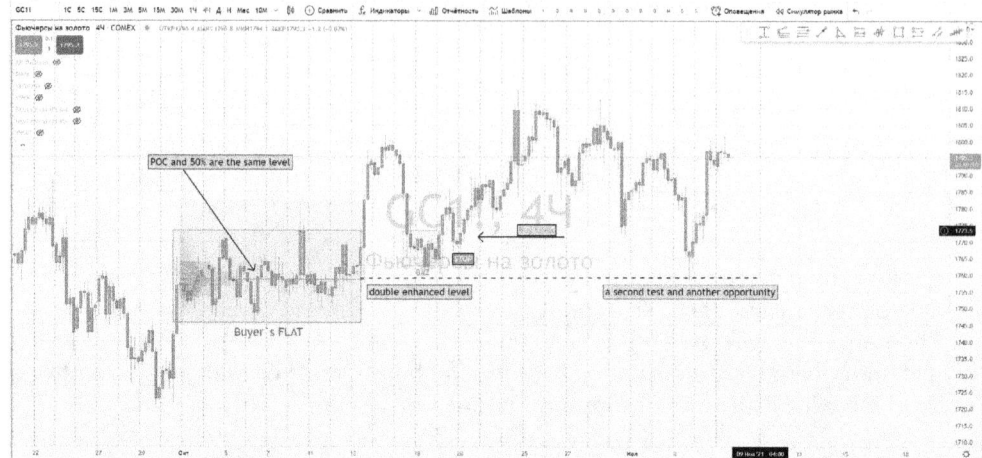

Here's a good example with the gold futures.

Pay attention to the entry method. I did not open a deal immediately on the test of matching levels, but on the test of the AZ that was formed later. I put stop loss under this test. And the second level test also gave a great trade. Always extend the levels to the right!

Chapter 2.1.3. Entry after consolidation.

Having mastered this entry, you will make a great progress in your trading.
You will have to:

- **Determine the flat,**
- **Find signs of its change,**
- **Find consolidation.**

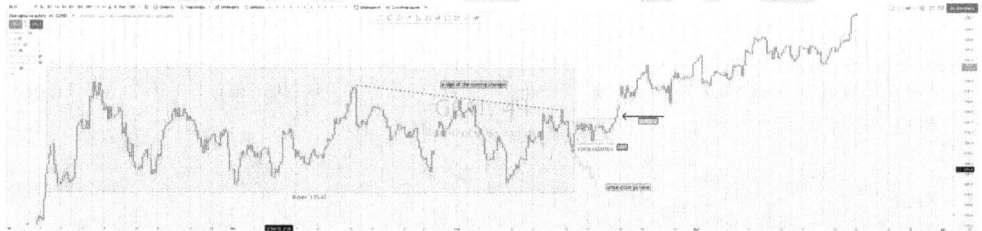

Look - the flat on gold has been going on for several months.

When I saw the first signs, namely a decrease in highs inside the flat, I waited to see how it would end. And after making sure that the price did not move to the support test, but formed a consolidation, I bought with a stop loss behind its lower boundary. It's simple!

Chapter 2. Accumulative Flat

And you already know that the longer the accumulation, the greater the distribution, and hence our profit!

Here's another example:

It's a wonderful example of trading the flat on CAD!!!

Look at this ultra-short stop entry!

And look at new Buyers' AZs following each other with a characteristic pull-up, which suggests that the trend is upward.

And how the resistances where you can top up break down.

It's a unique trade!

Here I have already taken a step forward and combined several elements of the strategy.

Chapter 2.1.4. Trading inside the flat.

Everything is much simpler here.

Buy from the support is made when there are several touches of this support, i.e. when the boundaries of the future flat are set.

Chapter 2. Accumulative Flat

Example:

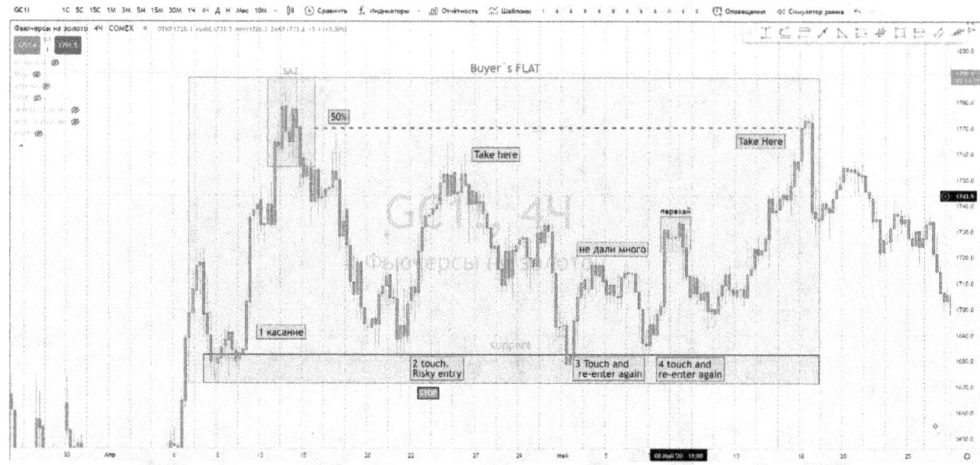

See how you could trade inside the flat.
Since we have the flat of buyers, we are buying from support.
In the future, as you get more experience, you'll learn how to sell from resistance.
I would recommend opening a deal at 3rd touch at first, after making sure that it is flat and there are boundaries.
The stop loss is put under support. And I put it a little further because burrs are possible.
I put take profit either on the resistance test, or, as in our case, on the test of 50% of the Seller's AZ.
It is not worth sitting in such a trade for a long time and waiting for a breakdown of resistance!
Also, look for an opportunity to re-open a deal on the support test again (3rd and 4th touch).
Do not worry if they do not show a good profit, without letting the price escape to the resistance test. In the flat, not all points are on supports and resistances. You can find it only in the ideal flat, which is rare to see.
And note that the difference between the flat boundaries is $100, by the way!

Chapter 2. Accumulative Flat

Example of sale:

Look at the wonderful opportunity to sell on the test of the flat upper boundary formed by the resistance.

It was possible to sell directly on the resistance test, and this would be a risky entry for more experienced traders.

But it is better to use the safe entry technique once the Seller's AZ is formed. In this case, the stop loss can be moved beyond the high of this area.

Take profit should be set on the lower boundary of the flat, i.e. on the support. And do not hope for the price to go lower.

An example of sales and buys inside a flat. For experienced traders.

Look. I just outlined our favorite Buyer's AZs and the 50% level. And I waited for its test.

The Smell Of The Cash

And considering that we are on important support, I bought using the early entry technique.

In this case, you need to put the stop loss either behind the Buyer's AZ low or directly under the 50% level.

It is advisable to set the take profit in the resistance test area.

And to sell from there!

That's how the major players accumulate their positions and allow us to make money by driving the price up and down!

CHAPTER 3.
Reversal levels.

Reversal Levels (RL) are another great formation of technical analysis that I use extensively.

The Reversal Level includes:

- Center of liquidity capture;
- Two or one AZs located slightly above or below, depending on the type of reversal level;
- Or several AZs in a row, the boundaries of which form support or resistance, and several smaller accumulation zones that are slightly higher or lower, depending on the type of reversal level (buyers or sellers). They should test the support or resistance level.
- Typical pull-up from the AZ;
- It is a reversal formation;
- In foreign literature, I read the name of the "Cup with Handle" pattern, but this is a simplified version.

Buyer's Reversal Level. It consists of two Buyer's AZs forming support and resembling an oval, as well as two tails to the left and right of this area testing the support. If you switch to a smaller timeframe, you can detect the buyer's AZ.

Above you can see the Seller's AZ and, by comparing them, understand what the difference is.

> **The trick.**
> RL can form vast areas, and like everywhere else -
> the larger the scale of RL, the greater the profit potential!

Chapter 3. Reversal levels

One RL can test the previous one and this is an amplifying factor.

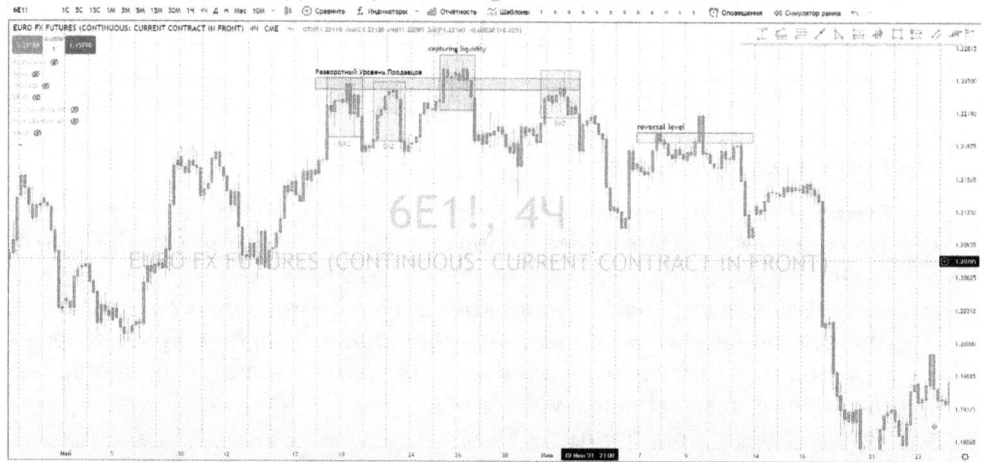

The chart perfectly shows the formation of one large RL of sellers, consisting of several AZs of sellers and the capture of liquidity in the middle.
As well as the formed second RL, which tests the first one.
You see the profit potential, right?)
Here is an example of the Buyers' RL:

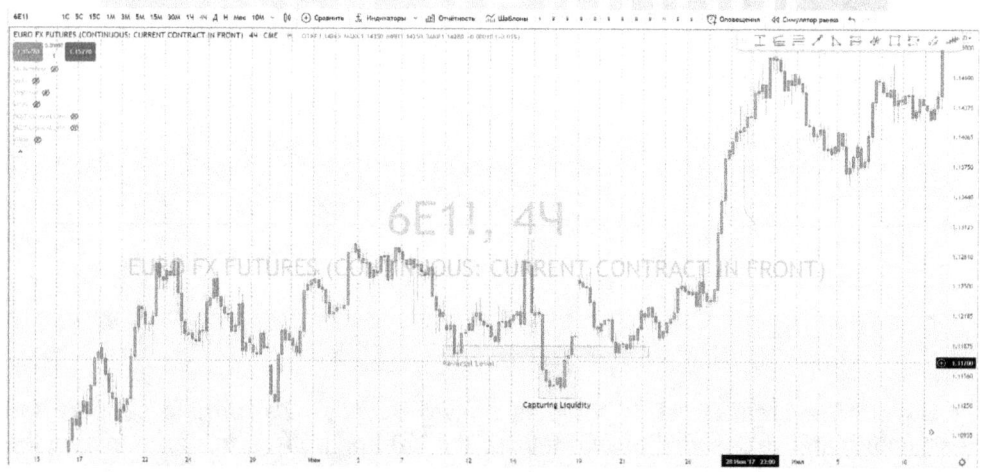

The example clearly shows 3 Buyer's AZs represented by the left and right shoulder and the capture of liquidity in the middle.
The early entry would have been made on a right shoulder test with a stop loss under it.

Chapter 3. Reversal levels

The right entry is at the resistance breakdown with a stop loss under the nearest low.

Chapter 3.1. Method of entry using RL.

If you have carefully read everything that was written by me above, then you should already see the regularities).

But I understand that you don't have 5 years of practice and so here are the examples:

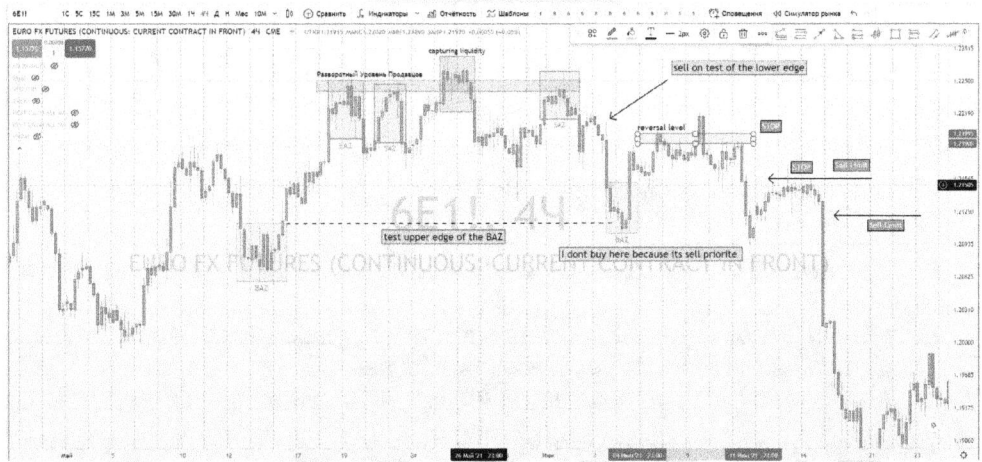

See how I would trade this case:

- **I would put the first sell on the lower boundary test of accumulation zone by performing the Right Entry;**
- **I would fix the position on the test of the Buyers' AZ upper boundary;**
- **I would not buy, because buys are corrective!**
- **But I would sell again after formation of a new RL, placing a sell order either right under it and a stop loss above it, or I would put it at the breakdown a little lower, and then the stop loss would be above the local resistance.**

Chapter 3. Reversal levels

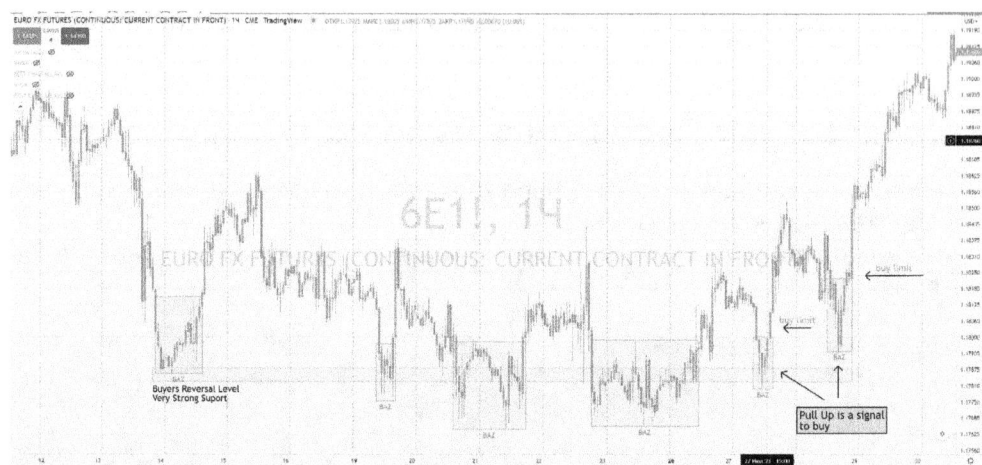

Here's an example worthy of being shown at an exhibition. Look:

- **The reversal level has been strengthened by 3 AZs of Buyers. It is a powerful level!**
- **I would buy by performing a safe entry, after I made sure that a new AZ was formed on the pull-up, i.e. a new low was set.**
- **And I would top up in buys at the Buyer's AZ upper boundary test.**

The potential is impressive, isn't it?
This is the power of reversal levels in action!
Join our school's *Private Chat* **to see more results!**

CHAPTER 4.
The use of indicators.

So, dear friends, it's time to show you my indicators.
I should point out right away that I've been developing this set and setting for many years, trying to find the right ones every day.
And now I can share a truly working option with you.
I will not go into the description of their work principle. You can easily find it on the Internet.
My goal is to show you the indicators and settings I use.
As well as entry points and logic of thinking.

Chapter 4.1. VWAP

In my opinion, it is a unique indicator I use every day and on any timeframe.
It is based on the calculation of the total amount of volume per session or more.
The main advantage is that it is widely used by institutions, which means that we should use it as well!
The main principle of trading is to sell on the test from below and buy on the test from above.
And it is alo very important to clearly understand that everything above the indicator has a buy priority and everything below it - a sell priority.

Now as for the entry points.
Even looking at the chart above, it becomes obvious where we could have opened the position.

Chapter 4. The use of indicators

Namely, on the indicator line test. That is, sales on the indicator test from above and buys on the indicator test from below.

I would like to stress that I see such tests and entries often and make them, because the VWAP test, as practice shows, is a very strong level.

Here is an example:

The trick.
It is very important that you understand that it is desirable
to open a deal on the indicator level test, but after
the pattern like 1-2-3 pattern has formed.
That is, this indicator, like any other, gives you only
a hint, but not an entry point!

Chapter 4. The use of indicators

Look - here I have returned to the euro futures chart again.

If you scroll up, you will see a chart without a vwap and an entry point just on the support test. But if we take it into account too, we will get additional support that intensifies the signal.

And again, we will get a point, after waiting a little for the test:

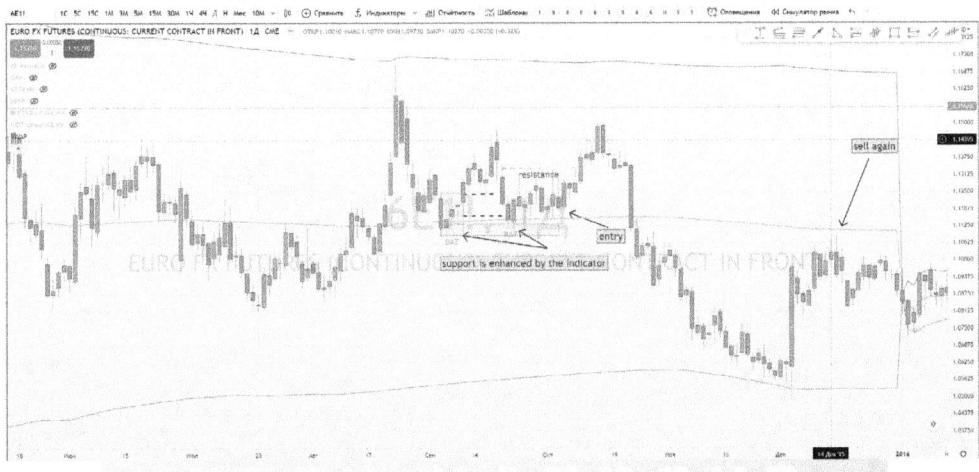

Here is an example of a situation when it was possible to buy on the indicator test after the priority change.

You probably noticed the yellow area and the two black lines below and above.

These lines form the channel effect area and are powerful support and resistance.

In the indicator settings, they are called standard deviations.

Now as for the indicator settings.

Chapter 4. The use of indicators

To analyze the charts, I use almost all timeframes, including the monthly one. So, below I will give the settings for each of them.

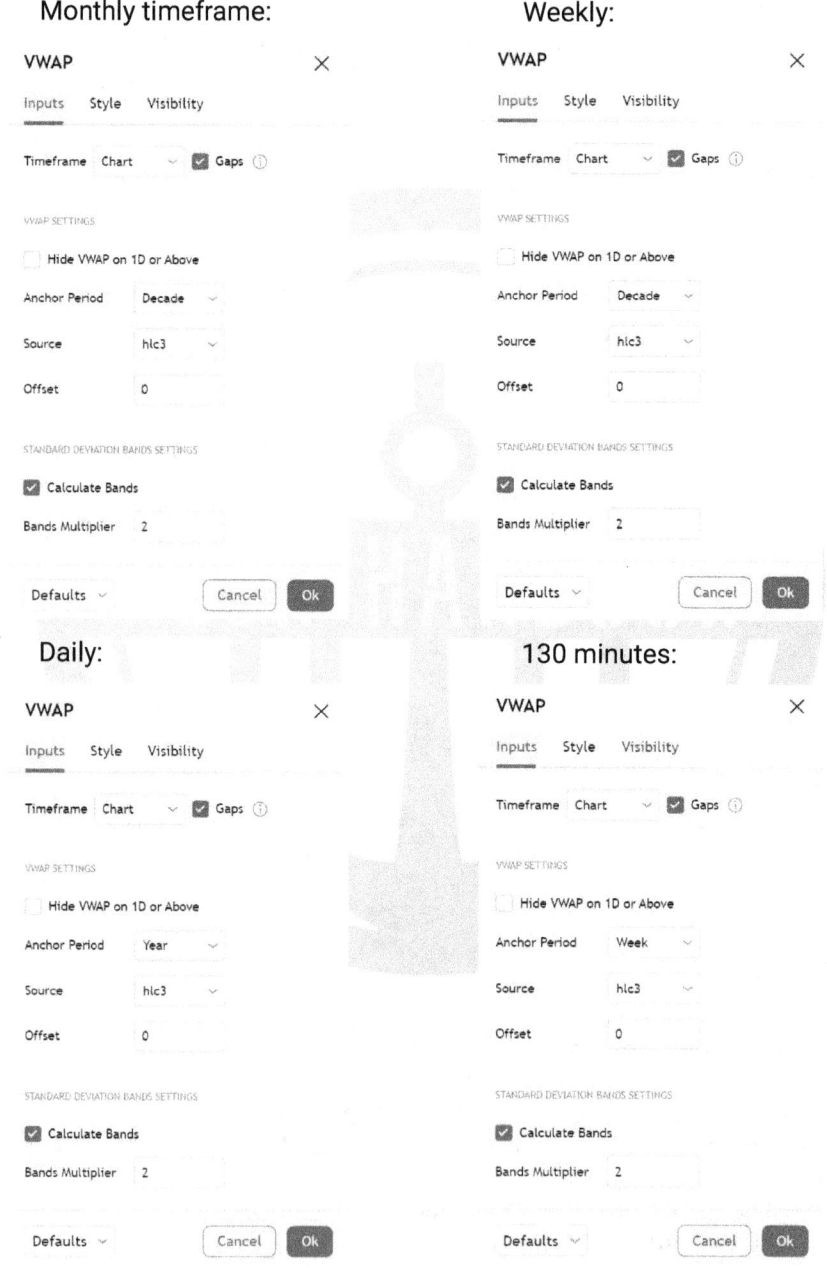

Chapter 4. The use of indicators

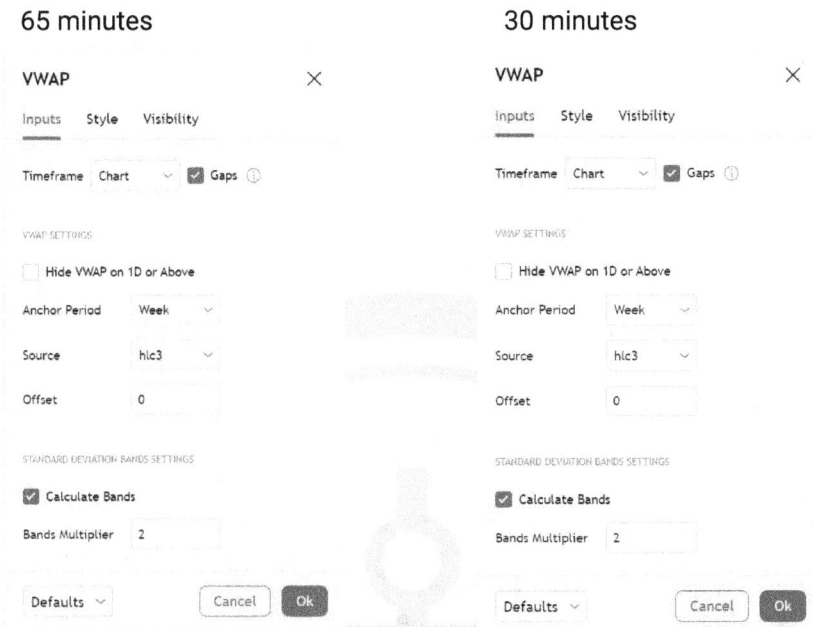

So, as you can see, the settings are slightly different for each timeframe. Namely, the time period. It is changing downwards because the timeframe is decreasing. And it is important for us to see the right tests only.
Play around with the settings and you'll understand what I'm talking about.

Chapter 4.2. AVWAP.

It's an equally important indicator, but you need to know how to use it. Its unique feature is that it does not count the entire volume on the chart, but only from the set point.
The points that can be used:

- **Beginning of the year or month,**
- **High or low,**
- **Maximum extreme point,**
- **On the GAPs.**

You can see 3 levels plotted from the extreme points and from the beginning of the year on this chart.
And of course, each level is valuable and important.
Testing these levels will tell you the right moments to find the entry points.

Chapter 4. The use of indicators

Here is an example of a successful trade on the test of an indicator cast off from the extreme point. We already know that there is a test of the upper boundary of accumulation or flat, so we would wait for the price there, but after seeing the additional confirmation in the form of an AVWAP test, we would get ready twice as much.

You will often encounter double levels that will form support or resistance. And do not expect that the test will be exactly on the level!
Don't forget - it shows us the search area.

Chapter 4. The use of indicators

Here's a good example.
Let's examine it:

- We set AVWAP on extreme points;
- On the beginning of the year;
- And we immediately found several entry points.
- Sell on the breakdown of resistance from double levels;
- Buy on the test of the upper boundary of the accumulative flat.
- Buy on the intensified level test from several avwaps;
- Sell on the double intensified level test.

And now we apply the knowledge about AZ we received earlier:

That's the picture you get! Cool, right?

Chapter 4. The use of indicators

But this is just the beginning and many exciting things are waiting for you ahead! I want you to gradually form the right view on the market.

I looked at the market with the eyes of many renowned traders and did not find a system cooler than mine. My only regret is that back then, five years ago, when I was just beginning to trade, I did not come across this book and the Rich Harbor project.

After all, it is fundamentally important to initially learn a profitable and easy system and not invent the Gann theory, the Mandelbrot channel, and other things that certainly work, but only when they are used by experienced trader and with lower probability.

Chapter 4.3. Buy on GAP and engulfing.

Now I want to confide a comprehensive trading strategy to you. Namely, trading on GAPs and on engulfing using AVWAP.

> *A gap is a price gap formed by high volatility due to news or due to emergence of a major player.*
> *It occurs mostly on Monday.*

The level formed by the GAP is very strong. According to statistics, GAP is closed in 80% of cases.

The first candlestick of the GAP is a reference point for applying AVWAP.
And in the future, it is necessary to monitor the reaction of the price to it.
It will act either as support or resistance.
Let's see:

We can hardly find a better example.

Chapter 4. The use of indicators

- We determined the first GAP. Set AVWAP on the first candlestick.
- We saw the second GAP. Set the indicator on the first candlestick.
- We plotted the Seller's AZ.
- If you want to take a risk, you can go against the trend and sell on the AVWAP test in order to close the GAP.
- Having taken profit, we should and must have bought after the formation of intensified AVWAP by RL.
- At the moment, we need to make sure that the price does not bounce back from the indicator.

And here is an interesting example of work on engulfing:

- We set the indicator on the engulfing candle.
- We identified the Buyer's AZ.
- Waited for the 50% test
- And safely opened the deal when the local resistance was broken.
- But all this happened before the entry using the indicator.
- Our entry was higher on the double intensified level test from AVWAP.
- Now we need to wait for the local resistance to break through and top up!

It's as simple as always!

Chapter 4.4. Guides.

I am often asked about the guides I use.
Here's my answer:
- I use the Best Cloud MA indicator, which has the following settings:

Chapter 4. The use of indicators

On D1:

On 130 min:

On 65 min:

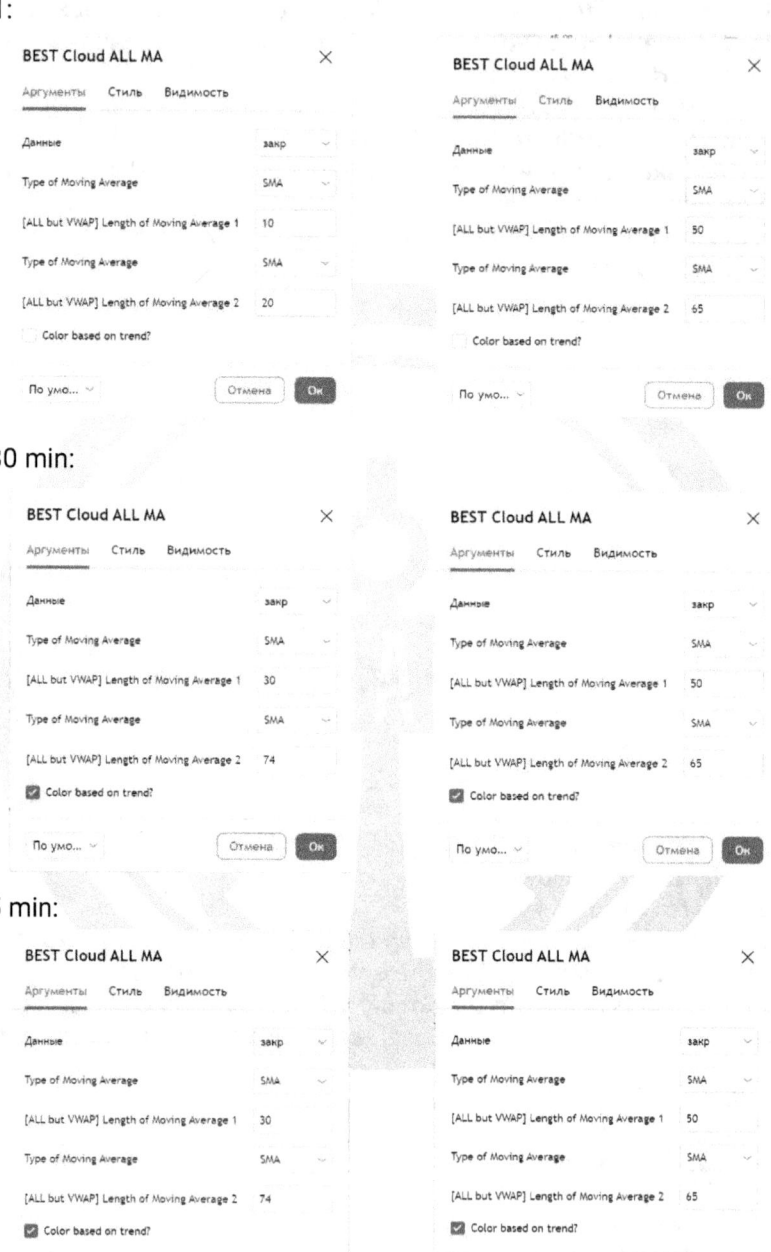

On 30min:

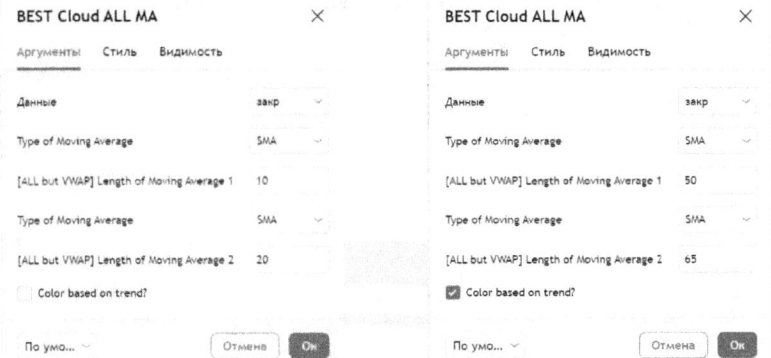

On 15min:

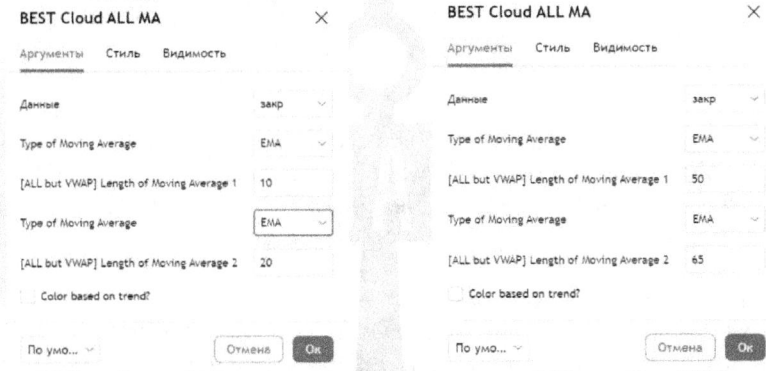

On all other timeframes, I use the same settings.
But on a 3-minute CScalp, I use these ones:

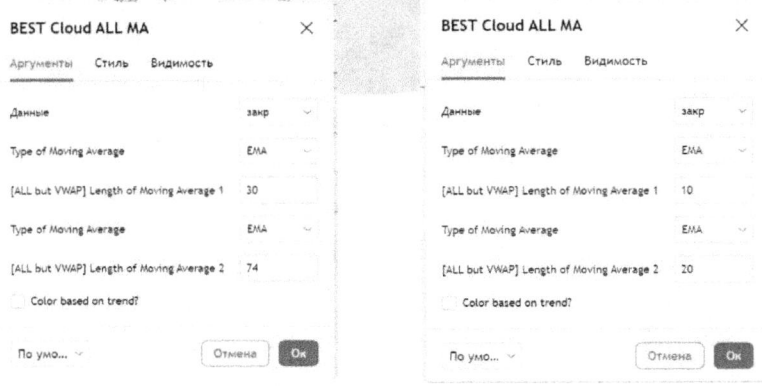

Chapter 4. The use of indicators

The point is that on a smaller timeframe, I use faster EMAs, not SMAs.
You can see clouds on the chart, but what limits them? Yes, that's right, it is these guides. I just turned them off!
Here:

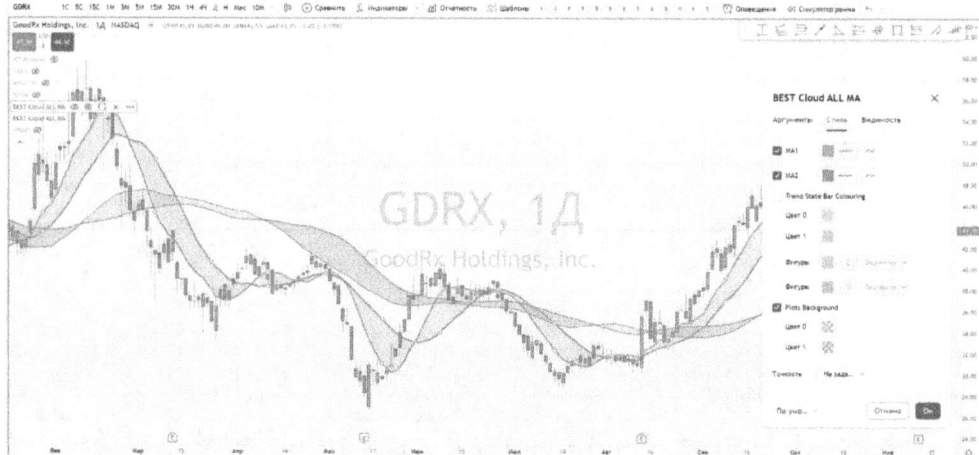

If it's more convenient for you, then you're welcome!
But the point is that these clouds will act as support or resistance for you.
And their intersection - as a possible signal!
You definitely need to learn how it works on your own!

And why two indicators at once?
Because the one with slower settings will show the main trend!
If the chart is in the red or under the red zone, then you have a sell priority.
And if it's in green zone, then vice versa!
That is, it makes sense to filter out the excess.
So, let's go:

Chapter 4. The use of indicators

The chart clearly shows how the two clouds work together.
If two clouds are in the red zone, then focus only on sell!
But if the trend changes, buys are also possible.
And pay your attention to how the cloud boundaries on the right support the price.

Look at how perfectly the clouds support the price. And if it was possible to open a deal at the very beginning of the priority change, then it was possible, by pulling up the stops, to make good money by leaving when the priority changes upwards.
And, of course, do not forget that these are only indicators, and they should be used together with all other elements of the system.
At the moment, there should be such a notion in your head:

Chapter 4. The use of indicators

How do you like this chart analysis using my system?)))
You should already be able to work like this.
And you see how each new element that I add strengthens the system and filters out the excess.
But this is still just the middle - the most exciting things will come!

Chapter 4.5. SMA guides.

Of course, in addition to clouds, I also use regular SMAs, which perfectly show the trend and will prompt you the areas to search for the entry points.
So, these are SMA 50, 150, 200.

Chapter 4. The use of indicators

Look - the use of only one indicator gives understanding of the trend and good entry points.
Now let's combine everything together again:

Chapter 4.6. Volume profiles.

Another integral part of my trading strategy is volume profiles.
I have two of them.
The first is the session volume profile.
The second is the visible area profile.
The session volume profile shows its trading levels for the entire session.
And volumes, as you know, are very important. They give us the most important knowledge about where the big trades occurred, which will act as support and resistance.
It is also necessary to observe the distribution of volumes within the session in order to have an idea of where to trade from the next day.
The maximum volume level of the previous day is a very strong level that can bounce the price!

Types of horizontal volumes:

1. P-shaped. It got its name because of the shape of the letter P.
The letter P can also be upside down. The maximum volume level always falls on the bow of the letter.

Examples:

You see - the level of max volumes in the form of the letter P gave us an excellent entry point.
Trading will almost always go in the opposite direction.

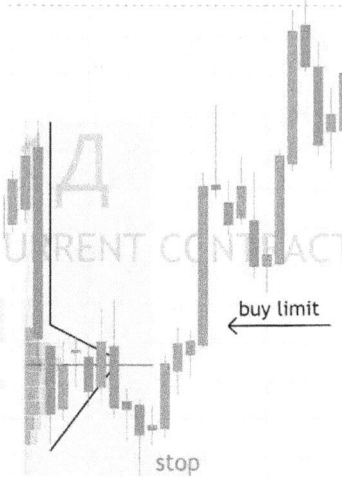

2. Arched profile.

It is characterized by a uniform distribution of volumes within the session. If the indicator shows the POC level, then it is rather conditional, and you should not rely on it.

The volume is relatively evenly distributed within the session.

It is the least helpful type of profile. It's hard to trade with it.

3. Wave-like

The volume is evenly distributed in the lower and upper parts of the profile. Both of these zones can become support and resistance. And most likely, the price will float between them.

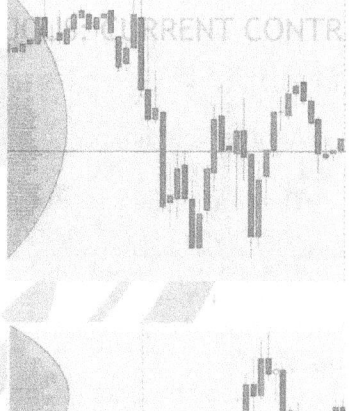

Chapter 4. The use of indicators

So, here are examples of use:

It's a great example. Look - after the sale and on the red cloud test, POC formed a strong resistance, which beat off the price twice, which means we could have made profit.

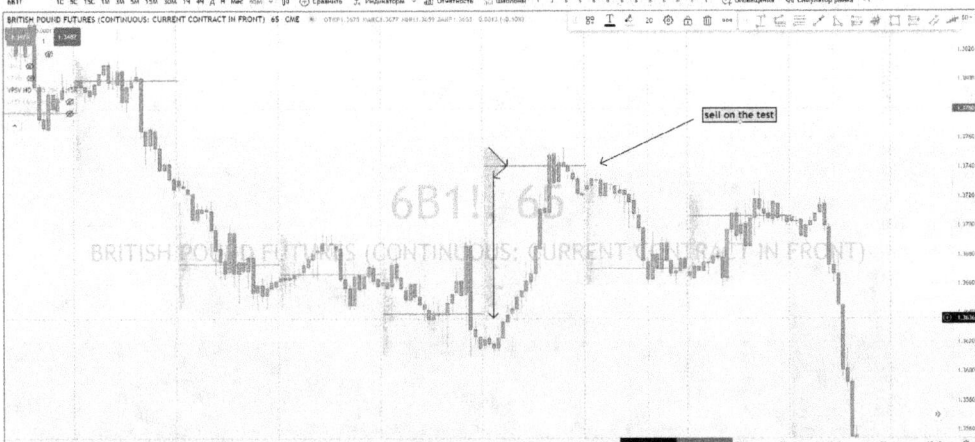

Here is a great example of how you can trade using only the POC levels, without using other indicators at all!

I suggest going back to our oil futures chart and adding this indicator.

Chapter 4. The use of indicators

Everything should be clear.

But I ask you to pay attention to the new levels of POC and working on them.

And here is how the P-shaped POC gave a powerful level, and the next day you could open a deal perfectly on its test. You see - the price moved in the other direction.

Chapter 4. The use of indicators

Here is a great example of sale on the POC level test. And the price moved down too.

And here is an example of how several levels line up in a row and form a more powerful double or tripple support level.
You should definitely expect a test and a good buy from this level.

Chapter 4. The use of indicators

And it's the same here, but already with sale. 3 profiles formed a powerful resistance and gave a level for retest sale.

4.7. Indicator of the screen visible area volume profile.

This is an equally significant indicator. It can also be used to easily find large horizontal volume levels.

P-shaped formations work here in the same way as on the profile within a day.

All in all, the meaning is the same, but the scale is much larger, which means that the levels are stronger.

This indicator shows the volume distribution on the visible part of the screen.

You can freely move the chart and see how the volumes are distributed.

Here is a great example of using the POC to determine resistance and subsequent buy.

Chapter 4. The use of indicators

I like using this indicator to determine entry points in a given segment of the chart.

Why look at the entire chart? It's not important to us! We are only interested in the last movement.

To do this, be sure to capture only the last price movement.

The profile will show you an important level from which you can continue to play.

Chapter 4. The use of indicators

4.8. Profile in the candle.

One of my favorite tricks is the entry on the POC level test in candlesticks of a large timeframe.

To see it, I left only this indicator in the settings and disabled the rest of the market profile.

The point is that there is no need to look for AZ of the Sellers or Buyers here.

We already have a ready-made maximum volume level in the daily candle. And this is a very powerful level, on the test of which we should look for the formation of AZs and subsequent entry points.

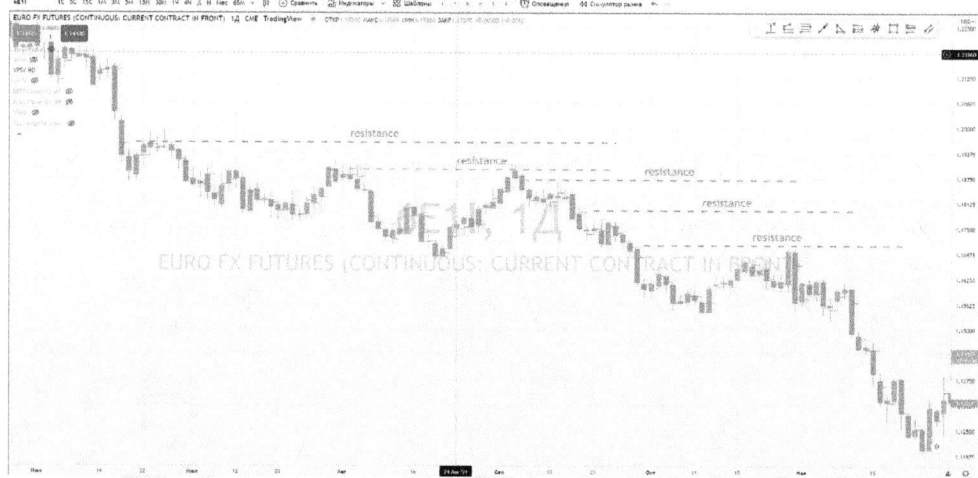

Look - I have marked 3 levels on the chart at once, from which it was possible to sell.

Chapter 4. The use of indicators

And here I have marked for you the levels from which it was possible to open a deal.
Study them!

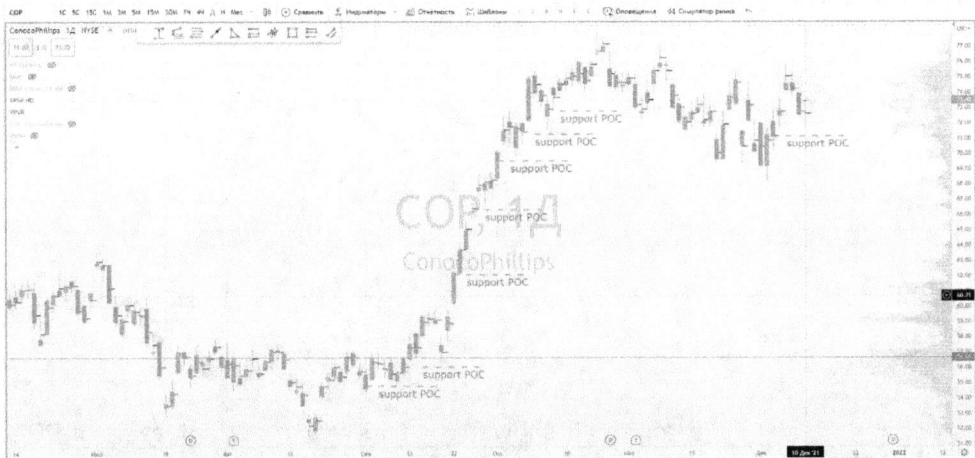

Look at how many supports were formed by this strong level I have marked. We could have opened a position directly on their test or on a smaller timeframe.

4.9. Using a fixed range

It is impossible to trade without this indicator at all!
It shows the POC level, which is so important to us, but on a certain section of the chart!
This is a unique ability, comparable to the AVWAP level.
If you want to see the volume distribution, just set an indicator!
P-shaped formations work here in the same way!

Chapter 4. The use of indicators

Let's examine them with the examples:

Look - I set the indicator and it showed me two very important levels of POC. Currently, the price is in the zone of uncertainty.

But, returning to our favorite AZ, the indicator showed an excellent level for searching for buys and sales.

The use of this indicator together with cluster analysis can serve as a basis for a dedicated book and a successful trading strategy.

Chapter 4. The use of indicators

Where should we look for the test without the indicator? It's unclear!
And with it? Everything is easier!
It should be used in the area we are interested in.
Namely, trades, AZ, descending and ascending movements.
Now let's apply all the indicators and knowledge that we have accumulated!

Look how nice it is.

- **We saw the huge AZ of the Buyer and, after waiting for the price to come out of consolidation, bought.**
- **We are watching how the price reacts to clouds. And we pull up the stop under the new low.**

Chapter 4. The use of indicators

- **We see that a flat has formed at the top and the price is being driven up and down. We are waiting for trading.**
- **We sell, after the price went below the POC level on the right, and this level became resistance.**

How do you like it? Can you smell the money?)

If you look closely, you can notice the resistance that is typical for this zone, forming the upper boundary, and the pull-up in its lower part.

Let me not comment on anything here!

Just look and you'll understand everthing. You already have certain experience in it.

And if you don't, then rush to my site www.richharbour.ru to boost your skills!

4.9.1. Vertical volume indicator, MACD, Stochastic

Of course, I also use the usual indicators with a delay. Such as the vertical volume profile, which will tell me exactly where the spike and climax were; MACD combined with Stochastic will tell me the entry point at their intersection. If you are already an experienced trader, then you do not need any explanations of how they work.

For everyone else, I'll show you some examples:

Look - in the first case, we received a signal only from Stochastic. But in the next two cases, there are already two stronger signals from the intersection of MACD and Stochastic.

Chapter 4. The use of indicators

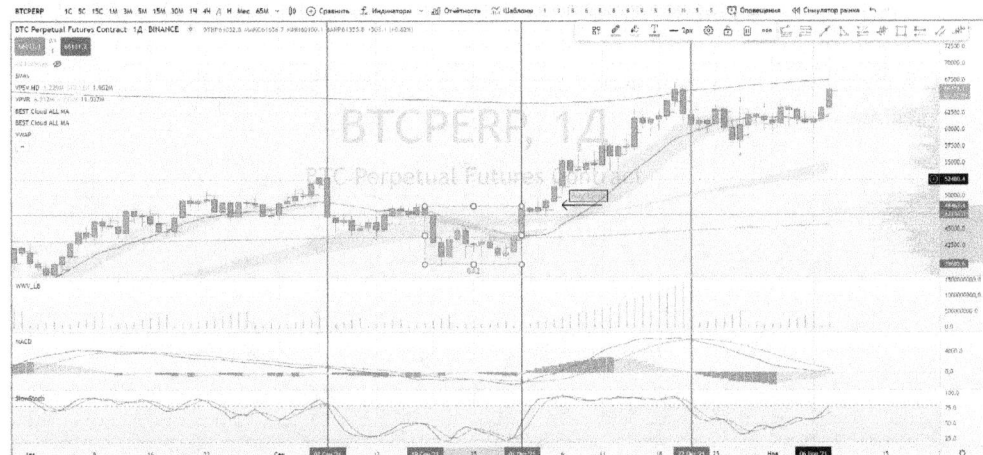

But by applying these signals within the entire system, we can filter and get one good buy point, which is in the middle.

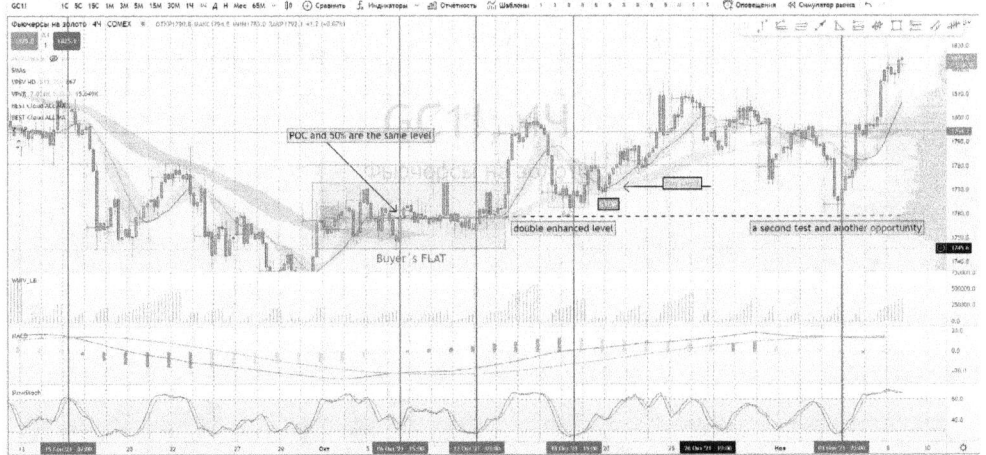

Here is another example of how well these indicators could be used together.

4.9.2. Climax.

This is definitely one of my favorite setups.
There are buy and sale climaxes.
It is marked by a sharp surge in volume at the end of the price movement.
It tells us that either buyers or sellers can no longer sell or buy. There's just no one to do it. Everyone is exhausted!
It's a strong reversal formation in the market.

Chapter 4. The use of indicators

We can see a tail, confirming the removal of all players and a sharp surge in vertical volume!

The level is very strong, and there are several ways to work with it.

See how the sellers have unloaded at this point. They collected all the buyers' limits.

Here is an example of trading. As you can see, we need to switch to a small timeframe. Determine the Buyer's AZ there and then open a deal according to our rules. And be sure to mark the level to the right for a possible touch.

> **Remember!**
>
> **The tail is a very strong level. And the price may slightly not reach its end and make an excellent entry pattern.**

Chapter 4. The use of indicators

> **Players almost always defend this level.
> There is a large accumulation of stops behind it!**

And sometimes the price can slightly tap the end of the tail.

Often, AZ will be formed after the climaxes. That is, in addition to the fact that you can earn on the movement after the climax, you can do it after formation of the AZ as well.

Don't forget to watch the newly released climaxes!

Here is a great example of oil trading. Look - the climax occurred at the top, the Seller's AZ was formed, and we could have waited for the test and sell with an excellent profit.

Chapter 4. The use of indicators

Well, in general, you should understand that the tails on the chart mean lack of interest from the parties. And there will be a reversal.

Do you remember the oil falling to minus marks?
This is how it looked on the chart.

And here is a newest sale climax of Bitcoin, which gave the opportunity to buy on 30 min. chart.

Chapter 4. The use of indicators

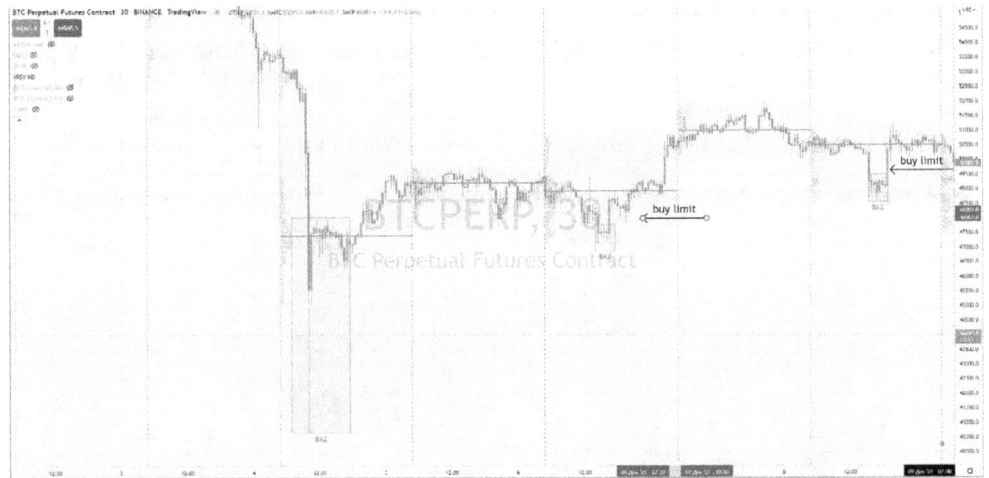

This is the image right after the climax and a recent trading plan.
I planned to buy after a breakout of local resistance or on a test of supports.

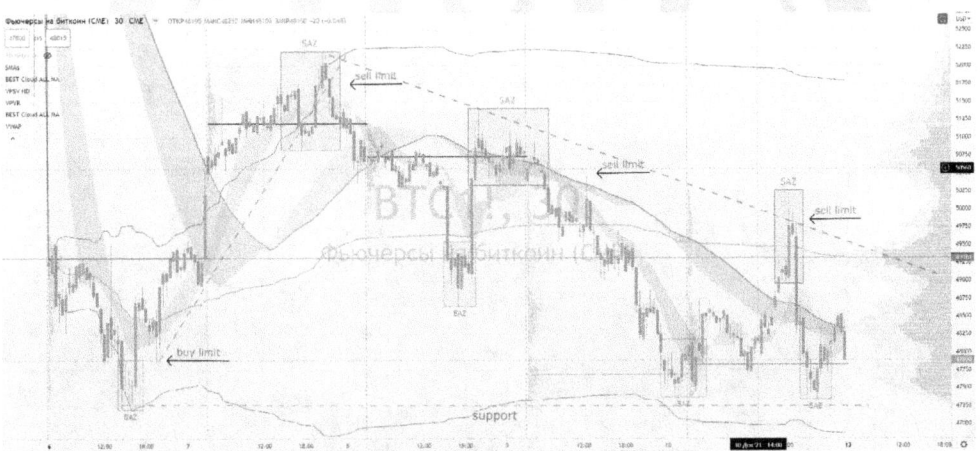

And that's what happened in the end. That's right, my students and I were trading during the climax of Bitcoin sales.

Since the candle before the gap down was red, it means that everyone who sold made profit and did not rush to close their positions. That means we should be expecting the continuation of sales. But considering that the price is on strong support even after the climax, I did not open short position. I waited for the formation of the Buyers' AZ and bought on its test. I was counting on the closure of the GAP. And that's what happened! I sold at its closing, which coincided with the AVWAP double level test. And as you can see, it was possible to sell more than once.

Chapter 4. The use of indicators

But most of all I want to draw your attention to how many times the price has tested the support level formed by the climax. As many as 3 times! And pay your attention to the picture. After the second test, there was already an attempt by buyers to break the downtrend.

At this point, I'm just watching and, as always, I'll join the strongest side!

CHAPTER 5.
Unscrambling and putting everything together.

Well, friends, I'm done with the highlights of TS. Or rather, with its technical part. In the following chapters, I will talk about the stocks I select and how I do it.

In the meantime, let's put our trading strategy together in your already tired head. I will just show my charts with final analysis and comments.

I will start with the largest timeframe and gradually, like a matryoshka doll, I will analyze the market in front of you.

Your task is to observe carefully and, if you have any questions, ask them me by email.

So, let's go:
Let's start with the pound-dollar pair.

In various sources, you will often see the ways for determining the trend. And in most cases, you will be prompted to use descending or ascending channel lines.

Like here:

Yes, you definitely need to use it.

But I'll show you another way!

It is absolutely important to understand that there is a concept of a timeframe of the higher and lower values.

That is why I start my analysis with the maximum possible timeframe, which will tell me the main priority and trend.

Your task is to find several unidirectional timeframes with the same priority at once. Thereby, you can significantly enhance your trade.

Chapter 5. Unscrambling and putting everything together

This is the key to success!
Do not stroke the fur the wrong way and against the higher timeframe!
If you have set sales on the daily chart, then you should not buy on 1 hour timeframe or less!
It is possible, but only with certain experience.

So, here is my step-by-step algorithm:
1. **Go to the maximum timeframe, in my case it is a Month;**
2. **We mark all AZs.**

The zones give us a hint about important resistance and support levels.

3. **Then we define all the levels that we see.**

The Smell Of The Cash

Chapter 5. Unscrambling and putting everything together

Not bad, huh?) So, what do we see and what do we need?

- Many levels of resistance;
- At the bottom, I see the first signs of a trend reversal. Namely, the formed large AZ of the Buyer after the climax of sales. Two AZs of Sellers form the resistance. This means that the formation of a flat is possible.
- It is very important to see the Seller's AZ that came out of the descending channel. This is an important point! The moment when the price leaves the figure, namely the triangle. Do you see it at the bottom?

4.   Now we begin to apply indicators.

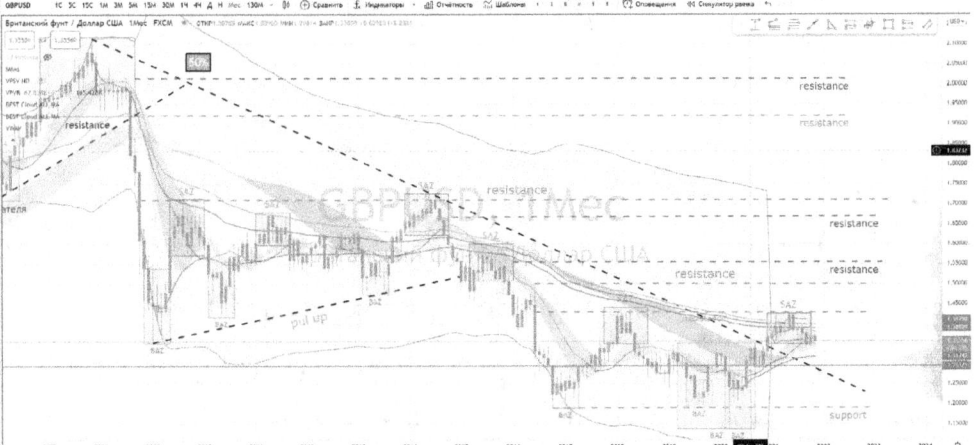

Namely, our favorite VWAP and AVWAP. And it is perfectly clear to everyone that the price is now testing a very important resistance of three guides dropped from different peaks. So, despite the price leaves the descending channel, it's still too early to buy!

We never buy when VWAP is the resistance!!!

Chapter 5. Unscrambling and putting everything together

5. And now we apply the remaining indicators:

What do we see here?

- The indicator of the POC horizontal volume level is at the bottom, which means that it is already the support.
- Clouds from the guides are already below the price too. Which means they are also the support.
- Preliminary conclusion - the price is squeezed between important levels.

FINAL Conclusion on the monthly chart of the pound-dollar pair.

**It is recommended to wait for the POC level test
and look for a pattern to enter buys there.**

**Or wait for the price to go above a strong level
from VWAP and AVWAP and buy there.**

**But you need to take into account the plenty
of resistances, each of which can stop the price.**

Let's move on! We turn to the analysis of the weekly chart of the pound-dollar pair.

But now we understand the exact area on the monthly chart where we work. When switching to a smaller timeframe, the area for analysis is significantly reduced. But it is necessary to remember the already defined buy or sell priority from the higher timeframe!

And again we move according to the same algorithm:

Chapter 5. Unscrambling and putting everything together

1. We determined AZ and levels.

And we immediately noted the Buyer's AZ, which is on the bottom right. It has a POC level. Why? Because there was a climax of sales there. Can you see the tail? The sellers unloaded there.

And from this zone, the price moved up very quickly. In such setups, the price is unlikely to fall on the test of the zone itself; most likely, the test will occur on the Buyer's AZ, which is higher. At least it would be good for an uptrend.

2. We applied VWAP

We made sure that it is under the price, which means that buys are a priority. And it would be nice to wait for a test of its level and buy on it!

3. We connect the other indicators gradually to see our picture.

By involving our entire range, we can see that price is both under the clouds and under the SMA's guide. So, we still have sales.

And we would really like to buy on a test formed from the levels of VWAP and POC.

According to the second scenario, which is worse for buyers, it is possible that the price will go lower for the POC test.

The FINAL CONCLUSION on the pound-dollar pair on the weekly chart:

It is recommended to wait for the test of an important level in the area of 1.32-1.3 and look for a point to buy there.

Or, if the price moves down, look for it in the 1.24 area

Chapter 5. Unscrambling and putting everything together

Well, aren't you tired?
That's how I see it on my PC. And I recommend you buying such a big monitor or preferably even 2 monitors!

We proceed to the analysis of D1:
This is already a truly working timeframe.

Now we are considering a smaller piece.)

So! Step 1

Everything is according to the rules. We marked AZ and important levels.

Step 2.

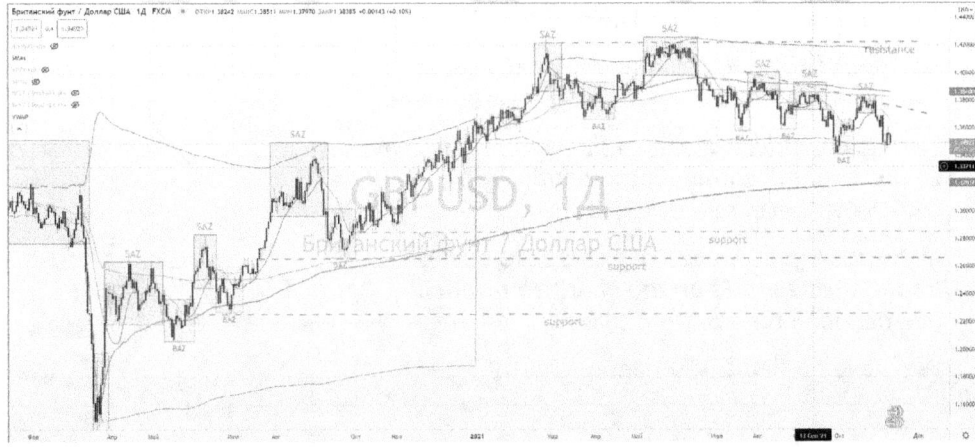

Chapter 5. Unscrambling and putting everything together

We added VWAP. We saw that it was exactly above the Sellers' AZ. So, there is the sell priority. And we note that the price is between two AVWAP levels.

But considering that there is a double level at the top, we can assume that sales are a priority.

Step 3.

Having added all the indicators, we see that the horizontal volume indicator does not have clearly defined boundaries. Only the POC level in the area of 1.2934 is of interest, but it is not as distinct as we would like it to be.

The intersection of clouds above the price says that we have sales.

The test of the lower boundary of the VWAP channel is confusing. A rebound is possible.

> **Final conclusion on the daily chart:**
>
> **The price is in a descending channel after the Seller's AZ test on the strong resistance.**
>
> **I would consider buys from the level of the lower edge of this channel and the intersection with the AVWAP level of the 1.32 area.**
>
> **If the price goes lower, then there are several important supports on the chart from which you can look for a pattern to buy.**

We move on to the 130-minute chart:

Chapter 5. Unscrambling and putting everything together

Step 1. We note AZ

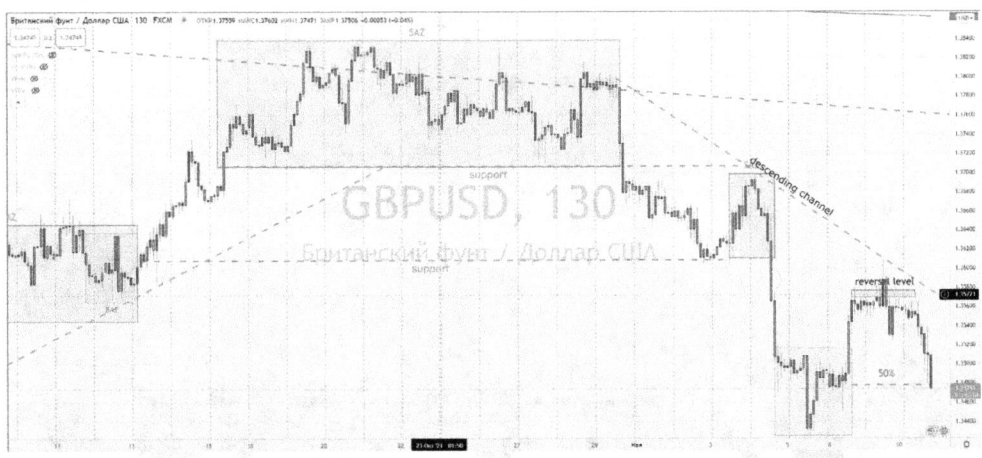

The ascending and descending channels are clearly visible.

Step 2. We apply VWAP

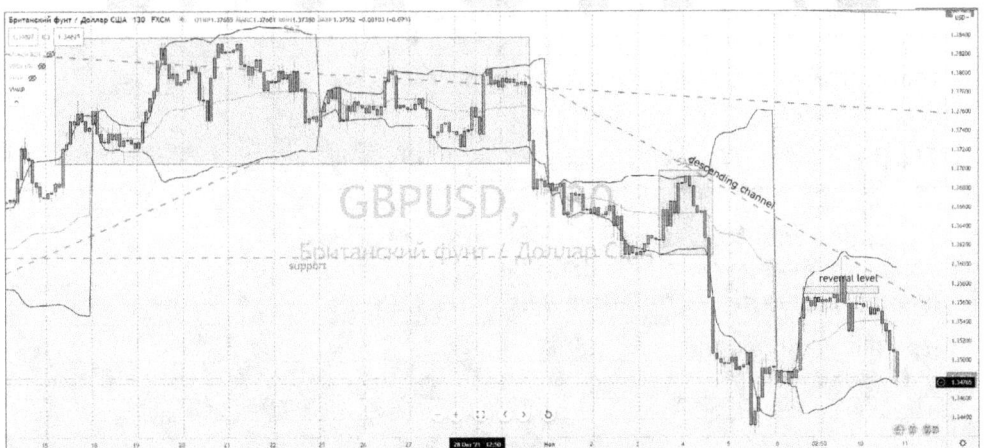

And we see that the price is just testing the VWAP level, which means there is a sell priority.

We continue to apply indicators:

Chapter 5. Unscrambling and putting everything together

And then it becomes obvious that the price is testing both the POC level and the clouds that are in the red zone.

So, we have sales.

> **The final conclusion on the pound on the 130-minute chart:**
>
> **The price is in the descending channel and below the POC level, but VWAP acts as a support. Both clouds are in the red zone.**
>
> **The price, having formed the Buyer's AZ in the area of 1.345, strengthened the support.**
>
> **The option with buys is possible only after the price goes above the POC level and the boundary of the descending channel on the higher timeframe, i.e. after 1.38.**

It's getting more interesting, right?

Chapter 5. Unscrambling and putting everything together

Let's move on to the 65-minute timeframe:

We marked the Seller's AZ and saw a downtrend. The Seller's AZ, which is higher, is much greater than the Buyer's AZ, which is lower. This means the distribution will be larger.

Step 2.

By adding VWAP, we see the support on the bottom. So, buys are possible, and the price may move up.

Step 3.

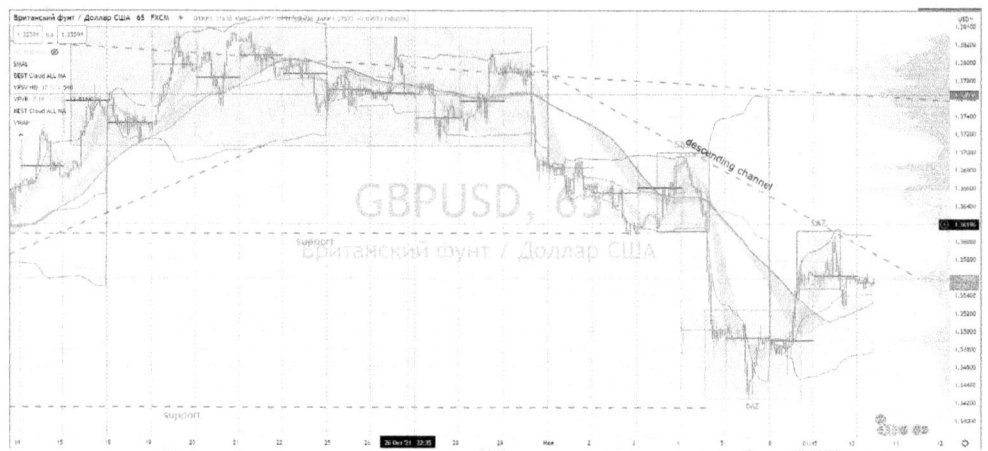

We see that the volume profile is high. So, it's pushing the price as a resistance. The clouds act as support.

We should expect the price to move up or down in order to test the Buyer's AZ POC, and perhaps we should look for buys there.

Step 4.

Adding MACD and Stochastic, we see that they gave a point to buy a little earlier. In the support test area. At the moment, their rates are insignificant.

Chapter 5. Unscrambling and putting everything together

Final conclusion on the 65-minute pound-dollar price chart:

The price has tested the upper boundary of the Buyer's AZ and VWAP; upward movement is possible.

But I would recommend buying after the price leaves the channel.

It is also possible for the price to move to the test of the Buyer's AZ POC, which is at the bottom of the chart.

And it would be a great point to look for buys.

We move further on the 30-minute chart:
So, here the chart is getting smaller and more interesting. We work with a matryoshka doll, don't forget it!

Step 1.

Two smaller AZs refer to the sellers, and the one larger - to the buyers. It's a descending channel.

Step 2.

We applied VWAP and saw that we had tested it. It would be nice if the price moved up.

Step 3.

The SMA guide still holds the price. Clouds are slightly below. To the right on the volume profile, I marked 3 important levels of support and resistance, from which a reaction is possible. As you can see, we are currently just at this level.

Conclusion on a 30-minute timeframe:

The price is caught between important support and resistance. It is at an important level of volume profile support. I would

Chapter 5. Unscrambling and putting everything together

recommend buying after trading the boundary of the descending channel or on the test of the POC level, which is lower in the 1.35 area.

So, we have come to the finish. Namely, the analysis of a 10-minute chart:

Step 1.

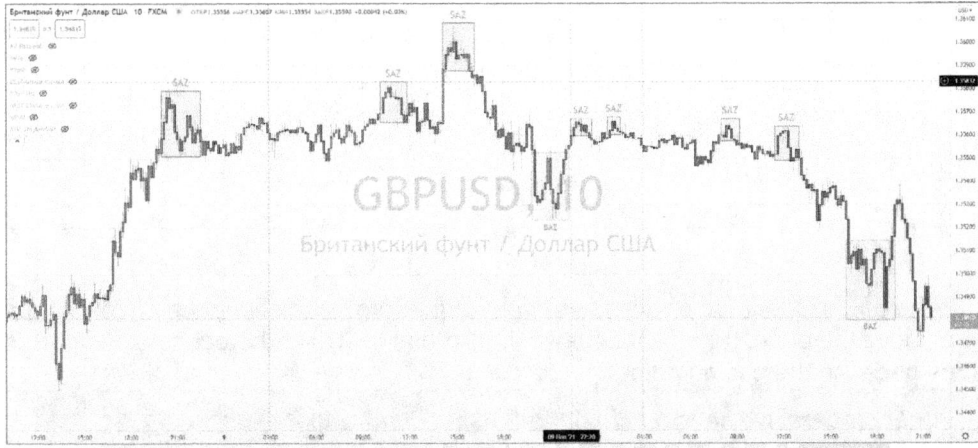

So? Do you see the formed reversal level of sellers? Capture of liquidity? What are we going to do on such a setup? We will sell!

Step 2.

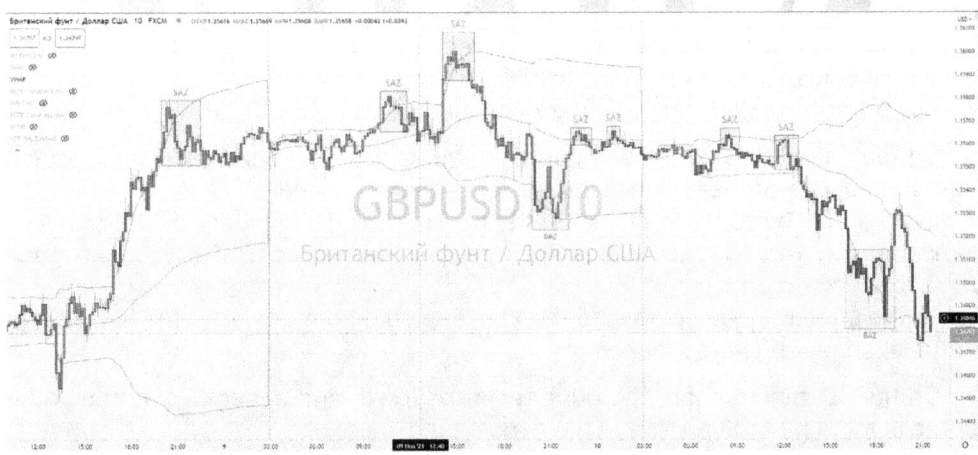

VWAP is already above the price, which enables to sell.

Step 3.

The guide is located above the price. Volume profile is above the price. Clouds are above the price. It's all about sales. I don't use MACD and Stochastic indicators here because there is no point.

Dear readers, we have reached the finish! I congratulate you.

Final conclusion on the pound-dollar pair.

**The pair is on a very strong resistance test in the 1.427 area.
At the moment, the price is going to test the POC level
on the monthly chart in the area of 1.35.**

**I recommend buying either from this area or after
a breakdown of the resistance, which is higher.
The points should be searched for on a smaller timeframe.**

On the 1 day timeframe, the price is in the descending channel. Having tested both boundaries of the channel, the price is still in the middle.

It would be better to wait for the test of the lower boundary of the channel, intensified by the AVWAP guide. But downward movement of the price is still possible.

Or the price may move up, and then buys should be made after the breakdown of the channel's upper boundary.

On the 65-minute chart, the price tests the lower and upper AZs. It should be borne in mind that the price is in the descending channel.

You need to keep an eye on the volume profile levels. They give 3 important zones.

I would recommend buying after breaking the boundary of the descending channel, or even better - after trading the level of 1.365. We would get the 1-2-3 pattern, which is good.

Chapter 5. Unscrambling and putting everything together

At the 30-minute chart, it is even more obvious that the price is squeezed between AZs. And they are of the same size.

At the moment, we need to wait.

I recommend buying after the Seller's AZ is traded in the area of 1.358.

This is how, dear friends, your analysis according to my TS should look like.

Here's what happened a few days later:

Our forecast worked perfectly. 3 declining highs were an excellent signal for subsequent sales. And it was possible to open a deal twice on the POC test of the previous candle in the area of 1.365 and 1.355.

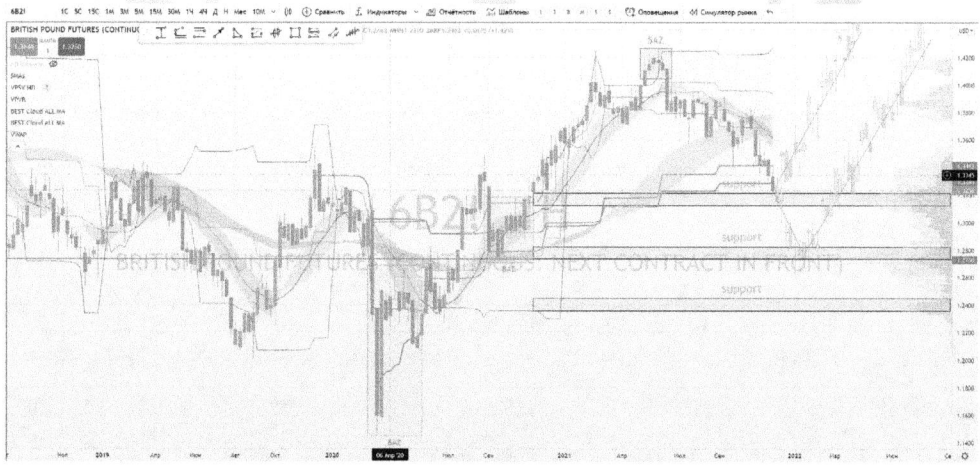

Within the weekly timeframe, the price is on the strong support, from which the price may move up. But it is possible that the price will move to test the support at 1.28.

Well, we would not want to see the price on the test of the support at 1.24.

I recommend that you once again carefully study all aspects and, if you have any questions, send them me through the website *www.richharbour.ru*

Chapter 5. Unscrambling and putting everything together

BTCPERP FULL ANALYSIS

And for the particularly curious ones, I have prepared one more review of the popular Bitcoin cryptocurrency!

Well, are you ready?
Let's go!
Monthly chart:

I didn't examine everything step by step here, because the candles are big.

But the Buyer's AZ is clearly visible on the test of the Fibo grid level and the VWAP.

This certainly indicates the upcoming growth of the pair.

The volume profile on the right shows support at 36,000.

Conclusion.

**The instrument is in the uptrend. A correction has occurred. After that, a 1-2-3 pattern was formed on the Fibo level test.
And the price renewed the high.**

Buys are recommended within this timeframe.

Chapter 5. Unscrambling and putting everything together

One week chart:

Step 1. We define the AZ and important levels.

More interesting details appear.
- Support at the level of 30,000;
- Buyer's AZ;
- Buyer's AZ that tested it;
- Seller's AZ, which has already been broken.
- And the important POC level is in the 62000 area.

Step 2. We apply VWAP.

As you can see, VWAP is a powerful support here. It means that we should only buy!

Step 3. We apply indicators.

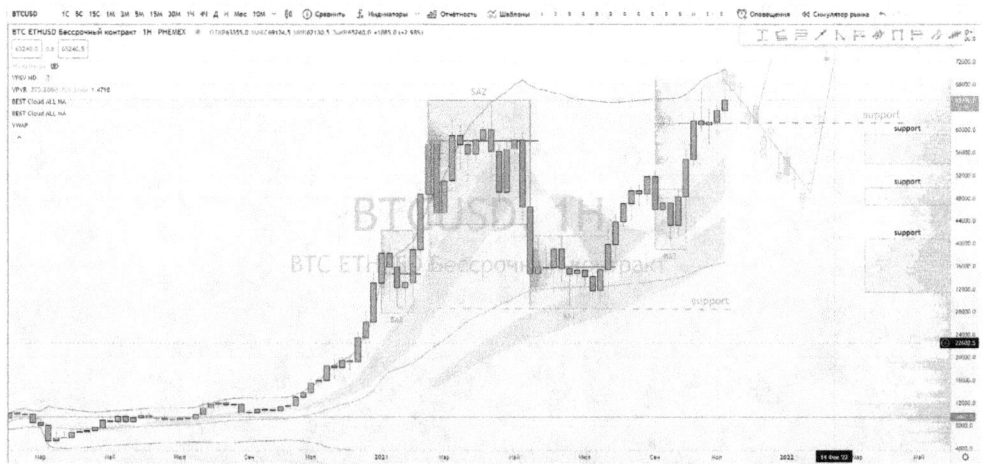

- The clouds have been down for a long time.
- Horizontal volumes are also a powerful support.
- The POC levels are at the bottom, which means they are also support.

Conclusion on the one week chart:

The price renewed the high, which indicates further buys. All the important levels and indicators are at the bottom, which also indicates the buys.

The only thing that happens quite often is a correction after the breakdown of the stops after the high. In our case, it can be in the area of 62000 or 52000. And it is possible that it is in the area of 48000.

Chapter 5. Unscrambling and putting everything together

Step 1. We move to D1:

Having marked the zones, we see all signs of an uptrend. Namely, the formation of a reversal level during reneweal of the high. Generally, it is a 90% successful signal. I have rarely seen such patterns break. Perhaps, only after the news is released.

Step 2. We add VWAP

Well, everything is unchanged here. We have buy priority.

Step 3. We add indicators.

- The clouds have been down for a long time.
- POC levels are also at the bottom.
- Horizontal support levels are also at the bottom.

Final conclusion on bitcoin on the one day timeframe:

The instrument has renewed the high. At the same time, it formed a fairly strong reversal level. I am almost sure that buys should be looked for right now on its test.

But the option of the price moving down to test the horizontal volume accumulation zones is not excluded. These are 52000 and 42000.

I recommend looking for a reversal pattern on the test of these levels.

So, friends! We analyzed the main and most powerful timeframes and came to the conclusion that we have an uptrend for the instrument.

So, if we work according to the system and want to strengthen our trade, we will only buy on smaller timeframes.

All sales that we will see there will be exclusively correctional in their nature.
And such sales are suitable only for more experienced and risky players!

Chapter 5. Unscrambling and putting everything together

Let's move to the 130-minute chart:

The zones are marked. DOes everyone now understand that this segment is exactly the reversal level from the 1 day timeframe, from which I expect the rebound?

And judging by the chart, i.e. seeing the tail, we can assume that the test has already taken place.

Step 2. VWAP

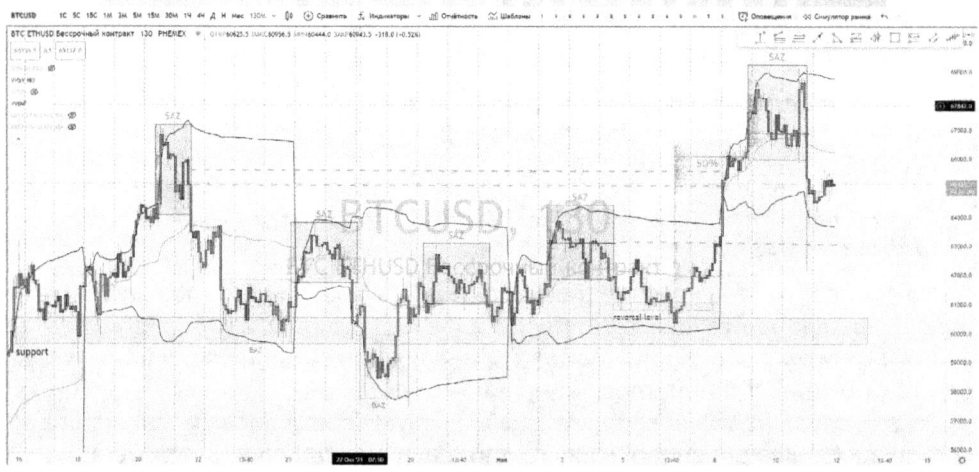

On this chart, we see that the indicator is above the price, which is resistance and indicates a prohibition of buys within this timeframe.

Chapter 5. Unscrambling and putting everything together

Step 3.

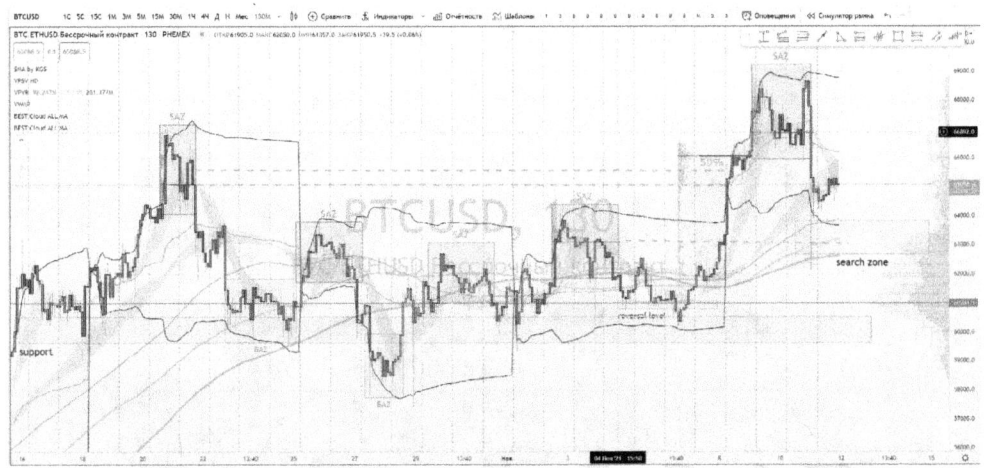

- Clouds are in the intersection, in a brown study
- All guides are slightly lower and support the price.
- And the horizontal volume POC is at the level of 61000.

Conclusion:

Obviously, the trend is upward. All the guides are below the Sellers' AZ, which is higher. Horizontal supporting volumes are also below. The only confusing thing is VWAP at the top.

I recommend buying with a 60,000 stop or wait for a more distinct reversal formation.

Chapter 5. Unscrambling and putting everything together

We switch to the 65-minute timeframe:

Step 1.

We marked all AZs and important levels. We see that the price is squeezed between support and local resistance. Pay your attention to the unusual setup at the top. It is the Buyer's AZ, which was not realized, and resistance was formed.

Step 2.

We apply VWAP. We see that it is at the top, so we have the sell priority.

Chapter 5. Unscrambling and putting everything together

Step 3.

Having added all indicators, we see that the clouds are above the price, the SMA guide is above the price too. Only the level of horizontal volumes is below it. And this is a very powerful level that has already pushed the price up.

> **Conclusion on the 65-minute timeframe:**
>
> *I recommend looking for buys on the support test in the area of 63000. Or open them after trading of the resistance in the area of 65600.*

Moving on to a 30-minute timeframe:

Step 1.

Chapter 5. Unscrambling and putting everything together

We mark all AZs and important levels. Now both local resistance and support are more clearly visible. We also see signs of flat formation.

Step 2.

By applying VWAP, we see that we have resistance, which means that the sell priority.

Step 3.

Having applied all indicators, we see that the clouds are above the price, and the level of horizontal volumes is at the price. The SMA guide is above the price. Therefore, we should wait for sales.

Chapter 5. Unscrambling and putting everything together

Conclusion within this timeframe:

I recommend waiting for the support test in the 63000 area and looking for a buy pattern there. Or wait for the breakdown of the local resistance in the area of 65000, which is unlikely.

Conclusion on Bitcoin futures.

Based on the uptrend on higher frames, I recommend buys. But corrective sales are also possible. Most likely, we should wait for a good correction to buy and stay there.

Look what happened a few days later:

    The price was corrected to the support level, which coincided with the level of the Buyer's AZ Lower Boundary, which happens quite rarely.

Chapter 5. Unscrambling and putting everything together

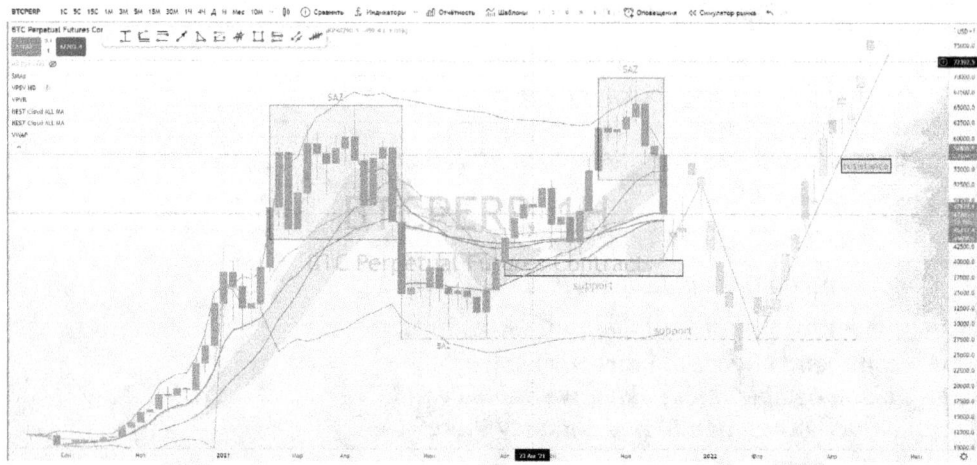

Within the weekly timeframe, the Seller's AZ was formed, which has not yet been tested. The level of horizontal volumes is already the resistance. So, it is quite reasonable to wait for a test of this level and sell. Moreover, the indicator guides have already been traded.

Apparently, we should wait for the price to move to the test of 50% of the Buyer's AZ in the area of $ 35,000 or even lower in the area of $ 27,500 and wait for the buys there.

And this picture was at the beginning of the 2022. My system works perfectly.

SO, FRIENDS!

I CONGRATULATE you on the completion of training in my system. I am sure that I have given you enough to make you feel confident and able to make good money.

> *But it is very important to secure the result by practicing with experienced traders on a daily basis!*
>
> *This book is just your beginning and the premise before something big.*

I also started from scratch many years ago and I did not know where to look first because of the abundance of information.

And take my word for it, if I had been shown this material I made for you 5 years ago, I would have been financially independent for a long time.

So, I'm waiting for you in my Private Chat every evening at the opening of the American session.

We will analyze your trades.

I will send you the most delicious and tasty morsels from my table. I really don't begrudge it, because I am very pleased to realize that I am making this world a little better!

ADDITIONAL MATERIALS.

TRADING OF REVERSAL PATTERNS USING OPTIONS.

This is one of my favorite strategies, because it is very simple. And I love simplicity)

I used to complicate matters unnecessarily and lost my money, but with experience, I came to the simplicity and became very productive.

So, do not overcomplicate and you will see the cash flow.

The tactic is to find stocks in the market with a strong potential for growth or decline with reversal patterns ready to go off. Find confirmation signals from the options market to help them do this.

I search for such stocks every day with the help of finviz and option activity scanner.

I use the following finviz settings:

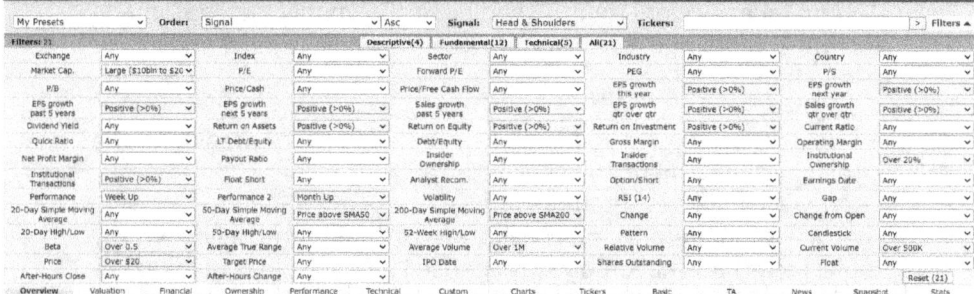

Of course, you can play around with the settings, but ideally you should look for a strong stock that can technically change the trend. And pay attention to the Signal field. I put the Head&Shoulders there. But I usually change signals to find a worthwhile stock.

And here are the settings of the option scanner:
- **The option premium should exceed $ 500 000**
- **The volume should exceed the open interest**
- **Options deep in the money should be excluded**
- **Search only for options outside of money**
- **Only co-directional movement with indexes**
- **Preferably, with a relative strength index of more than 90**
- **Preferably, above ask or bid**
- **Preferably, single-leg options, i.e. not spreads and butterflies.**

Here is a good example:

Additional materials

In the option feed, several large trades on TSLA took place at once.
I immediately realized that this was a bullish signal and switched to the chart

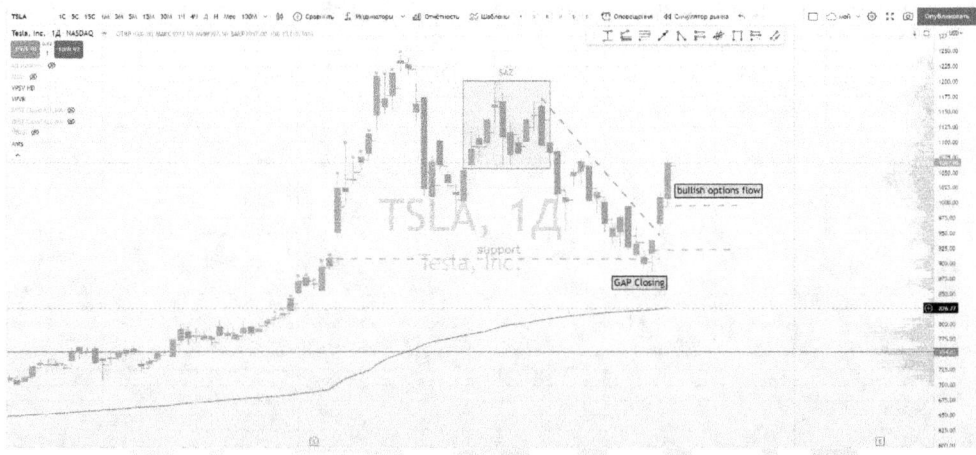

And this is where the wonders of technical analysis happen. Namely, the GAP was closed, the descending channel was broken, and the market was flooded with about 10mln with a strike above the spot price.

In this example, support became a reversal moment, and the option flow became the signal.

Here is the same day for CRWD:

In the option feed, there were two bullish signals at once about buying a call with strike outside of money and selling a put with a strike below the spot price

I immediately rushed to look at the chart:

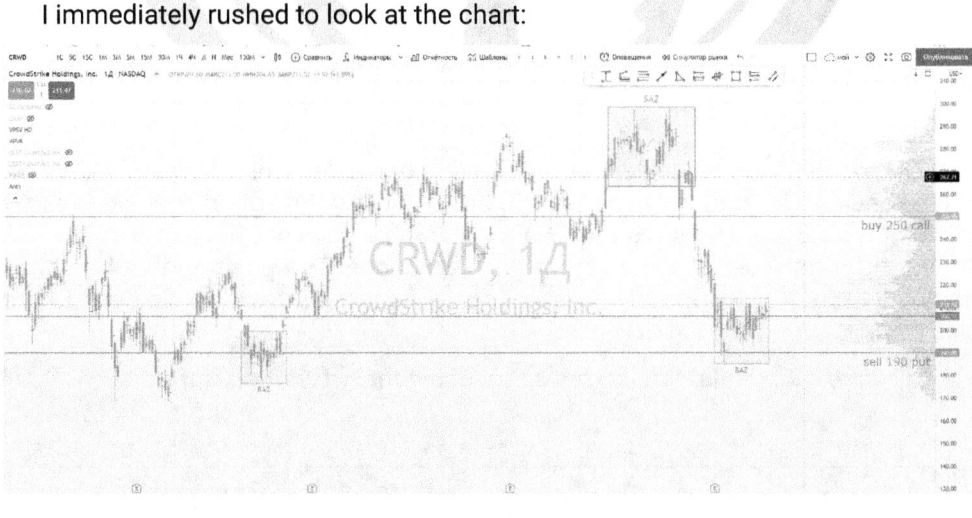

The Smell Of The Cash

Additional materials

And here is a great picture suitable for our conditions. A new Buyer's AZ was formed on the support test, which is undoubtedly a reversal factor, and a bullish option mood will only strengthen it. As a result, a great trade with a high level of stop loss and take profit.

And here is an example of a trade that is not worth taking:

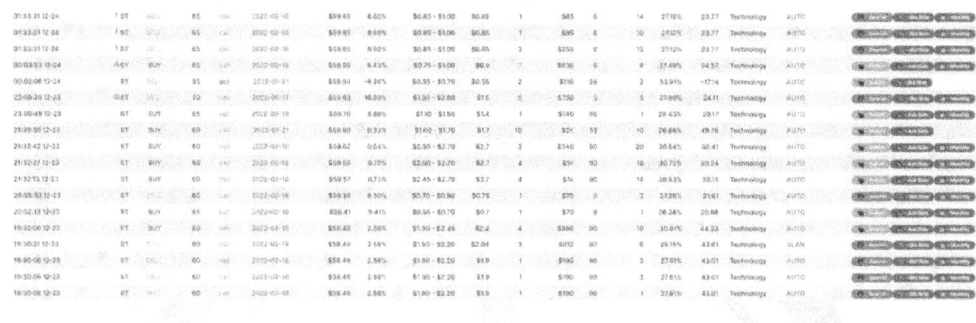

Look, on the chart we see an excellent cumulative flat, which looks like it will be traded and the resistance will be broken. But looking at the option flow, we see that it is empty. There are no big trades. So this example does not fit our criteria.

But it fits the rule of breaking the flat resistance. The position that has been spinning inside it for so many days will surely bear good fruit. So we need to put this stock in the watch list.

As I said, it's simple! You just need to follow the rules of selection.

THE PRINCIPLE OF TRADING ACCORDING TO THE INDEX.

When making a decision, you should keep an eye on major indexes such as the SP500 and Nasdaq.
And when trading cryptocurrency, you should follow the situation with Bitcoin.
These instruments should become markers for you.
What do I mean by that?

> **You should follow the principle of unidirectional trading according to these markers.**
>
> **That is, buys or sales with all instruments should be made in the direction the marker moves.**

Here are the examples:

Bitcoin has been falling for the last few days, which means no buys in the entire cryptocurrency market!
Yes, there will be a few coins that will live their lives, but this is the exception rather than the rule.

Look - the same movement happened on Ripple:

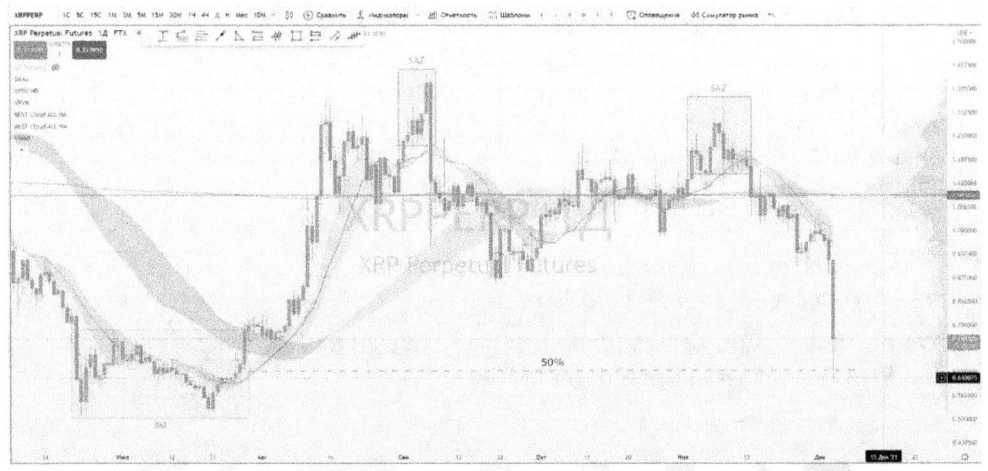

And on Doge:

Additional materials

The same rule applies to the stock market. In recent days, the main indexes have been falling:

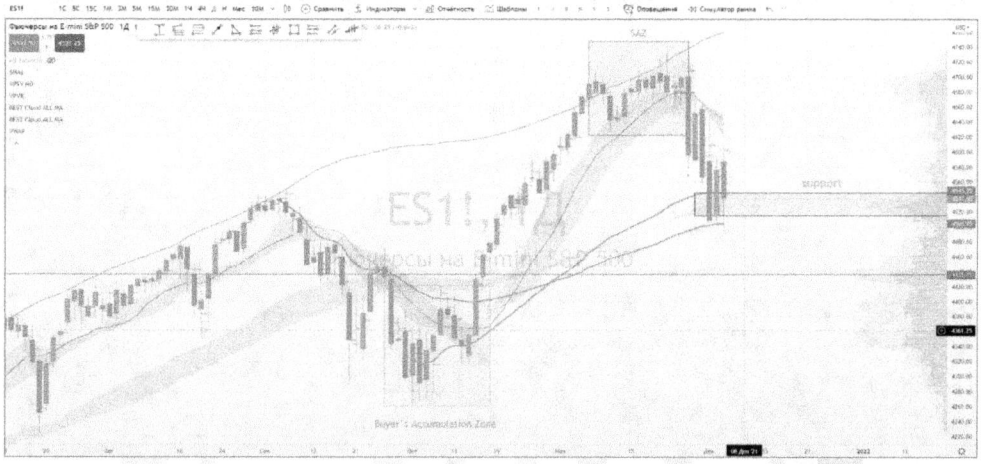

The SPY index has fallen to strong support and is testing AVWAP.

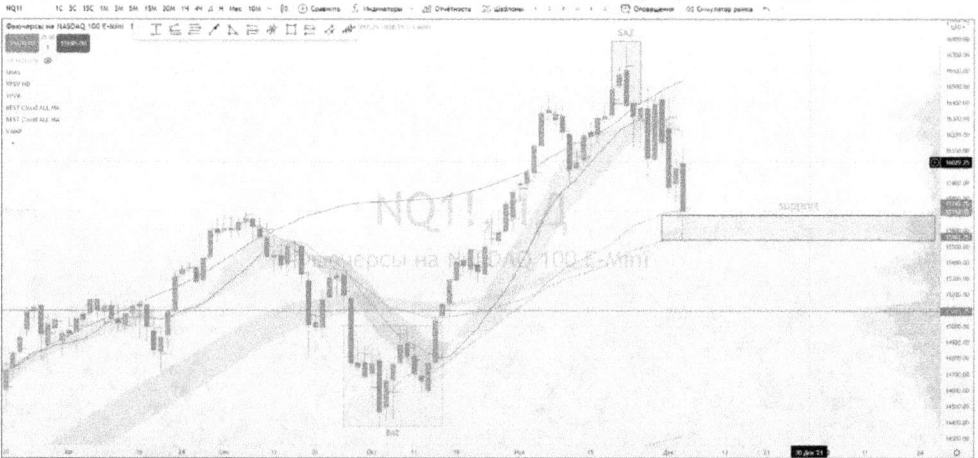

The Nasdaq index did exactly the same thing.
You will observe correlation of these indices in 99% of cases.
But I want to tell you that, in these days of correction, we should look exclusively for sales in stocks!
And especially in the stocks that are included in these indexes!!!

Additional materials

Here, look:

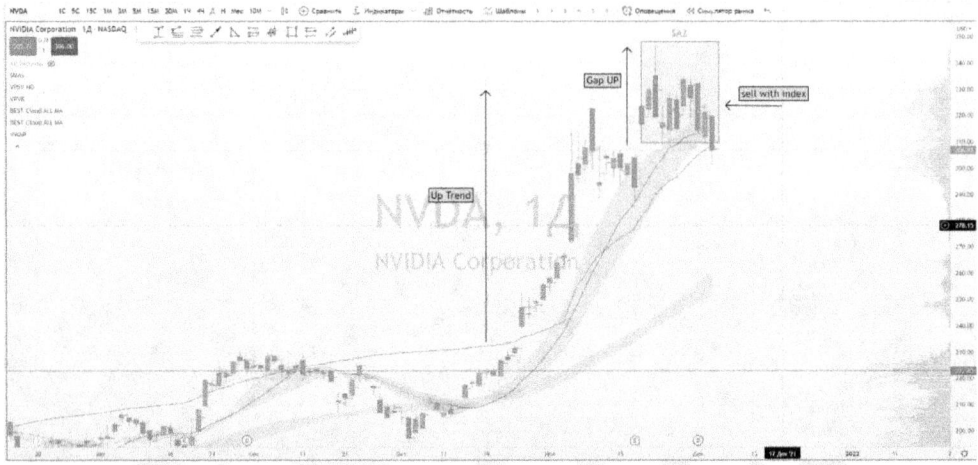

NVDA stocks, despite a strong uptrend and a Gap Up, still fell along with the indexes.

And here are the stocks of Apple, one of the market leaders. And look - they also followed the main indexes.

Remember!
Always follow the index.

And remember that there are only a few stocks in each index that move the entire index. These are the so-called FANG Stocks.
Facebook, Google, Netflix, Amazon.
These are the 4 stocks that move the market. Just imagine.

Additional materials

And these stocks will copy the movement of the index as well:

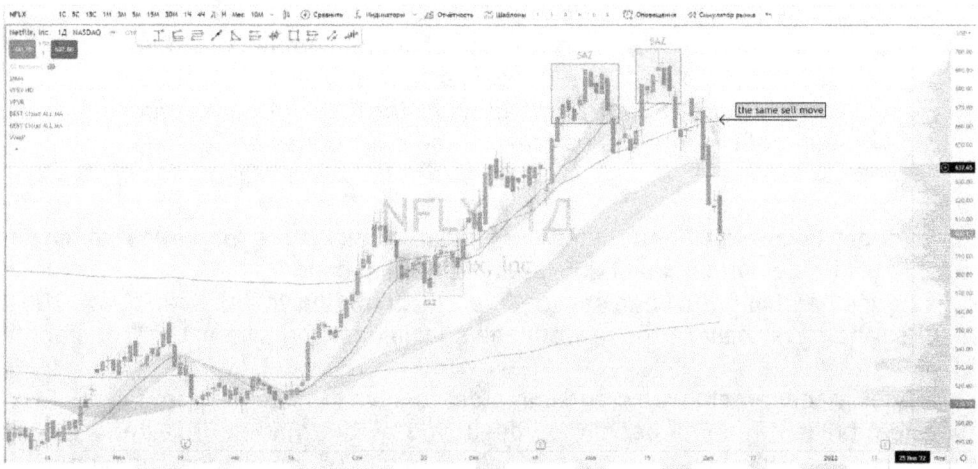

You definitely need to keep an eye on them!
But since they are very expensive, not everyone can buy them.
Therefore, use them as markers and trade on other, cheaper stocks.
Look - the same sell priority was observed on stocks with a much lower capitalization:

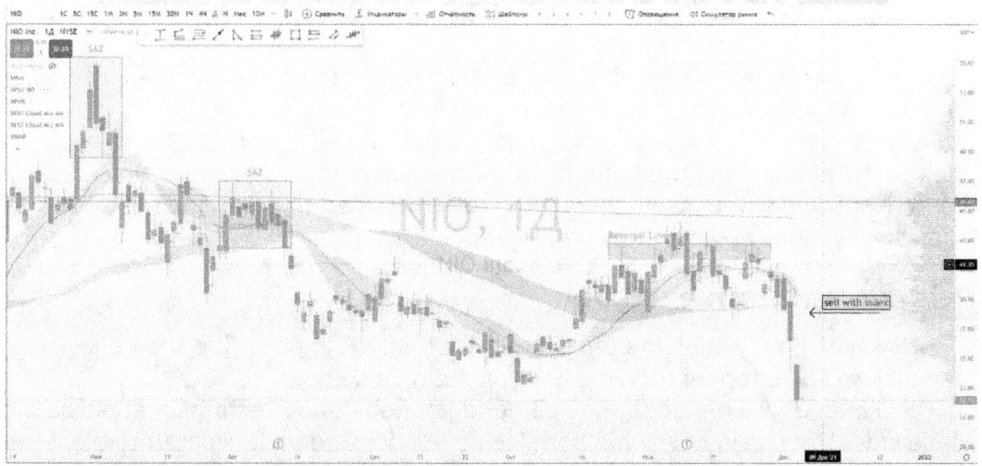

FUNDAMENTALS WHEN CHOOSING STOCKS

The market leader is not the biggest company and the most popular brand. The leader is a company that has the best quarterly and annual profit growth, the best price/earnings ratio, profit margin, sales growth, and price behavior.

William O'Neill

So, today I want to talk about how to choose stocks in the market. What stocks provide the holder with at least 80% confidence in success?

Yes, you heard it right! I can say for sure that in trading you just can't have 100% results. And never believe those would-be specialists who give a 100% guarantee of success.

Money management was created in order to save the traders from failure. Even the most brilliant idea can easily be destroyed by the market. It is important to remember this. Only naive simpletons believe in a 100% result, opening a position with a 50% deposit.

Relative strength

What is meant by the concept of "relative strength"? This means that in a falling market, the stock is holding up better than the corresponding index or is growing at a faster rate in a raising market.

The key principle of my trading is that the best return will be provided by buying the stocks that have the greatest relative strength.

At the beginning of a new trade, I sometimes take former leaders in order to analyze them, study the pros and cons. I don't see anything reprehensible in such a practice. But it's not worth spending a lot of time on this, because you need to invest in new leaders who show greater growth.

Relative strength example

As I have already said, the term "relative strength" implies that the behavior of the stock will be stronger than the corresponding index.

This concept will be most relevant during periods of corrections and pullbacks of the index. Its use is advisable both inside the day and on low timeframes. If the index makes a pullback, it is important to look for stocks that continue their growth or pull back, but at a lesser rate than the index.

In such situations, I always say that the stock does not want to fall, there are not enough sellers in it, or it has already been oversold. The stock itself does not want to fall, but it is forced to decline due to the pressure of the broad market.

The idea is that when the market turns up again, the stock showing relative strength will grow at the maximum rate.

This principle works in the opposite direction as well: relative weakness is lagging of the stock behind the index. Sometimes it happens that the index moves up, but a certain stock, for some reason, falls or grows slower than the index. This can be a sure signal to either withdraw profits or trade the stock short in a bear market.

The concept of "wedge-shaped movement" is often used. It refers to a situation when a stock rises to the maximum, but then falls down. This continues for several days in a row: there is no real upward movement together with other stocks. This is very disturbing. This sign indicates that, for some reason, buyers do not want to raise the stock higher.

Volume

Volume refers to the activity of trading a particular stock. When you see a volume that is noticeably larger than usual for a given stock, it is a sign of institutional buys. A small investor should look for stocks in which institutions are picking up positions in order to join them and participate in a big movement.

Therefore, when large volumes come across your eyes, take a closer look at them and look for the entry with minimal risk.

Stock idea.

The growth of the stock happens when there are more buyers than sellers. There are many reasons to buys the stocks. One of them is the idea or theme of the stock. Long-term investors often invest in the future of stocks as they imagine it. If the prospects are promising, then the number of buyers grows. The company's task is to meet or even exceed the expectations of investors.

If it succeeds, then the stock growth will be long and strong. It is also worth noting that a strong idea will provide investors with confidence during periods of pullbacks during the upward movement.

Some examples

The main topics of recent times include transition to digital technologies, remote work, green energy, e-mobility, as well as work on platforms:

- *Topic: E-Mobility and Green Energy (Tesla: TSLA)*
- *Topic: Transition to home gyms: (Peloton: PTON)*
- *Topic: Telehealth (Teladoc: TDOC)*
- *Topic: Work from home (Zoom: ZM)*
- *Topic: E-commerce (ETSY, PINS, SHOP, AMZN)*

- *Topic: Cloud Technologies (FSLY, NET)*
- *Topic: Cloud Security (CRWD, ZS)*
- *Subject: Freelance (FVRR, UPWK)*

Sales growth

The companies that showed the biggest stock growth in history increased sales by 25 percent or more per year. The conducted research demonstrates that sales growth projects the future behavior of stocks as accurately as possible.

If a company has the opportunity to increase its revenue, then it is quite capable of changing the distribution of costs in order to achieve maximum profit in the future. Therefore, the main indicator for finding market leaders is revenue growth.

Profit growth

According to statistics, the market leaders have a high profit growth. Peter Lynch explained his idea in the book "Strategy and tactics of the individual investor." In this book, he outlined the idea that, in the long term, the dynamics of quotations is directly correlated with the level of earnings per share. The principle of "the higher the better" applies. The point is quite clear: if a company puts all its energy into generating revenue, its stocks will naturally rise. The more it earns, the more the quotes increase.

Trade what you know

Remember: you should trade what you know. When you find a strong stock with good profits and sales volumes, relative strength and a fresh and relevant topic, and you understand it well - this is the perfect combination, the best idea.

High beta and liquidity

I advise everyone follow my example and deal only with the most liquid stocks, because there are clearer movements in them. I need to be able to open/close a position with minimal slippage, because my system uses different signals and is not about "buy and hold." Usually my choice falls on securities with daily trading volumes of at least 1,000,000. This is important for the uniform behavior of the stock.

It's hard to put into words, but I literally feel when the stock behaves correctly. If there is no such feeling, then I do not trade it.

In addition, the stock should have a high beta index, so that if a strong trend is found, the price can make a big move in a short period of time.

Avoid cheap stocks

There is an opportunity to make a good profit on cheap stocks BUT only if you are right. If you make a mistake, you can lose a lot. It's important to me to keep the main capital safe. Therefore, I never deal with stocks that have a price less than $ 10. I usually prefer securities with a price of more than $50.

Most financial institutions have rules that do not allow them to trade stocks, the value or capitalization of which is less than the established level. I want to rely on the support of institutions in the process of trading.

It is worth noting that mathematical models are often used on Wall Street to analyze the stocks. They are not suitable for the fastest-growing stocks. Such securities can show spontaneous results and go further than the model predicts.

I believe that new brands and innovative companies are much better understood by today's youth than professional analysts, hedge fund managers, and graduate financial experts.

This is a significant advantage, by means of which you can successfully select stocks for long-term growth. The renowned Wall Street professionals will not be able to plant doubts in me if the price behavior, the opinion of my key analyst, and consumer sentiment clearly indicate the opposite.

It should also be noted that the classical evaluation parameters are not very suitable for emerging companies are currently exposing our lives to radical changes.

I prefer to be on the same wavelength with the trade. At the same time, I try not to pay attention to the falling knives. Therefore, I advise trading stocks that have been in the trade for a long period of time.

The trick is not to know for sure what stocks will do next, but to know what they should do. Buy only the stocks that are at the distribution stage.

Selection criteria.

There are 13 criteria you should always keep in mind:

- The price is above the 150 and 200 day moving average.
- 150 moving average is above 200 day moving average.
- 200 day moving average is under the price for at least a month or more.
- 50 day moving average is above 150 and 200 moving averages.
- The current stock price is at least 25% above the 52-week low.
- The current stock price is within at least 25% of its 52-week high.
- The relative strength rating of RS from Investors Business Daily is at least 70 (preferably about 90). Thus, the RS line should not be in the downtrend for at least 6 weeks of upward movement.
- The current stock price is above the 50-day moving average.

- When the cost moves to the distribution stage, there should be large volumes that indicate the interest of major players.
- Option activity.
- Good news as a growth driver.
- A positive powerful movement in the sector to which the stock belongs for at least a month.
- Alignment with the main indexes.

The trick.

Remember! We should be like a stick fish that sticks its mouth to the shark's body and eats what is left.

We don't have enough money to move the market. But we have the knowledge that allows us to find sharks.

NOW LET'S TALK ABOUT RISK MANAGEMENT

This chapter probably should have been put at the beginning of the book, because it is very important.
Without following these rules, it is impossible to succeed in the market.
But it's easy to lose all money!
Let's first make terms that you should never trade using using borrowed, credit, or any other money that does not belong to you!

> *I do not risk more than 2% of the deposit amount in 1 trade.*
> *And many gurus do not risk more than 1%*

Think about these figures now, please. Professionals with many years of experience do not take risks. They competently diversify their trades. Believe me, any trade can let you down, even if it is 100% correct in your opinion. And if you opened it with a large lot?

Why do you need this? The market provides excellent opportunities for work every day. Several dozen first-class trades can be found every evening.
And get the result like this:

Or:

Additional materials

NOW AS FOR CALCULATING THE POSITION SIZE.

I told you that I do not open a deal of more than 2% of the deposit.

But how to calculate the position size? How many stocks are there at a particular stop?

The answer is simple – you can use mathematics or special utility software.

Since I am a fan of tradingview, I use its trading panel on a demo account equal to my real account.

And every night in my Private Chat I start trading with a demo deposit of $100K. And all my subscribers can see the daily results on my website.

This is how the panel looks like. It is quite easy to use. You should simply determine the direction of trade and set the risk for a trade. In my example, it is 2% or 27 contracts with a stop of 1.14285. By changing the stop size, the platform will also change the position size.

Look at this:

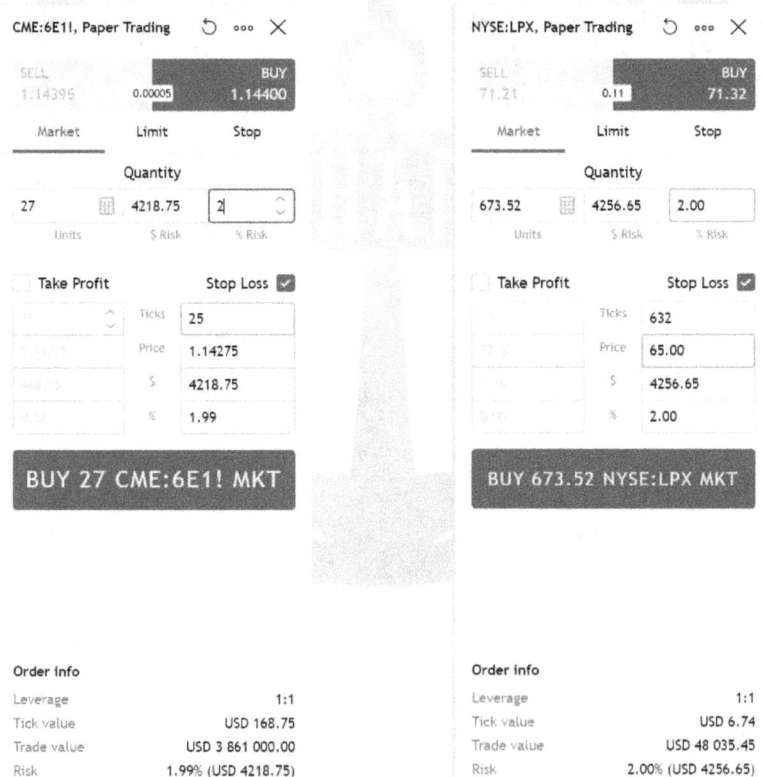

With a stop of $65, I will be offered to buy only 673 shares.
I highly recommend this tool!

The Smell Of The Cash

Additional materials

NOW AS FOR HOW TO SUPPORT THE TRADE.

It is not enough to find and open a trade; you should skillfully support it afterward.
But at the beginning of this book, I said that trading is easy!)))
And this is really the case when you accumulate certain experience.
I support my trades or pull up my stops on new accumulation zones along the way of the stock movement.
Let's examine it with the examples:

Look, I opened a deal at the resistance breakdown and set a stop under the local trading, because I knew perfectly well that the price was unlikely to return there.

Additional materials

Now look, I've pulled up the stop under the local support.

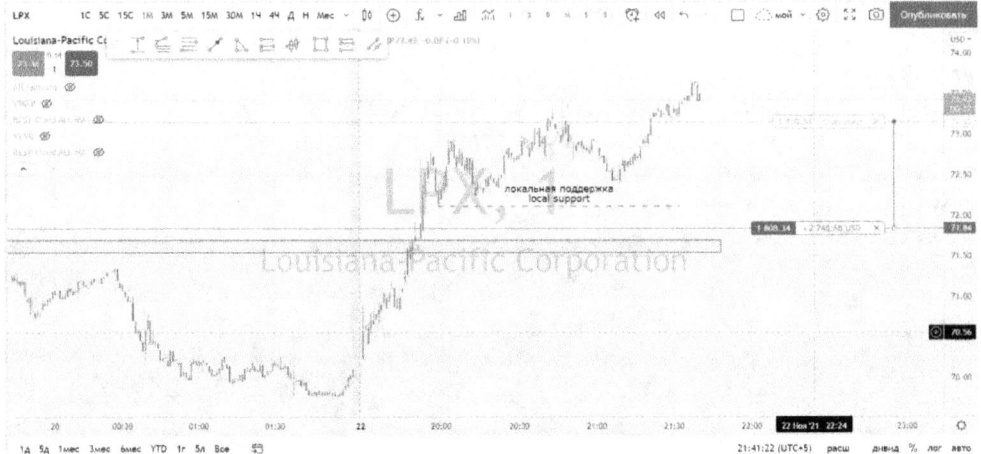

And here's the result it brought me after only 30 minutes. And pay your attention to how I pulled up the stop again.

It is very important not to constrain the price with a stop, but to let it breathe, because the price will be corrected during its movement.

When trading under the control of ATAS, I use the big trades indicator, which accurately identifies a major player who first opens a position and then closes it.

Simple charts and platforms do not enable you to see such moves.

SETTING A TAKE PROFIT.

A correctly set take profit level is less important than the correct stop loss level.

I use several reference points to set it:
- Lower or upper boundaries of the Accumulation Zone
- 50% level of the Accumulation Zone
- VWAP test
- AVWAP test
- POC level test
- Test of the maximum horizontal volume
- Resistance or support level test
- SMA guide test
- Profit taking after formation of a new divergence, convergence.
- Profit taking when a large option position of the opposite direction is detected.
- On fibo levels.
- At the climax

I often divide my take profit into several parts as the price moves, which is logical, because it is necessary to let profits flow and take at least a piece from the market, if not the whole pie.

I apply full profit taking when waiting for important news, during formation of reversal patterns, emergence of a large option counter-trade, a 200MA test.

Here are the examples:

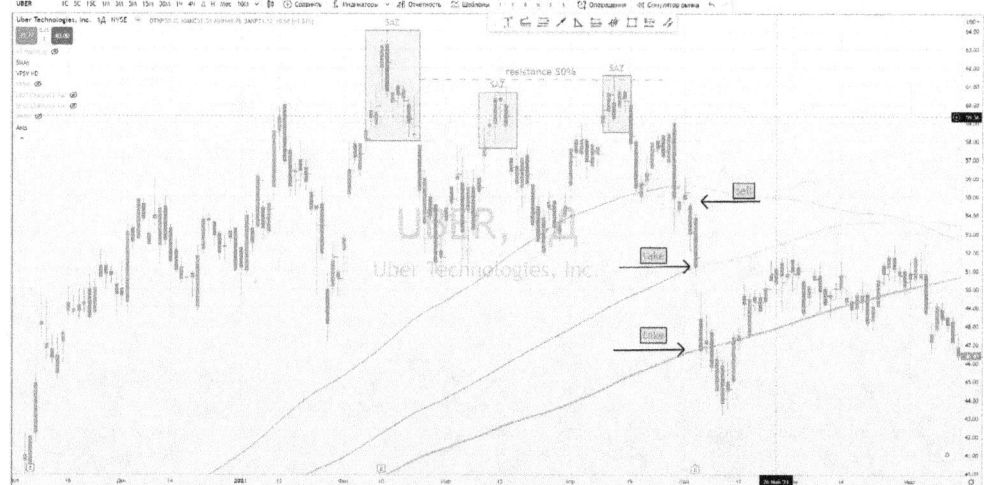

Additional materials

Here is an example of partial profit taking on the tests of two guides.

And here is an example of taking profit at the test of Seller's AZ lower boundary.

Additional materials

Here's how you could have taken profit on a test of 50% of the Buyer's AZ level.

An excellent example of taking profit on the test of the maximum horizontal volume level.

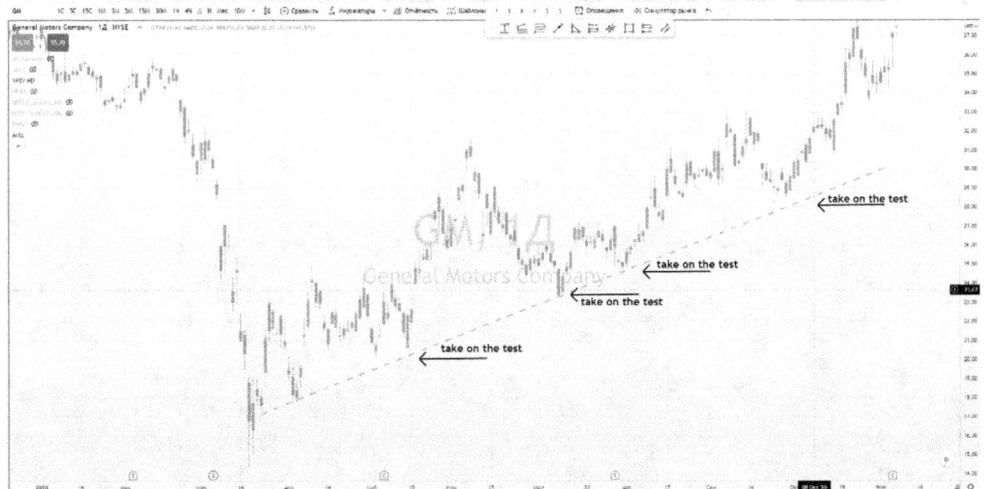

Additional materials

It is a great example of how it was possible to take profit multiple times on the test of the ascending channel lower boundary.

Naturally, take profit should be set according to the trading plan. That's how I would act in reality. Of course, I would buy on the test of the descending channel lower boundary and would do it when VWAP is under the price.

Here is an example of profit taking on the VWAP test.

Here is a great example of profit taking at the resistance level. Please note, as I said earlier, levels are not an exact concept and very often it is better to close a position either a little earlier than the test, or after a new AZ has formed, placing an order under its boundary or the next candle after the engulfing candle. Or to switch to a smaller timeframe and work there.

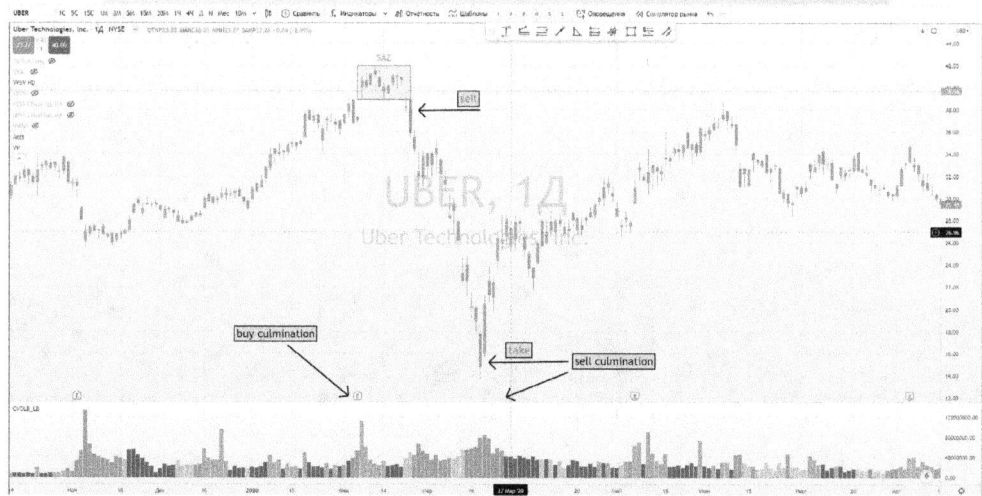

An example of profit taking at the selling climax.

Additional materials

The trick.

You should understand that profit taking is not always a reversal of the trade in the opposite direction. More often it is necessary to simply take profit and stop and look for the entry point only after analyzing the situation!

See how well the fibo level has worked as a take profit for selling.

Take a closer look at the divergences of the price and Stochastic. Profit taking of buys should have been done after detecting the divergence and immediately after the engulfing candle.

Look, after a long rally, there was a large put option buy transaction of $ 2 million in the option scanner. This stopped the movement and created a correction. This is where it was definitely important to take profit.

Additional materials

TRADING ON DIVERGENCES.

I started my trading career with trading on divergences and convergences. And, honestly speaking, they are still a very informative method of trading.

The principle of getting the signals is related to the divergence of price and indicators like Stochastic, MACD, and RSI.

This divergence is a result of imbalance in the market.

And the signals received in this way are reversal or correction.

The zones from which the movement began as a result of the divergence will perfectly beat off the price in the opposite direction during further testing. Always mark them and wait for the price to come back to make a good profit.

> **The rules for finding the divergence are very simple.**
> **In order to determine it, it is enough to have at least two ascending highs on the price chart and two descending highs on the indicator chart. Visually, it looks like a divergence.**

Let's find some divergences:

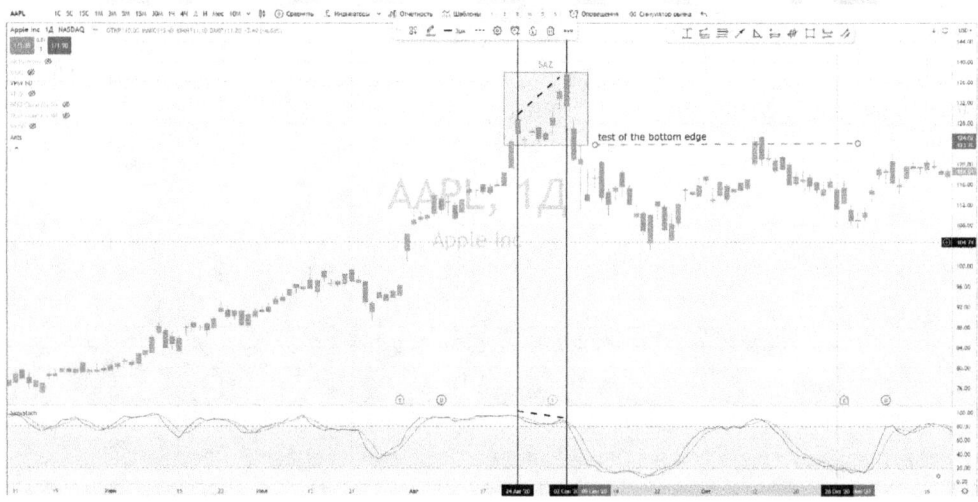

Pay your attention to how the points of highs and lows diverge on the indicator and on the chart. This is a sure sign of a reversal. Having marked such a zone for yourself, you just need to wait for the test and join sale.

Additional materials

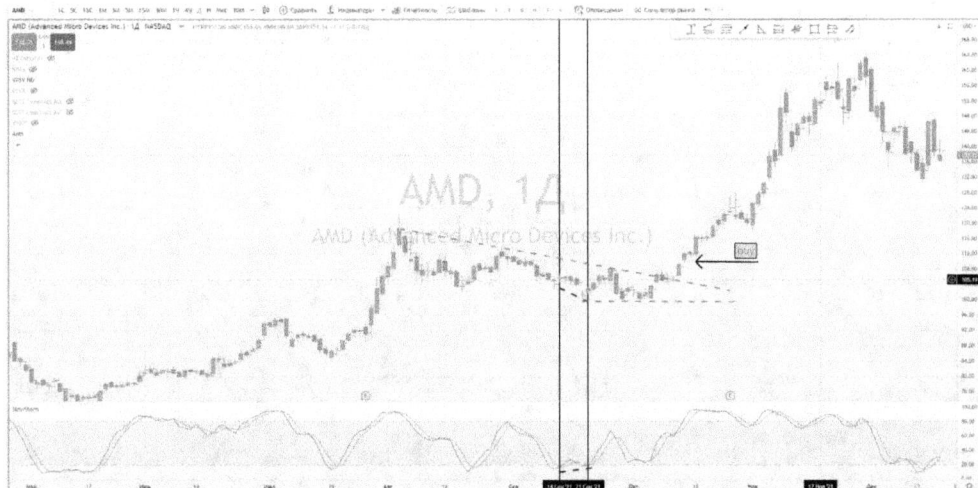

And here is the convergence on the correction, which indicated that another upward impulse was about to begin.

In trading, convergence means convergence of the price chart with the indicator chart. That is, when each subsequent low is lower than the other on the price chart and higher on the indicator.

There are several entry algorithms:

Additional materials

Determining the AZ by divergence and then implementing the correct entry technique after its test. It is more reasonable to set stop loss here not under the low, but under the test.

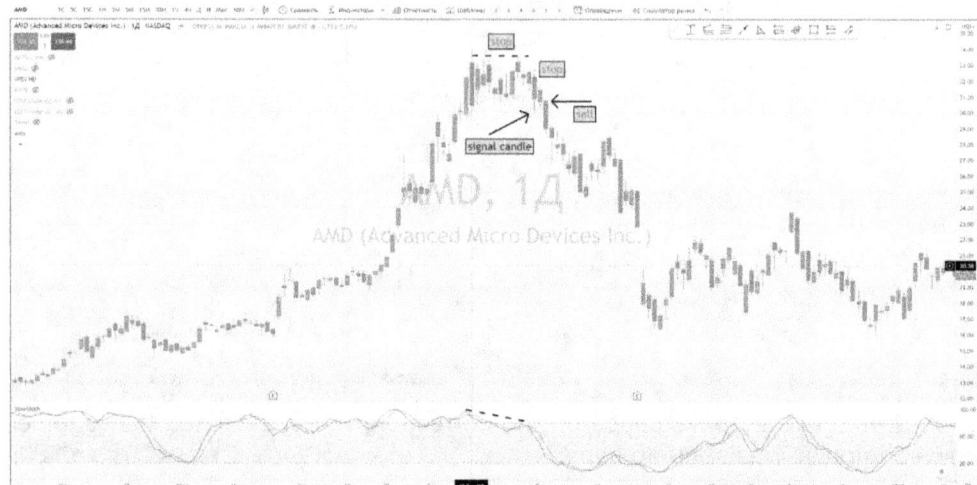

You can open a deal by a signal candlestick, which follows the divergence detection and engulfs the price by breaking the local support. Stop loss is set either after the high of this candle or after the extreme point.

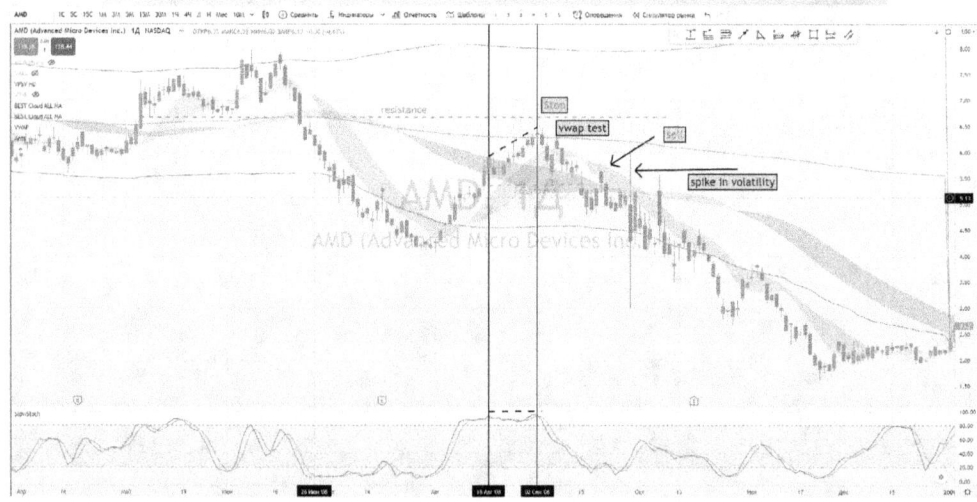

And look at this interesting case. Several elements of the system that indicate a price reversal coincided. Firstly - the resistance test, secondly - the VWAP test, thirdly - the divergence. The perfect sell! These are the points I post in my Private Chat.

Additional materials

Pay your attention to the surge of volatility, which would knock you out of a great position if you pulled up the stop. Always let the price breathe. The price needs a space for moves.

When detecting divergences, you should always use only the nearest points to connect, and not several points or points at a long distance.

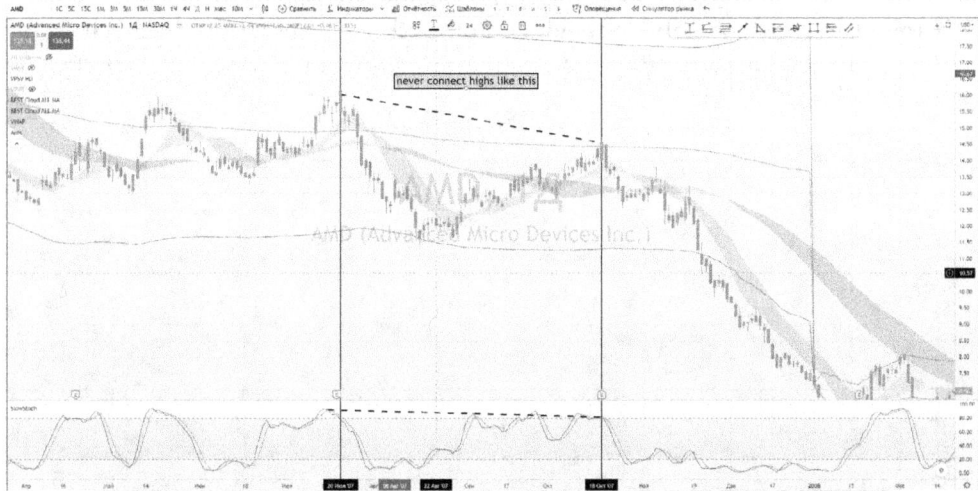

Here is an example of a wrong connection of highs on the chart and the indicator. Of course, it is obvious that the search for divergences and convergences can be carried out on any timeframe. It's just that the indicator settings need to be changed to faster ones. On the daily timeframe, I use the standard settings. But when trading within a day on a 3-minute timeframe, I use "9" and "3" Stochastic settings.

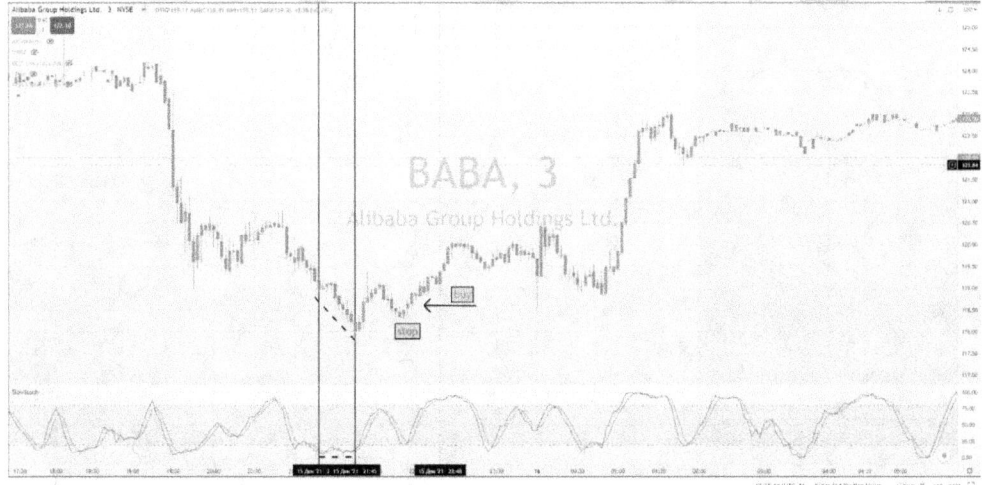

Here is a good example of an intraday buy after the convergence.

As you can see, even trading using only this simple strategy can bring substantial profits. And using this knowledge as part of my trading strategy significantly strengthens it.

Remember the 70% of successful entries at the beginning of the book? This became possible thanks to the synergy of all elements within the system.

Gradually studying each element separately, you will surely soon learn to apply all the elements at once and see the market with the eyes of an experienced predator sitting in ambush.

Additional materials

THE FIRST TOUCH RULE.

I derived this rule simply from many years of experience observing charts.

I noticed that if the price touches an important level or zone several times and the second and subsequent touches are below or above this level or zone, depending on the buy or sell priority, then this indicates cancellation of the scenario.

What I mean:

Let's say we wanted to buy BABA after the fall. We found the Buyer's AZ and opened a deal at the first touch of 50% of the level. According to the first touch rule, the second touch should be either at the same level or slightly higher, as in our example. Because if the second and subsequent touches are lower, then this will prompt you to close the deal with the least loss. In this case, the second touch in the form of a new Buyer's AZ was slightly higher and the trade took place.

The Smell Of The Cash

Here is an example:

Look, 2 touches were a bit higher than the first one, while the subsequent ones hit exactly the level, which, in theory, should indicate its strength and the price should bounce down. But that didn't happen. Therefore, be careful whenever you see such setups.

Example of the correct second touch:

Ideally, you should get such a picture. Thus, pay your attention to the large sales before the setup suggesting that they should continue. And why you should not pull up the stop early, but rather move it to breakeven. But I would recommend partially closing the position as the price moves.

Additional materials

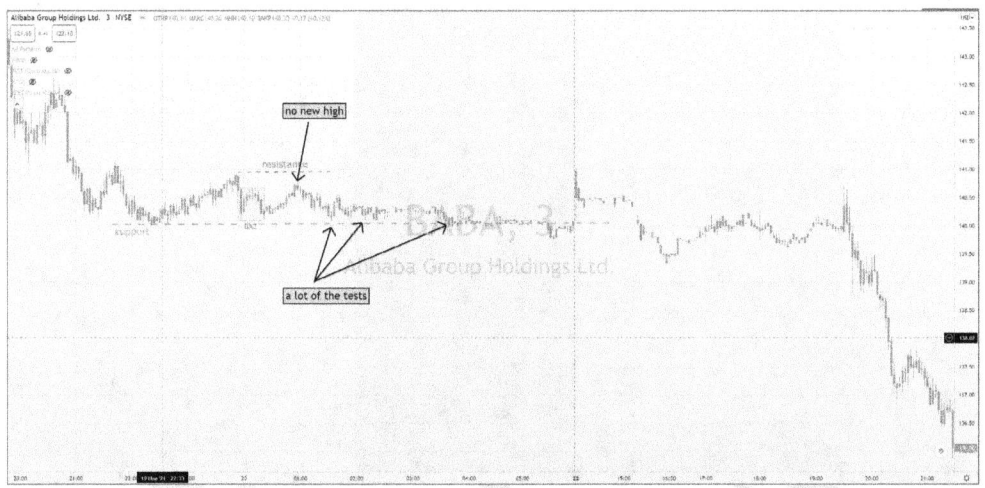

Also, the many support tests after the failed high renewal should be alarming. Basically, after formation of the Buyer's AZ, we should wait for its test and buy at the breakdown of the local resistance. But this did not happen, which certainly indicates the weakness of the stock.

Look, in the first case, everything went as planned. If we had bought at the Buyer's AZ test, we would have made profit by closing the trade after the Seller's AZ was formed. But in the second case, after 1 touch, the high was not renewed and the resistance breakdown and the second touch were lower than the first one, which would indicate cancellation of the buy scenario.

And here is an example of how to look at the situation in context and not in small parts. If the price is on the strong support, then the first touch rule does not apply, because the support beat off the price and holds the level. In this example, 1 touch was followed by several other that were slightly lower, but as a result, the support resisted and it was possible to buy.

The first touch rule also applies for normal transactions. Like here, for example. Look, it is very important to make sure that after the rebound from the resistance, the price touches a little lower and does not move to the top, which would indicate cancellation of the scenario.

TRADING ON GAPS. ADVANCED VERSION.

Trading on GAPS is certainly an interesting and profitable process. I know traders who do nothing but that. And they have achieved great success.

> *A GAP is a gap in the price on the chart caused by increased volatility as a result of the released news or for another reason. As a rule, it occurs on the Monday after the Friday market closes. That's why many traders close their positions on Friday. Simply pulling up the stops is not enough, because they will not work due to slippage, and you can lose most of the deposit.*
> *It can be either the Buyers' or the Seller's GAP.*

Here are the examples:

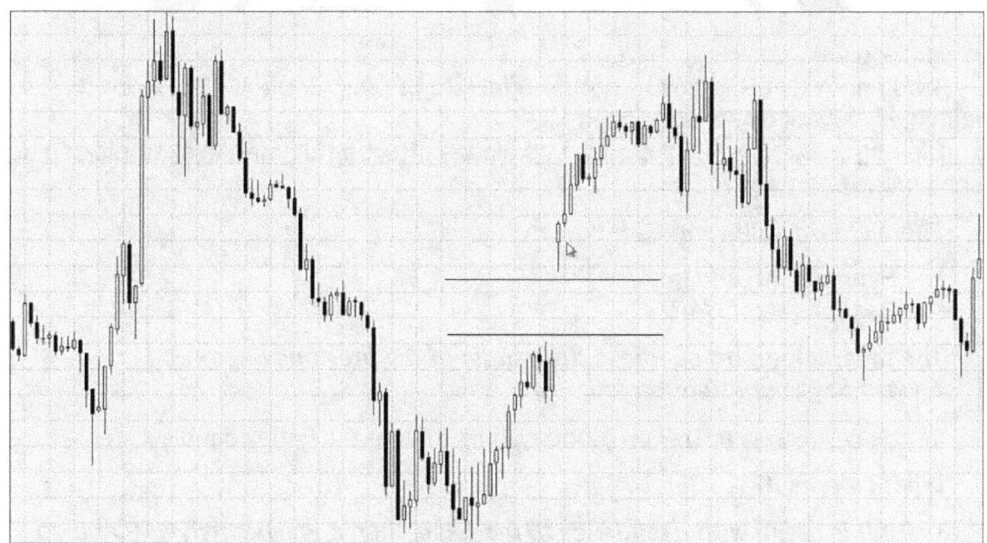

GAP up

GAP down

Trading on GAPS is based on the principle of closing the GAPS. According to statistics, 90% of GAPS are closed.

Closing a GAP is when the price gap closes after some time. An example can be seen in the chart above.

There are the following GAP types:

- Bearish GAP and go,
- Bearish retest GAP.

The most important candle is the candle of the previous day. Always pay your attention to it.

Let's say you saw a GAP on Monday, then look at the Friday candle.

What color is it?

- **If it is green with a tendency to increase, then it is a bearish GAP and go**
- **If it is red with a downward trend, then it is a bearish retest GAP.**

In the basis of trading on GAPSS, it is important to answer the question - WHY?

Why did the gap go downwards when the previous candle is green with an upward trend?

You should understand that if the candle was green, the traders have probably bought there and these buyers are now suffering from losses. Because GAP went down!

And what do they do to get rid of this pain?

That's right - they close their positions, which will lead to an upward pullback of the price, and there will be a retest of the level from where the GAP occurred or to the level of the nearest resistance.

So our tactic is to wait for this retest and opened a position with a small stop, counting on the continuation of the price decline.

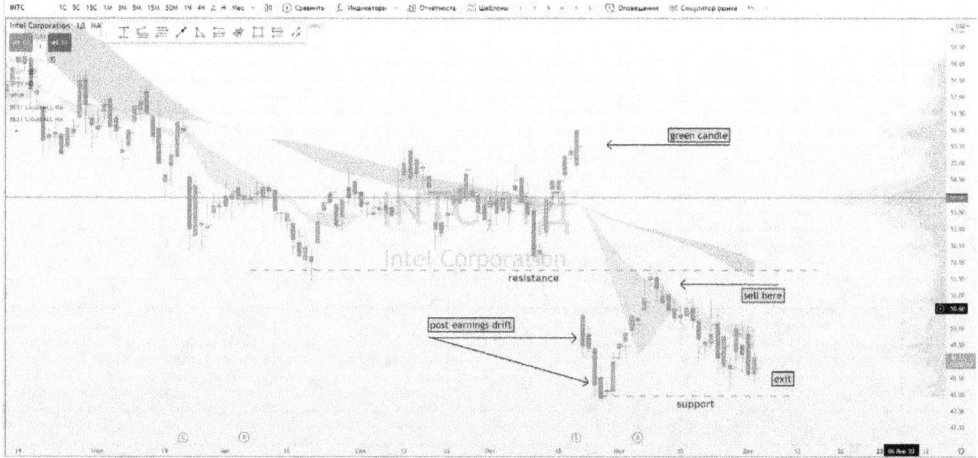

Look at this interesting example. It is non-standard, because it occurred on the report. Do not forget that after the report, the so-called Post Earnings Drift occurs quite often, and the price moves away for a few more days. And that is what happened. In theory, taking into account the rules of the system, a retest of the resistance level should have taken place right on the first day. But this did not happen because of the negative report.

But, as you can see, it's okay, you could safely wait for the retest in a few days and open a position.

Additional materials

Here is another interesting case. I do not know why, but it's a fact that the price will almost always test the resistance, which is closer and with high accuracy. In the figure, I marked two resistances. As you can see, the first one worked.

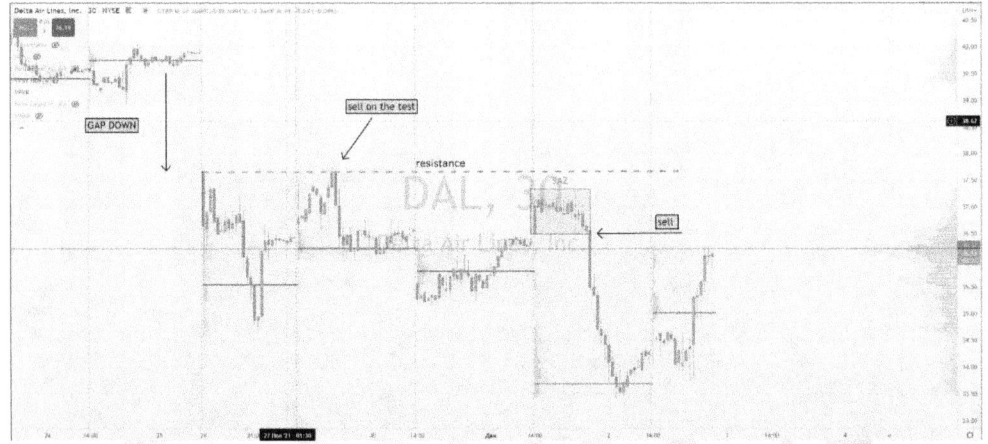

You will also often encounter strong resistance over the first candle after the GAP. Look - it was possible to sell with a very short stop twice after the GAP Down on DAL.

Additional materials

BEARISH GAP AND GO

Another option is when the candle of the previous day was red with a downward trend. Which means the traders must have been selling there.

And, therefore, today these sellers are happy, because they have earned great money by doing nothing.

This means that no one will close their positions, but rather, on the contrary, more sellers will join.

And, consequently, the price will run even lower.

In this case, our tactics is to set a sell order under the low of a new candle for a breakdown, hoping for further downward movement.

Here you can see a vivid example of how the price ran lower after the GAP, because the candle of the previous day was red, which means that everyone who sold did not want to leave and remained in position. Therefore, there was no retest. It was possible to open a position on the breakdown of the daily candle low. But it is better to do it on a smaller timeframe.

Like this:

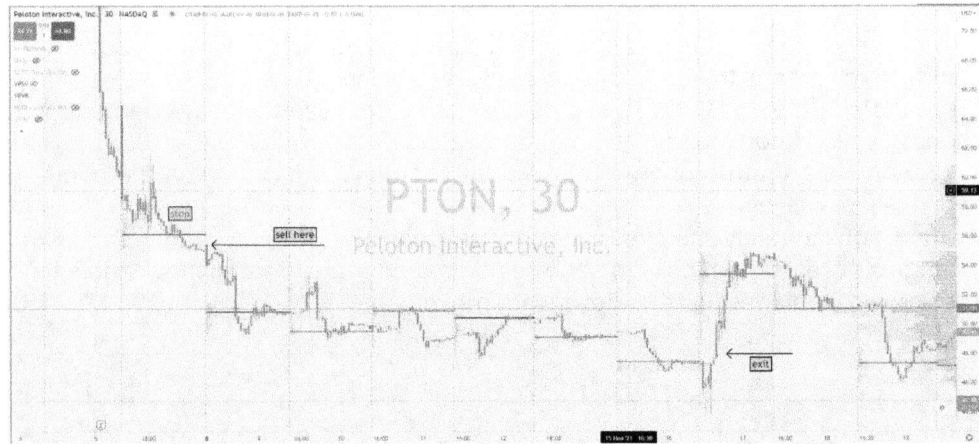

I would sell the next day with a stop after POC.

SO, HOW I TRADE BEARISH RETEST GAP.

1. I look for stocks in the premarket that have made a GAP down from 3 to 10% and a volume of 1 million shares.
2. I determine whether the stock is on support or under resistance.
3. It is fundamentally important not to trade for the first 30 minutes. It is necessary to wait for the retest
4. I use 10 EMA on a 5-minute timeframe. I wait until the price tests it and a reversal candlestick pattern is formed.
5. I open a deal with a risk of no more than 2% of the capital and pull up the stop after 30 minutes or according to the rule of new accumulation zones.

NOW AS FOR THE BEARISH GAP AND GO:

1. We repeat all the steps from the instructions above - step 1 and step 2.
2. It is mandatory to have a red sell candle on the previous day.
3. Lack of support at the bottom.
4. I put an order of no more than 2% of the deposit on the breakdown.
5. I follow the trade and try to move it to breakeven as soon as possible.

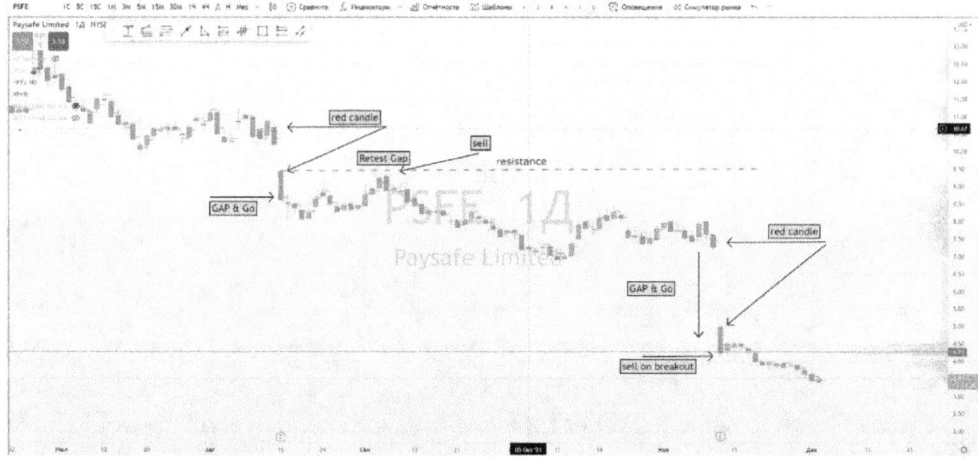

Here is a case when both setups get along on the same instrument at once. First GAP&Go, then Retest GAP and GAP&Go again.
Always mark the high of the first candle after the GAP. This is a strong resistance. Wait there for the test and sell.

Additional materials

The first case on the 30-minute timeframe:

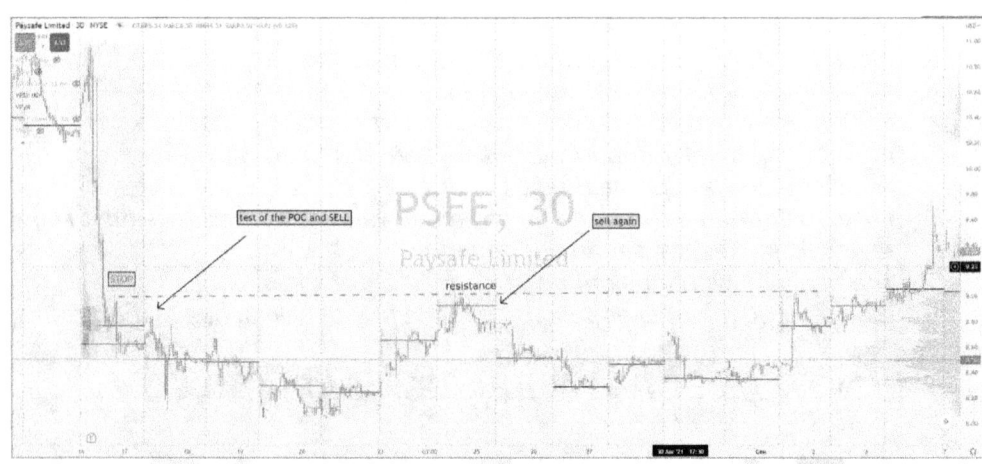

Do not forget to apply Fixed Volume Profile.
And here is the second case of GAP and GO:

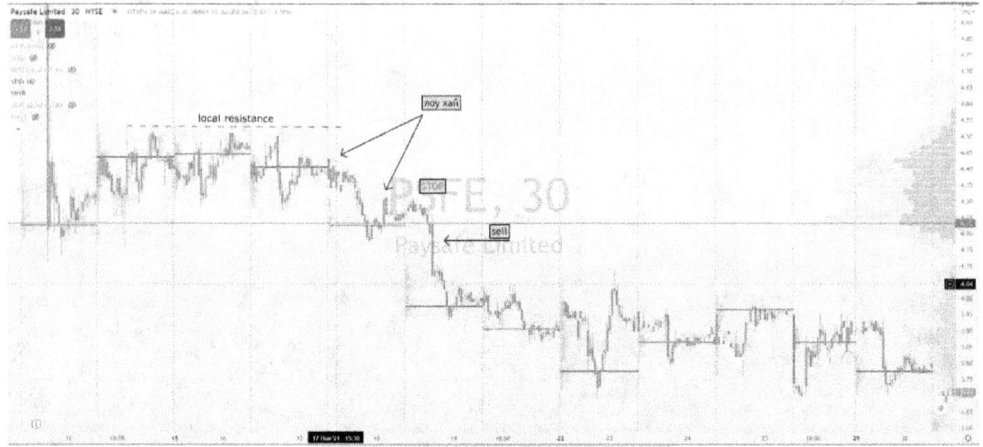

It was enough to set a sell order for a low breakout - and everything would have worked out.

BULLISH RETEST GAP UP AND BULLISH GAP AND GO.

And everything is also simple here!

We look at the candle of the previous day. It should be red. The candle in which the sale occurred.

The logic is simple. All sellers are now at a loss due to the GAP and will probably want to close the position, which will lead to a retest.

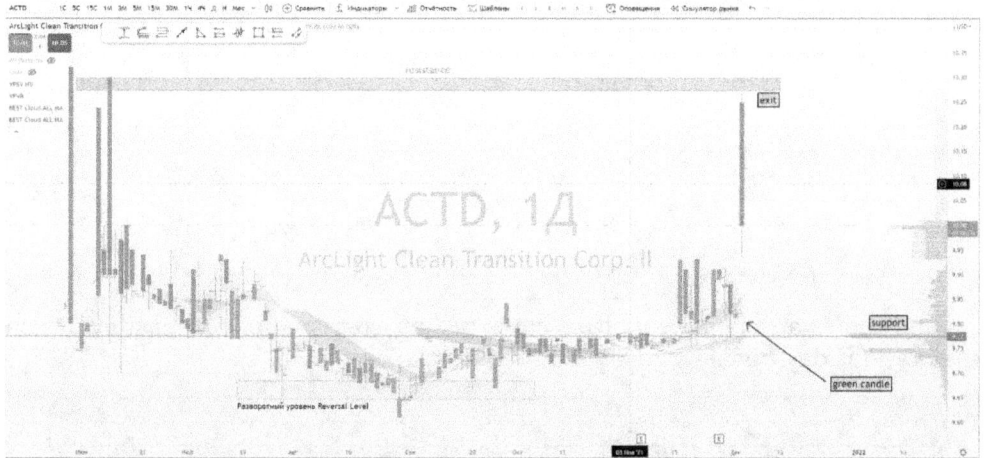

This case does not apply to the operation of the system, because profit taking occurred on the resistance test.

Here's a good example. Look - the stock was actively sold on the previous day. This means that today these sellers are incurring heavy losses. And we should expect a retest of the support level, where it is worth looking for purchases on a smaller timeframe.

And here is an example of how a stock makes a retest after successful buys on the previous day, because buyers decided to take profit.

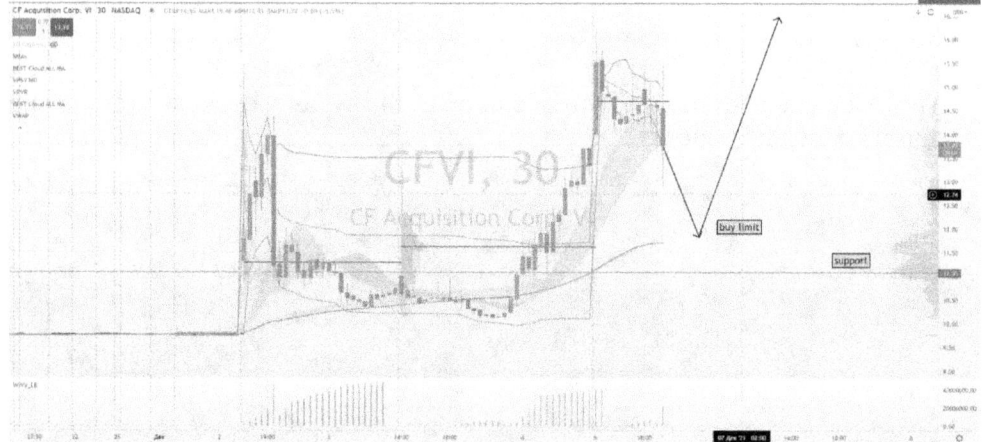

This is the kind of a trade I would be looking for on a 30-minute timeframe after rollback ad profit taking of all buys of the previous day.

Additional materials

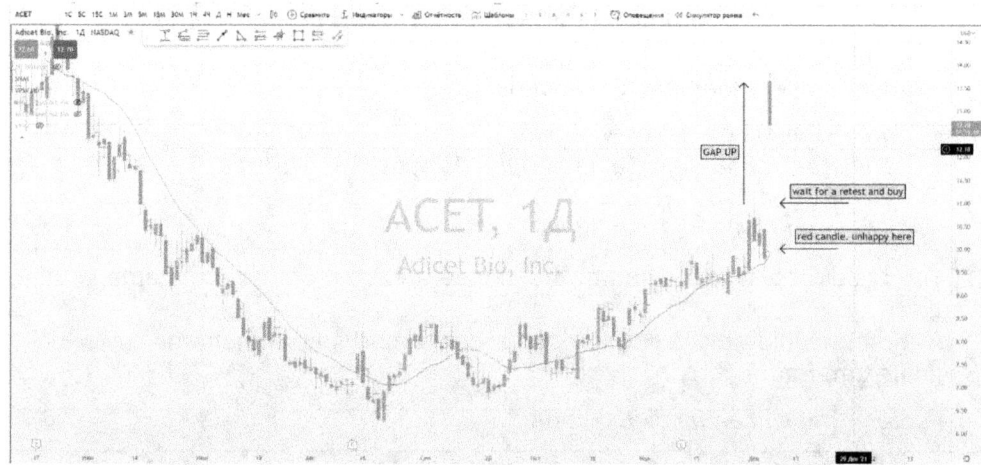

Here is a great example of how sellers are fleeing from a stock that gave a GAP up.

BULLISH GAP AND GO.

Its mandatory characteristics include:

- green candle on the previous day,
- The stock should give a gap on the day you discovered it,
- GAP from 4 to 12%,
- Premarket volume from 500K.

You should open a position at the candle breakout on the timeframe you are trading.

At first, I would advise you to open a deal on a higher timeframe. Let's say a 5-minute timeframe.

Factors that will enhance the setup:

- the candle of the previous day is on support,
- large volumes,
- good news.

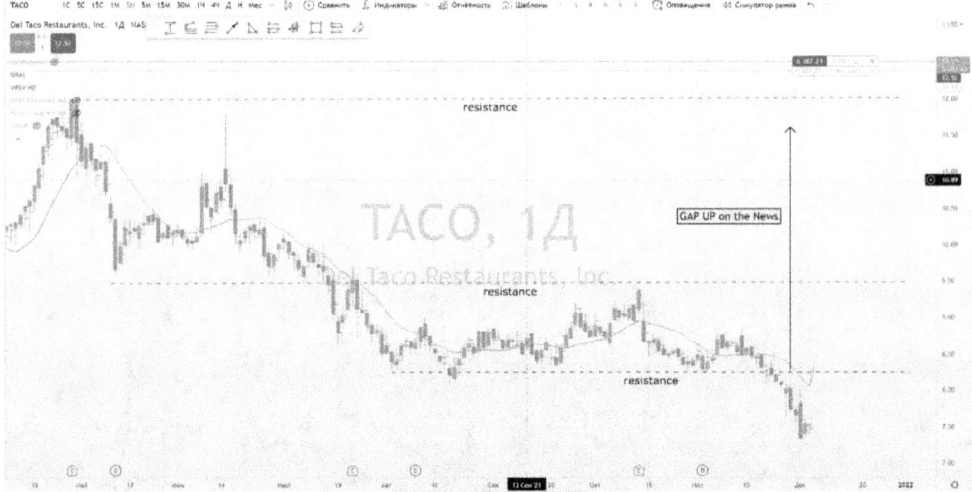

Look - on the good news, the stock has made a powerful GAP Up. And the previous 2 days were green candles. This means that it is likely that the buys will continue.

Here, see how I opened a position on the 3-minute chart:

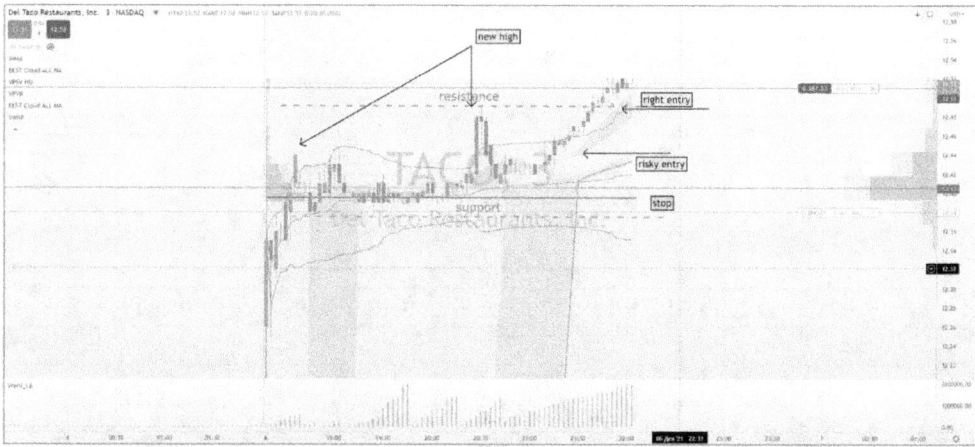

Always open a deal on breakout of a high, whether it's on the premarket or not. It is logical to put the stop under the local support.
Here is another unusual case:

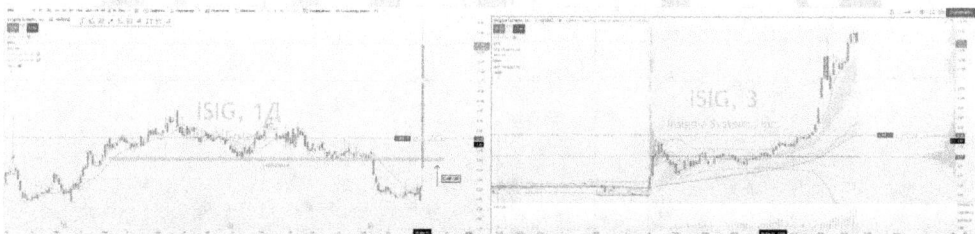

Look, I usually don't take such GAPS because of the resistance over them. But in this case, the news was so strong that it gave the stock a powerful boost, and I managed to make great money!
Therefore, buys at the breakout of all resistances are quite acceptable.

MISTAKES ARE POSSIBLE.

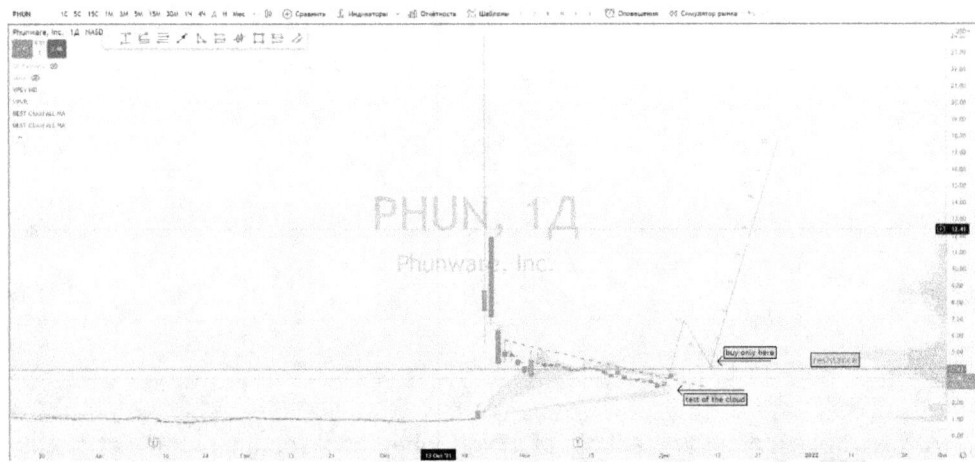

See why I didn't buy in this situation. Everything is simple! Because there is a powerful resistance at the top from the horizontal volume level. And I would buy only after its breakthrough.

And here, despite the GAP Up, I would not buy either, because there is a powerful resistance at the top.

Additional materials

Always watch out for resistance, which can easily beat off the price and break your hopes of profit.

NOW I WOULD LIKE TO TELL ABOUT HOW I USE AVWAP FOR TRADING THE GAPS.

- I use AVWAP for the first candle after gap. That is, I wait for the end of the trading day after the gap first. Or better - I wait for a few days for the test of this indicator.

- It is desirable that the test is intensified by some other level or guide.
- I opened a position on a smaller timeframe.
- I observe the trade, following the new accumulation zones.

Example:

As you can see, the AVWAP level coincided with the POC level in the candle next to it. This strengthened the setup.

Here's how it was on a smaller timeframe:

Additional materials

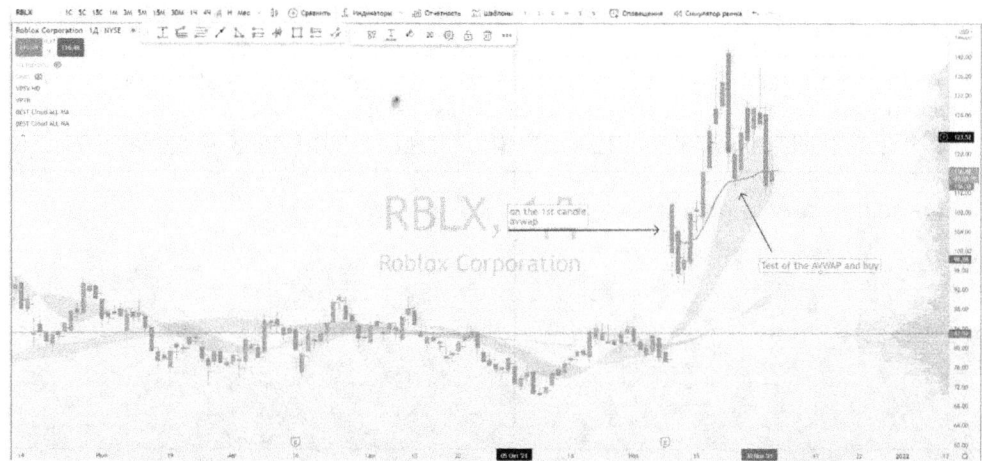

Take a look at a great buy on the Buyer's AZ test, which coincided with our indicator. And we should have left on the test of the lower boundary of the Seller's AZ, which is on the left.

Thus, it was possible to take about $ 20 profit.

Another example:

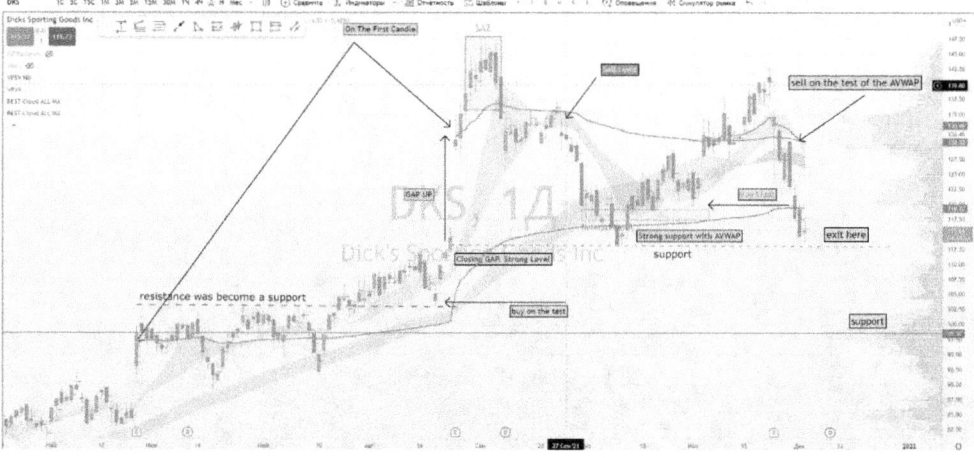

DKS is just a quintessential example of how you can make a fortune on one stock.

See, first we could buy on a retest of support, which was the resistance. And take profit of as much as $ 50.

Then we could sell on the test of the lower boundary of the seller's accumulation intensified by the AVWAP test. Of course, we should have left at closing of the GAP. This would have added another + $20.

Then, after formation of the Reversal level intensified by the AVWAP test, we should have bought with the test targets of 50% of the Seller's AZ. And another $20.

And, of course, sales after the GAP Down on the reverse test of two AVWAP levels at once with support targets. That's another $15.

In total, it was possible to take profit of about $ 100 on one stock using my system.

I regularly post similar trades in my Private Chat.

So, join us).

In this book, I want to share my favorite strategy for trading options. It has proven itself well and will really bring a lot of benefits when used skillfully.

TRADING DOLLAR OPTIONS.

Ordinary people are distrustful of stock exchanges. Many believe that the play on them is faked, so a small investor will not be able to succeed. This is partly true: banks and insiders have better access than we do to research, analytics, computing resources, contacts, and capital.

However, I see one way to equalize the odds in options. The strategy I have developed allows you to quite ethically "steal" the best ideas of Wall Street and use them.

How is it possible?

Whenever someone opens an option transaction in the American options market, they are obliged to notify the Options Price Reporting Authority (OPRA) within 90 seconds.

This is true: when you open an option transaction, whether for 10 or 10,000 contracts, you need to inform OPRA about your buy/sell orders, their volume, and time.

For several years now, I have been following unusual activity in the options market and recently began to earn decently, adopting it as a predictive indicator.

The results are simply tremendous. And this is coming from a man who was already making good money in the stock market.

Imagine that you are trading ideas the others give you every day. And these are not the ideas of some average guy who trades from a room in his parents' apartment, but the ideas of experienced institutional traders and insiders who show you the stocks they like, the possible direction and time of their movement.

A specially designed real-time options scanner shows me the option contract that is being currently traded by "smart money" and the price with which it opens a position. Some of their lucrative trades are so crazy (millions of dollars are invested in very risky trades and bring huge returns) and flawless in implementation that it seems as if these guys were playing with marked cards.

A fool would be quick to part with his money. But why do informed traders choose the positions that even an idiot would avoid?

Let's put aside the conspiracy theory. However, it's no secret that Wall Street professionals and company insiders have better access to information than we do.

In addition to publicly available information that everyone can see, they can afford to hire an army of analysts and traders to increase their opportunities to earn quickly. One can find a "hot" signal in something that seems like market noise to you and me.

Trading Dollar Options

How else can you explain the perfect choice of the moment of opening/closing a position? Who of us wouldn't want to know about the movement in advance, too? It's like reading the financial section in a newspaper the day before it's published.

Here are some more advantages of trading based on unusual option activity:

- **No need to generate ideas (you are told what and when to trade)**
- **You follow BIG MONEY – not all trades become profitable, but all of them are generated by major players**
- **Explosive profit potential – profitability of a trade often reaches three-digit values in an hour**
- **Wide range of trades – there is unusual option activity every day when the market is open. This is perfect for active traders and anyone who likes to trade some ideas, but selectively.**

I like the profit potential in such trading – the risk/potential ratio here is one of the best in the market. Besides, it's really exciting. It's like you're looking over the shoulder of the most astute minds on the Wall Street and trading with them.

I will be happy to show you how it works and how I use this niche and profitable style of options trading. But first let me introduce you to the basics of options. If you already feel confident with options, then you can skip the next section.

EXPRESS COURSE ON OPTIONS

An option is a contract between two parties - a buyer and a seller. There are two types of options: call and put. A call option gives the buyer the right to buy shares at a specified price before a certain date.

Remember:
The buyer of a call option gets the right, but not the obligation, to convert their options into shares. In other words, you are not tied to an option transaction and can open or close it as often as you wish, until the deadline for execution of such a contract comes.

Example:
Starbucks $88.37

I started trading options only in my third year as a trader. Although this article is not intended to serve as a guide to options trading, I think it's worth highlighting the

Trading Dollar Options

main points before delving into the details of unusual option activity and my unique approach to trading based on it.

Above you can see the register of $90 call options for June 2020 (the execution date is June 19).

On the left, there is a list of exchanges offering such contracts.

Bid is the price that the buyer is willing to pay for the option. For example, on the AMEX exchange, someone submitted a bid for 5 contracts (BS) at $6.50 (Bid).

Ex	Bid	BS	Ask	AS
COMP...	6.50	30	8.35	107
AMEX	6.50	5	8.35	14
BOX	6.50	30	8.35	30
CBOE	6.50	8	8.35	25
ISE	6.30	20	8.35	46
NYSE	6.50	4	8.35	15
NASDAQ	6.50	12	8.35	17

On the other hand, the buyers are offering 14 contracts (AS) at a price of $8.35 (Ask). These contracts expire in 264 days.

If buyers and sellers agree on the price, a transaction will take place.

Within 90 seconds after such a transaction, you need to notify the OPRA.

Each option contract is concluded for 100 shares.

Let's suppose you bought one contract. It would cost you $8.35 (if you pay at the ask price).

Multiplying this price by 100, we get the total value of the contract - $ 835.

Of course, $835 is a considerable amount that needs to be paid for some kind of contract. I usually trade options that are worth no more than a dollar.

But we'll discuss it later.

Now, as a buyer, we have the right to convert an option contract into shares, but we are not obliged to do this.

If you keep the contract until June 19, 2020, its execution date, and it closes "in-the-money" for at least one cent, it will be automatically executed, and shares will be given to you.

The trader's task is to open and close positions with profit as often as possible.

The trader does not need to hold an option in order to convert it into shares later. But if you are going to trade options, you should be aware of the existence of such a rule.

Given that the purchase of a call option is a bid on an increase, let's consider how such a transaction can bring profit.

Options are so-called depletable assets. When the execution date comes, they either end with a loss of value or are closed in the money.

$90 call options are out-of-the-money. If the date of their execution had come today, they would have ended in a loss of value.

Where does the $8.35 premium come from?

The option is a secondary security for the underlying asset, in our case, Starbucks shares.

In options trading, only the price behavior matters.

If you buy a Starbucks for $89 and the price rises to $90, you will earn, and if it drops to $88, you will lose money. Everything is simple.

But option prices are formed according to a probability model. Thus, you should take into account the factors like stock price, option exercise price (strike price), execution date, dividends, and volatility.

All these parameters can be entered into the formula for calculating the option price, except for one - volatility.

The option price is determined by supply and demand, which also affect the hidden volatility.

If the activity of buyers of a call or put option is high, this can lead to a sharp spike in the option volatility.

This is the reason for the difficulties that many people experience when trading options.

For example, you can buy a put option, the stock price will rise, but the option will still lose value.

How is it possible?

Due to a sharp drop in hidden volatility or due to temporary erosion.

This can also happen if the strike price is too far away and does not have a significant impact on the option.

Thus, the $8.35 premium for the $90 call option is caused by the time factor. Even the out-of-the-money share has a chance to reach the desired level in 264 days.

Now let's consider options with the same strike price, but expiring after 12 days.

As you can see, the premiums for them are much lower. And this is also mainly due to the time factor.

When trading options, you need to monitor the hidden volatility, the time left to expiration, and the behavior of the stock itself.

∨ .SBUX191011C90		SBUX 100 (Weeklys) 11 Ot		✕
Ex	Bid	BS	Ask	AS
COMP...	.84	11	.89	30
AMEX	.78	7	1.06	4
BOX	.84	10	.89	30
CBOE	.79	18	.92	2
ISE	.79	42	.98	22
NYSE	.81	2	.90	2
NASDAQ	.82	7	.90	8

> **My trading based on unusual option activity is very simple – I only trade call and put.**

WHAT SHOULD YOU KNOW WHEN BUYING AN OPTION?

Buyer call: Bid for increase. The value of such a position increases when the stock price rises and hidden volatility increases. Time works against the buyer of the call, as we have seen in the examples with $90 call on SBUX.

Buyer put: Bid for reduction. The value of such a position increases when the stock price declines and hidden volatility increases. Time works against the put buyer, as in the case of a call buy.

But if the buyer has an open long position and buys a put, it may be not a bid for reduction, but hedging of the position. This behavior makes it difficult to trade based on unusual activity by buying put options.

Other types of orders that you need to know to trade based on unusual option activity.

Selling call options. When a trader sells call options, they are bidding on a price decrease. The value of such a position increases when the stock price remains in place or decreases. The option seller receives a premium, and time works in favor of the premium seller. The profit potential in the transaction is fixed, but the risk is not, so this is one of the riskiest option strategies.

But if a trader has a stock in long positions and sells call options on them, this does not necessarily mean a bid for reduction. That is why it is more difficult to recognize unusual actions in transactions in which there is a call is sold at the bid price than in the case of other types of orders.

Selling put options. When a trader sells put options, they are bidding on increase in the stock price. The value of such a position increases when the stock price rises or remains in a certain range. Since a premium is obtained with this strategy, the profit potential is fixed. Time works to the advantage of the premium seller. And so does the drop in hidden volatility.

Of course, there are many other option strategies, such as spreads and trading based on volatility, but you don't need to know them to trade based on unusual option activity, as I do.

The exercise price of options can be classified as follows:

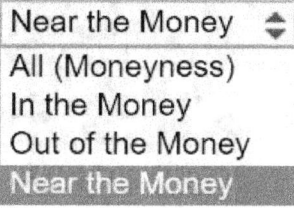

In-the-money: such options have intrinsic value, that is, at the time of execution they will be converted into shares.

Trading Dollar Options

Example:

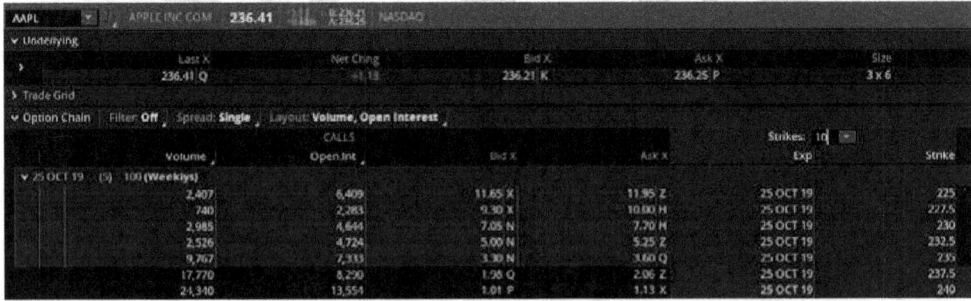

Call $232.50 and call $235.in the figure above are in-the-money options.

The stock is trading at $236.41. If we subtract this price from $235, we get $1.41 – this is the intrinsic value, the value of the option at the time of execution.

But if we look at the bid-ask spread of call options of $235, we can notice that they are sold at $3.60 at a bid price of $3.30.

Where does a premium of $2 come from?

In options trading, this is called a time value. When option prices are formed, the time and probabilistic components that affect the premium are taken into account.

Another example:

If we subtract $232.50 from $236.41, we get $3.91.

We look at the bid-ask spread of these options and see $5 and $5.25.

In other words, in the premium of such options, a time component makes approximately $1.34 and intrinsic value is $3.91.

Advice from a professional dollar options trader

The further "in the money" the option is, the more its movement will track the movement of the stock, since it will consist mainly of intrinsic value.

Out-of-the-money: Such options have only a time value and end in a loss of value at the time of execution.

In the example above, the $237.5 and $240 call options are considered out-of-the-money.

The $240 call is sold at about $1.13, but the shares need to move to $4.72 before the execution to make such a trade at least break-even. A bid is considered risky if there are less than five days left before the execution date.

But it is these bids that I pay most attention to. Big money usually doesn't make mistakes. Therefore, when I see significant activity with out-of-the-money options, I ask myself the question: "Maybe they know something?"

I am also interested in at-the-money options. Why? Because they have a big time premium.

In other words, if a super-powerful at-the-money options trade pops up, it tells me that traders need to notice the movement and need to act quickly, because at-the-money options are sensitive to time and volatility changes as well as movements in the underlying share.

WHY OPTIONS?

It's no secret that options give you the opportunity to get financial leverage. Few instruments offer such a great opportunity for earning as options do.

Starbucks calls (see below) allow us to work with 100 shares for just $89 (the cost of one contract).

✓ .SBUX191011C90		SBUX 100 (Weeklys) 11 Oi		✗
Ex	Bid	BS	Ask	AS
COMP...	.84	11	.89	30
AMEX	.78	7	1.06	4
BOX	.84	10	.89	30
CBOE	.79	18	.92	2
ISE	.79	42	.98	22
NYSE	.81	2	.90	2
NASDAQ	.82	7	.90	8

It would take $8,837 to buy these 100 shares directly. Yes, the shares are not limited by the term of execution. But options are a very powerful instrument in the hands of a sophisticated and informed trader. They give incredible leverage.

Do you know the other reason "smart money" likes to buy options?

When buying an option, the risk is limited to the premium paid. That is, you can take a giant position and sleep with a calm mind, since the risk in the transaction is fixed. Take any competent trader, give them a leverage, and you will see their account starting to grow.

Market sharks - pension funds, hedge funds, banks, and very wealthy investors like to trade options because it is one of the fastest ways to build a position.

Imagine a billion-dollar hedge fund that wants to form a position on a stock with a daily trading volume of just 300,000 shares. It is difficult to make a big bid on such a sophisticated instrument without attracting attention and without affecting the price. Of course, there are computer algorithms that allow you to buy stocks slowly throughout the day to make it look natural. But why bother if you can call a broker and make a large option transaction - quickly and simply.

Options provide excellent returns on capital, and Wall Street professionals know this. I'm not kidding. We are unlikely to see Netflix shares double in value overnight. But with NFLX options, this happens all the time.

And here's another thing options are useful for: they give us the opportunity to trade anything. Having a small account, you will most likely initially abandon the idea of trading Microsoft, Apple, Amazon, and Facebook shares. With the options, you can trade shares of these and thousands of other companies.

In addition, options give incredible flexibility. For example, the most active stock options are expiring every week, and the most popular ones - even every few days.

Why is it important?

When buying options, you can limit the size of the time premium by trading contracts with closer dates. This also allows you to play on the expected movement more accurately.

None of this was available ten years ago, but improvements in technology and increased market efficiency have made options a viable trading instrument.

Gone are the days of liquidity problems - millions and millions of option contracts are traded every day. Some of them have such narrow spreads that bid and ask prices can be separated by only one cent!

UNUSUAL OPTION ACTIVITY: PAST, PRESENT AND FUTURE

Options used to be traded mainly on the Chicago Stock Exchange by means of so-called open outcry. This procedure remained dominant for several decades until everything went digital.

Although I have not had a chance to observe these processes firsthand, I have seen films and heard the stories of traders who shared their experience.

Men and women screaming in the "pit" in search of response bids from institutional buyers and sellers... at the top of their lungs... in an incredibly dynamic environment. They had quite an honest advantage. And some even managed to get rich just by following the flow of bids.

For example, if they saw that a large bid was about to come out, they simply stood in front of it or made the same trade immediately after it. Makes sense, doesn't it?

If you see someone making an astronomical option trade right in front of your eyes, you will probably think that this trader knows something. You can try to find it out, or you can just join and catch a wave. That's exactly what many of them did - they followed the flow of bids.

As technology improved, so did trade. Today, most option trades are made electronically and through an intermediary who is not in the "pit." But this does not mean that it is impossible to follow the flow of bids.

In fact, technology has made it easier to identify the actions of market sharks and the ability to swim alongside them.

I use an options scanner developed by experienced traders from New York. It allows you to create custom filters and search for unusual option requests. In particular, I am interested in options with a price of no more than a dollar. Read more about my dollar options trading strategy below.

But before that, let's decide what to consider an unusual option activity.

UNUSUAL OPTION ACTIVITY

We live in a world of data. In trading, information gives an advantage. Option orders whose current volume exceeds the daily average are considered unusual. On average, about 23,000 contracts are traded per day for McDonalds (MCD), and more than 200,000 for Netflix. Unusual option activity is a relative term. Size matters, but the main thing is the relative size.

For example, there is a flurry of options on NFLX. But since it is known that 200,000 of them are sold every day, for unusual activity, we should see this value exceeded.

WHAT IS THE VOLUME OF OPTIONS?

Each completed trade is taken into account in the daily volume. Not all trades are closed on the same day. Unclosed contracts are called open interest. We'll discuss it later.

Let's look at some examples of unusual option activity.

On Friday, September 27, 2019, more than 57,000 contracts for MSG Networks (MSG) were traded. On a usual day, only about 4,400 option trades are made on MSG. The volume this Friday exceeded the usual 12.9 times.

On the same day, 1,220 option contracts for Retail Properties of America (RPAI) were traded, although the average volume for this stock is only 13 contracts. Despite the fact that 1220 contracts is not a lot, such an activity for RPAI is simply gigantic, since it exceeds the usual one 94 times!

Thus, when talking about unusual option activity, we are talking about comparison with the average value. A large volume in itself is not an unusual option activity.

For example, more than 2 million SPY options are traded every day. If 2 million contracts are traded today, there will be nothing unusual about it. In fact, this will be the usual average value.

On the other hand, when on October 17, 2019, someone bought up more than 2,000 contracts on Investors Bancorp (ISBC), it was a relatively large volume of bids, as only about 100 ISBC contracts are traded on a normal day.

WHAT IS THE OPEN INTEREST?

Every time a buyer and seller agree on a price, a trade is made. In the case of options, each strike price level represents a different volume.
Example:

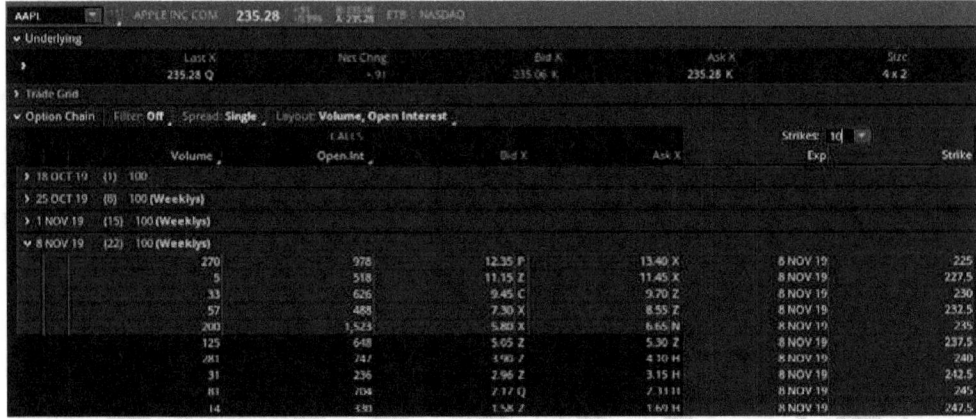

The picture above shows a chain of options for Apple Inc. (AAPL). On the left, we see that, on this day, 200 calls 235 were traded with the execution date of November 8. There is an open interest column on the right.

All outstanding contracts are taken into account in the open interest. We see that, in addition to the 200 traded 235 calls, there are also 1525 calls in the form of an open interest. The natural question arises: were these 200 call options the opening of new positions or the closing of old ones?

Every morning, the volume indicators are reset to zero, and the open interest is corrected. If these were new positions, then the open interest should increase. If these were closing trades, the open interest should decrease. Of course, there could have been both types of trades.

VOLUME AND OPEN INTEREST IN RELATION TO UNUSUAL OPTION ACTIVITY

If someone buys 10,000 call options 235 on AAPL, it will attract everyone's attention. But when there is a figure of 15,000 in the open interest column for call 235, we do not know whether it is an open position or a closing transaction.

> **Advice from a professional dollar options trader**
>
> **When trading on the basis of unusual option activity,
> it is better to look for options with the volume exceeding**

the open interest. This will allow us to trade positions for which there are new actions.

All this information can be found in the options chain window of the trading platform.

The options chain shows all the option contracts available for a particular stock and the corresponding strike prices. It also provides information such as bid and ask prices, volume and open interest.

For more sophisticated traders, the values of hidden volatility and the so-called "Greeks" will be useful.

There are options not only for stocks. And not all stocks have weekly options (with an exercise period of no more than a week). However, weekly options are issued for many companies that are popular among traders.

But keep in mind that for successful trading based on unusual option activity, such data must be obtained in real time.

Why?

Because institutional traders act very competently. They know that if they make a big deal, all other market participants will have their alerts triggered. So they break up their bids into smaller ones to make sure they go unnoticed.

For example, on October 21, 2019, my options scanner, specially designed to detect unusual activity, caught a relatively large deal on Twitter (TWTR).

Someone bought 3200 December 42 calls on TWTR at $1.83. An incredible premium of $590K was paid for these out-of-the-money options.

But here's the interesting thing: the bid actually looked like this:

Several small bids were distributed on different options exchanges.

Most platforms will display such trading as a series of small bids. My scanner recognizes it as one big bid, the so-called sweep. A sweep is a bid that places trades on several exchanges in order to mask their impact on the market. My specialized scanner is quite complex, so it recognizes such activity as a single bid, and not several small ones.

TWTR Dec 42.0 Call

Price	Volume	Pct
1.85	1554	43.9%
1.80	526	14.9%
1.84	402	11.4%
1.83	340	9.6%
1.79	274	7.7%
1.81	215	6.1%
1.75	118	3.3%

Exchange	Volume	Pct
AMEX	7	0%
ARCA	23	1%
BATS	787	22%
BOX	21	1%
BXO	1	0%
C2	10	0%
CBOE	1656	47%
EDGX	16	0%
EMLD	2	0%
GEM	26	1%
ISE	1	0%
MIAX	11	0%
MPRL	115	3%
MRX	21	1%
NOM	820	23%

Let's look at two examples of the sweep and what they tell the trader.

Sweep, example 1:

2500 SE Dec 28.0 Calls $2.15 At ask price [MULTI] 09:31:19.622 IV=54.5% +3.9 PHLX 161 x $1.70 - $2.15 x 608 PHLX Sweep/ Opening Vol=5001, OI=106

Trading Dollar Options

At the time of the transaction, the bid/ask spread was $1.70 to $2.15. Someone bought 2500 call contracts at the ask price.

What does this tell us?

- *This is an aggressive bid. The trader is willing to pay the top price to get these options. Keep in mind that institutions have access to the best execution in the market. They can call a broker (exchange or curb) and ask them to arrange a reasonable price for their bid. But here they just bought, paying a high premium.*
- *Most likely, this is a buy, since the tranaction took place at the ask price.*
- *Hidden volatility (IV) has increased. It always increases with increasing demand for options.*
- *It was opening of a position, since the volume exceeds the open interest (OI).*
- *The trader spared no money, laying out more than $537K to pay for the option premium.*

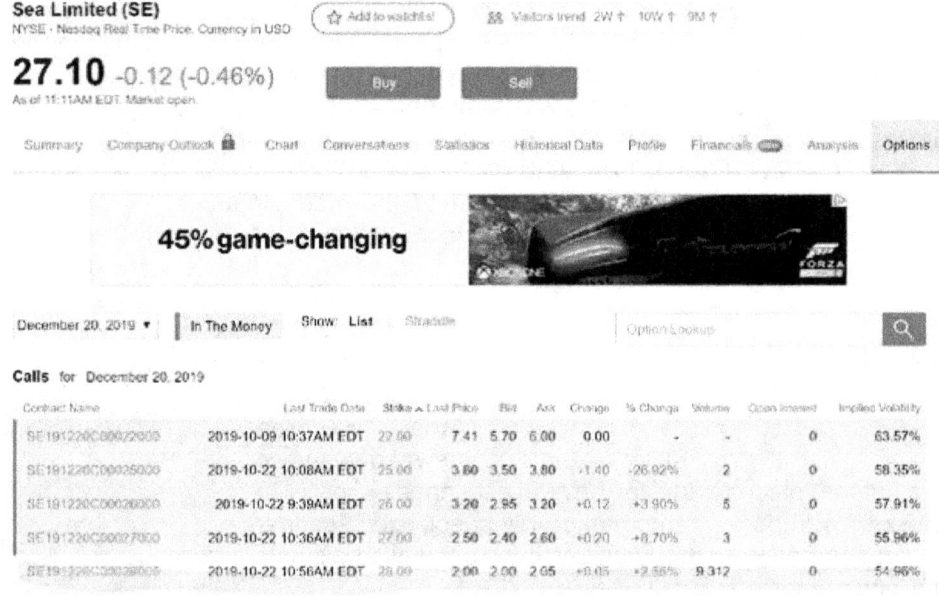

Sweep, example 2:
2000 FRPT Nov 50.0 Puts $2.086 Above ask Price! [MULTI] 09:50:40.710 IV=59.7% +5.6 ARCA 3 x $1.70 - $2.00 x 31 NOM Sweep/ Opening

Wow! This trader acted so aggressively that they paid a price above the ask in order to get the desired volume guaranteed. At the time of the transaction, the spread was $1.70 to $2.00.

Although it was a put transaction, you can notice some similarities with the SE transaction from the previous example:

- **Surge of hidden volatility**
- **Aggressive bid**
- **Big money** – more than $417,000 was paid as a premium

UNUSUAL OPTIONAL ACTIVITY: HOW TO DISTINGUISH GOOD FROM BAD ONE?

Despite the fact that I use an options scanner, which helps me to notice unusual activity, this is not enough to make a trade.

There are several thousand transactions with large blocks of options per day. If you trade on the basis of each of them, your purchasing power will be exhausted in a few minutes.

In addition, not all unusual option activity is speculative. For example, traders buy put options, which looks like a bearish operation. But we don't know what they have in their portfolio. What appears to us to be a huge bearish position may actually be just a hedge if the trader holds the same stock long.

You never know for sure why "smart money" takes certain actions with options. But there are a number of signs that distinguish the best unusual activity. Let's consider them.

Size. Speaking about unusual option activity, we compare the volume of option transactions with its average value. Look, for example, at this bid for ZAGG Inc. (ZAGG):

570 ZAGG Dec 7.0 Calls $0.676 At ask price

At first glance, the numbers are small, but usually about 178 contracts a day pass through ZAGG. On October 22, this volume was exceeded 46 times by noon – as many as 13,000 contracts were traded.

However, if activity has increased 40 times for one stock and 3 times for another, it does not mean that the first one is better.

Option strategies. Option transactions can be made for various reasons. I am only interested in speculative unusual activity. As a rule, this is a simple call or put buy. I don't pay attention to combined trades and strategies with premium sales.

Interesting: 9000 ET Jan 14.0 Calls $0.24 At ask Price; 1500 ALLT Nov 7.5 Puts $0.45 At ask price

Not Interested: 360 MO Oct 25th/Nov 45.0 Call Spread $0.73 BID CBOE vs 7200 MO $46.1390 QD 13:33:16.317 MO=46.13 SP_500 = 360 Oct 25th 45.0 Calls $1.23 (FT Theo=$1.24) MID 13:33:16.317 = 360 Nov 45.0 Calls $1.96 (FT Theo=$1.97) BID 13:33:16.317 = 7200 traded in a block at $46.1390 13:33:17.839

I try to avoid anything that looks complicated, and only work with clear and understandable long or short trades.

Opening. Although it is impossible to know the intentions of "smart money" for sure, we can determine when they open new positions. To do this, it is enough to look at the figures of volume and open interest. When the volume exceeds the open interest, a new position is being opened.

Example: 9500 MRK Jan 87.5 Calls $0.95 At ask price Vol=10k, OI=8383

Execution price (strike price). When choosing the strike price, I prefer the at-the-money and out-the-money options. Why? In-the-money options are sometimes used as a stock substitute, and they already have intrinsic value.

On the other hand, an out-of-the-money option should end in a loss of value unless something unusual happens to the stock. I like it when informed traders make risky bids; it can mean they know something others don't yet know.

Example: 500 KODK Jan 5.0 Calls $0.10 At ask price KODK=2.69

Such a trader needs a large movement of KODK so that their options go "into the money". Such speculative transactions are of the greatest interest for trading based on unusual option activity.

Time. You can buy an option that expires tomorrow, or you can buy one that expires in two years. For trading based on unusual option activity, the closer the execution date, the better.

Why?

Because the movement will either happen in the near future, or not. Who is interested in sitting in a position for several months in the hope of emergence of a catalyst? I need a quick return, and options with close dates are best suited for this purpose.

Example: 6098 CRM Oct 25th 145 Calls $1.40 Above ask! Expires in two days

Do not trade on reports. Large option deals can often be seen before the release of the company's report. Such activity may seem unusual at first glance, but it is not.

It is risky to hold shares during the reporting period. There are only two options - you will either earn well or suffer great losses. "Smart money" does not trade like that.

It is more likely to buy put options for hedging (which will look like a bearish operation). Alternatively, it can reduce the size of the position or close it completely and buy call options with a fixed risk (which will look like a bull operation) as a replacement for stocks.

Example: 1192 SNAP Oct 25th 11.0 Puts $0.12 At ask price [MULTI] 12:53:23.187 IV=214.1% +11.8 Before the report Report today after closing

Nature of the bid. The buyer can either buy options at the ask price or place a limit order, which will be executed only if the price drops to the desired one.

I am not interested in orders that are executed at the bid price or within the spread. I am looking for buyers, especially aggressive buyers whose orders are executed at the ask price or higher.

Example: 500 MGM Nov 1st 29.0 Calls $0.39 Above ask!
Fluctuations in volatility. Option prices are determined by supply and demand. When the demand for an option increases, the hidden volatility and the price of such an option also increase. It's no secret that traders who trade large blocks of options increase volatility.

For me, a spike in volatility is a sign that this is a buyer.

An impressive amount. Although it is the relative size that is important, sometimes there are bids so large that they simply cannot be ignored. I'm talking about cases where gigantic six- and seven-figure amounts are invested in risky positions.

6098 CRM Oct 25th 145 Calls $1.40 Above ask! The premium is $854K.
One last thing: there has to be a corresponding chart. If all of the above criteria are met, but are not supported by the price movement on the chart, I will skip such a trade. Let's talk about this in more detail when we consider specific examples.

And now I want to tell you about one of the most important decision-making criteria for me - the option price. I ONLY TRADE OPTIONS WITH A PRICE OF NO MORE THAN ONE DOLLAR.

WHY I TRADE OPTIONS WITH A PRICE OF UP TO ONE DOLLAR

Remember, all the options I trade are worth no more than one dollar. This allows to take the maximum position using leverage. Why exactly up to a dollar?

I will explain this with a clear comparison.

The stock costs $20 and you want to buy 500 pieces. It will cost you $20 X 500 = $10,000. If the price rises by a dollar, you will earn $1000 - simple math. But if you notice unusual option activity in this stock, you will easily find options that cost less than a dollar.

Let's say you see activity with a $1 call (as a rule, I manage to find contracts much cheaper). You can get control of a position of 1,000 shares for just $1,000, which is significantly less than when buying directly.

For some reason, traders like to talk about their positions in dollar terms, for example: "I want to make XXXX dollars in this trade." But this way of thinking is not suitable for trading. You need to rely on percentages here.

Why?

Let's say you decide to buy shares. A movement of 10% (which is considered pretty big for a stock) on a $20 stock will bring you a profit of $2000 on a position of 1,000 shares. At first glance, it's not a bad amount.

But with the same movement of only 10%, call options can rise in price by a significant amount... in percentage terms. A move from $1 to $2 may make you skeptical. But think about it - the price has doubled. Next, I will show you movements of 100% or more, which are quite common for options. Therefore, by investing $1000, you will earn $1000.

This is the efficient use of money. Thus, you will still have purchasing power. If you find 10 more trades, you can make all of them and get the corresponding profit.

If you have little capital, buying stocks will directly devour your purchasing power. If you have $25K in your account and spend $10K on stocks, you'll spend almost half of your money.

And it's a whole different story, when you have a $25K account and buy stocks worth $1,000 - there's still plenty of money left to work with.

For those who have not yet realized that profit should be expressed as a percentage, I will give a small example.

This is the daily EXEL chart. To buy only 1,000 shares at $19.50, we'd have to spend $19,500, but at the maximum of the day, we would not have earned even $1,000.

Call options are a completely different story.

I bought a $22 call on EXEL with a maturity date of October 18, 2019 for less than a dollar, to be exact - just 48 cents.

You may ask: "How much can you earn on options at 48 cents?"

Let's say you bought 50-cent options for $ 1,000 - these are 20 option contracts that allow you to control 2,000 shares.

On that day, the share traveled 4.5%. By investing $19,500 in shares, we could earn about $900. That is, we needed a decent capital to get such a profit.

On the same day, the options just exploded and could easily bring a profit of 150% (if we had managed to buy them for 50 cents)! A small investment of $1000 would bring us ($1.15 - $0.50) X 100 X 20 = $1300.

The idea is that options priced up to a dollar provide a huge percentage of profitability and allow you to successfully make a profit in any market.

The next time someone says that they earned X dollars, ask them how much money they invested and what was the payback as a percentage. This information allows to accurately assess the effectiveness of trading in comparison with the market and other traders.

Now it's clear why I prefer to trade options that cost less than a dollar, isn't it?

Let's analyze some real examples so that you can see that my method works not only in theory and you can use it in your practice.

REAL EXAMPLES: OPTIONS PRICED UP TO A DOLLAR CONSISTENTLY PROVIDE HIGH RETURNS

After all of the above, you might ask, "Does this really work?"

Sure! Moreover, I trade cheap options and am not afraid to invest my own money in them. I will show you what I am guided by when making such transactions.

But first I would like to say that it is important to record all cases of unusual option activity that you come across. The fact is that you never know what is going to rocket up.

WHY IT IS IMPORTANT TO HAVE A WATCH LIST

According to statistics, in 2018, more than 13 billion option contracts were traded worldwide, and their number is increasing from year to year.

You can imagine how many smart, well-informed traders bet on cheap options based on non-public information. The scanner I use analyzes the actions of market sharks and gives me contracts that are worth watching.

Since several potential opportunities may appear during the day, it is better not to rush. But you should not forget about them either. To do this, it is useful to have a list of positions you monitor (the so-called "watch list"). I enter into it all cases of unusual option activity that I see, accompanying them with short comments.

As I said before, you never know which of these cheap contracts will shoot the moon. The Twitter (TWTR) contracts from my watch list gave a great explosive deal. I know that other traders who bought these call options also made good money.

When opening a trade, traders often show hesitation, and you need to act quickly. The presence of a watch list allows you to make a plan in advance.

However, in addition to the watch list, you also need to understand what you are doing. Let's move on to the consideration of real examples.

A SEVENFOLD SURGE IN VOLUMES IN EXEL GAVE A THREE-DIGIT PROFIT IN A FEW HOURS

I have already mentioned the unusual option activity in Exelixis Inc. (EXEL). Let's take a closer look at how this trade developed.

For about a week, I was watching activity of call buyers in EXEL. They bought a large number of options with different strike prices. After that, the stock price dropped a lot and, based solely on the chart, I assumed that it should rebound. Plus, someone bet a lot of money on the raise - maybe they know something. Will the company be bought out? Will the news about the beginning of the trial come out? Nothing could be said for sure, and there were no guarantees, but someone invested much money into this share.

At that time, on a typical day, there were approximately 6,500 option contracts traded on Exelixis Inc. (EXEL), including strike, exercise, call, and put.

But my scanner revealed an active call buy – 43,000 contracts were traded, which exceeds the average volume more than seven times.

I didn't need to be a major options specialist to understand that something was brewing there. It was enough just to notice this behavior, which I did. It was an impressive buy, to put it mildly.

At 10:47, such a transaction took place:

647 EXEL Oct 22.0 Calls $0.605 Above ask!

And a few minutes later - such a transaction:

929 EXEL Oct 22.0 Calls $0.80 At ask price

Buys took place almost continuously, and although the price of these options doubled by 12:58, some major players continued to buy them.

488 EXEL Oct 22.0 Calls $1.25 At ask price

In total, 25,000 call options were traded with an exercise date of October 22!

Such behavior could not go unnoticed and soon it was already being talked about on CNBC.

But before the general public heard about the EXEL call, I managed to take a position to get my share of the profit.

Three hours later, I sent my subscribers the following message:

"EXEL continues to grow, and they just talked about it on the TV. Therefore, I did the prudent thing by closing half of the position. I sold 25 of my 50 contracts at $1.15 – a profit of 150%! I'll leave the rest for the weekend; perhaps next week will bring even better news. And most importantly, I'm not risking anything, since I've already taken my initial investment."

That's what prompted me to make this transaction:

- *Aggressive buy of call options throughout the day; almost all transactions took place at the ask price – the trader wanted to get these contracts.*
- *Several call lines were bought up (with different prices and exercise dates). I bought closer contracts since they are cheaper.*

Trading Dollar Options

- **Out-of-the-money options were bought up. For the buyer to earn, the share had to make a good and quick move.**

My scanner caught a large order – 8000 call options of $22 were literally swept away, after which the trader began buying options of $23, $24, and $25. Considering that the share was trading at $20 at that time, it was a rather risky bid.

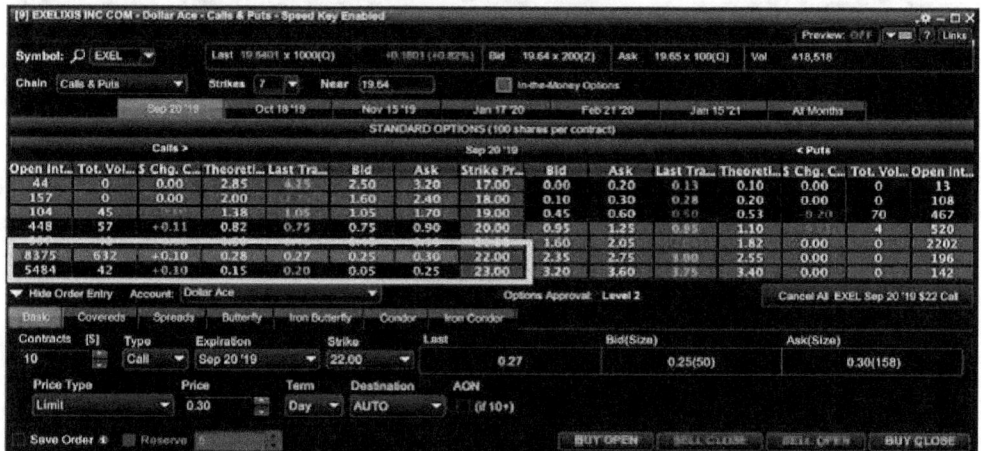

In this example, I bought call options not because they simply cost less than one dollar.

Given the wide variety of option contracts available, everyone should choose what they like best. For example, the mentioned options, which were bought by the bigwigs from Wall Street, had exercise dates in 3 weeks. If you need more time, you can easily find such contracts.

The closer the exercise date, the riskier the transaction. But if such a transaction works, then its profitability will be higher. On the other hand, options with a later exercise date are safer, since it is more likely that the stock you bought contracts on will manage to reach its destination.

In any case, we are only interested in the direction of the stock price movement. If the movement starts, any options will rise in price (provided that nothing else changes).

Look at the EXEL options from my real trade. At the time of buy, there were about 6 weeks left before the exercise date. When 7340 call options changed hands that day, I realized that the stock price could rise soon.

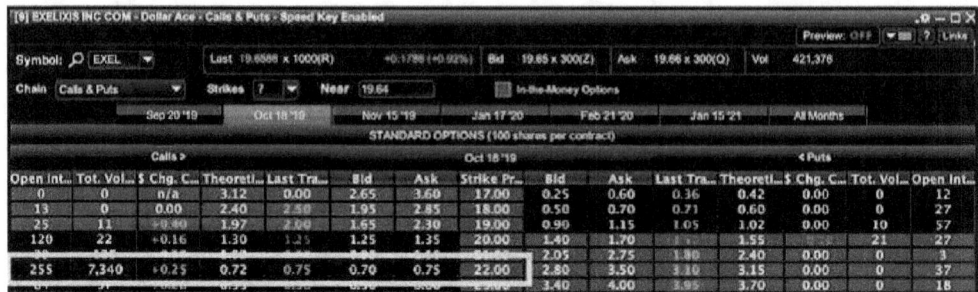

The chart also looked favorable for buys.

The day after I bought the options, the stock bounced off the support level, completing the formation characteristic of the oversold state.

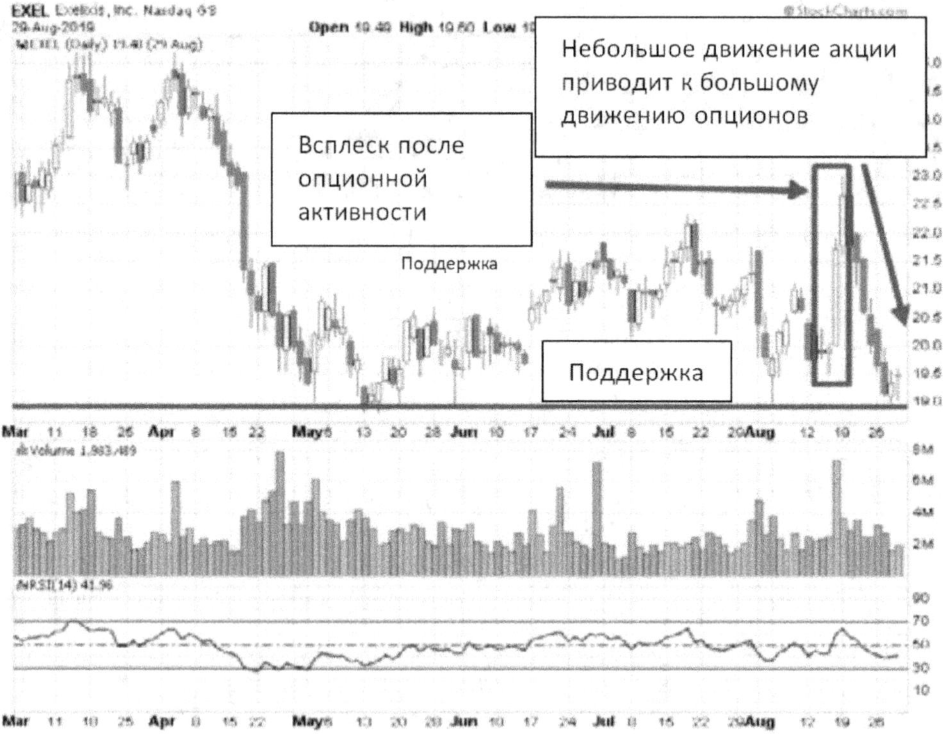

Taking into account the unusual option activity and the presence of a support level, call options looked very attractive, since the probability that buyers would enter the game and drive the price up was high.

You can see what happened to the stock the day I traded it in the chart above.

I sold the first half of the position with an excellent return of 150% on the invested capital, and the next day I covered the rest with a profit of 117%!

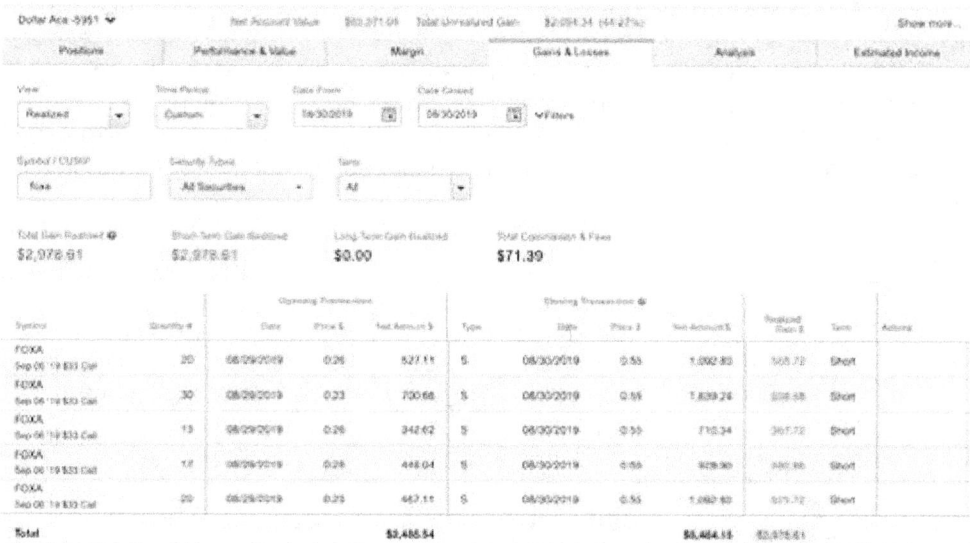

Of course, you are interested in whether you can also use this strategy.

Sure! I know that many traders who trade options with a price up to a dollar also earn well. Trades like the ones I showed above are not unique; they appear regularly. Another example:

CHOOSING THE RIGHT TIME, OR "WHO KNEW?"

An unusual option activity on Medtronic (MDT) attracted my attention.

What was special about it?

On a typical day, about 11,000 call contracts are traded on MDT. But that week, a trader came and bought 5,000 October call contracts for $115 in one order. My scanner also revealed many other transactions.

I decided not to rush to buy. Soon, the open interest on the $115 call increased to 11,000 – this is a huge value.

On October 18, 2019, I started buying a $115 call at $0.32. I took 100 contracts, spending a total of $3,200 (excluding the fee). That's what I call a good leverage!

For $3,200, I got the opportunity to control 10,000 shares of MDT. At the current market price, it would take more than a million dollars to buy them directly!

There was another attractive feature in this MDT trade. The options I bought were out-of-the-money. In mathematical terms, for most traders, such a bid looked very risky. But here's an interesting thing: someone with a lot of money just devoured this $115 call. And I'm sure they didn't do it based on mathematical calculations. I don't want to say that it was an unfair game, but I'm also not so naive as to believe in the randomness of what was going on. No one will make such a big bid without first conducting a thorough analysis.

And in fact, these options shot the Moon very soon. On Monday morning, a serious game began, which promised a good profit. And I took them.

That day, the $115 call on MDT was trading incredibly actively. The volume exceeded the volume of the previous day 22,000 times. I closed the position with a profit.

39 Days to expiration on 2019-10-18

Calls

Strike	Last	% From Last	Bid	Midpoint	Ask	Change	%Chg	IV	Volume	Open Int	Last Trade
65.00	N/A	-59.78%	40.35	42.83	45.30	unch	N/A	0.00%	N/A	N/A	N/A
70.00	N/A	-35.14%	35.55	37.93	40.30	unch	N/A	0.00%	N/A	N/A	N/A
75.00	N/A	-30.51%	30.60	32.98	35.35	unch	N/A	0.00%	N/A	N/A	N/A
80.00	27.90	-25.88%	25.55	27.90	30.25	+27.90	N/A	0.00%	2	N/A	08/28/19
85.00	N/A	-21.25%	20.65	23.03	25.40	unch	N/A	0.00%	N/A	N/A	N/A
90.00	17.75	-16.61%	15.75	17.98	20.20	-0.27	-1.50%	0.00%	2	3	09/03/19
95.00	12.56	-11.98%	10.90	12.95	15.00	-0.64	-4.85%	0.00%	1	6	09/03/19
97.50	10.59	-8.66%	10.55	10.88	11.20	+0.28	+2.72%	21.77%	1	18	09/04/19
100.00	8.33	-7.35%	8.30	8.45	8.60	-0.67	-7.44%	18.56%	22	378	09/09/19
105.00	4.55	-2.72%	4.25	4.38	4.50	-0.30	-6.19%	19.34%	25	230	09/09/19
110.00	1.73	+1.91%	1.70	1.75	1.80	-0.17	-8.95%	17.91%	1,202	6,277	09/09/19
115.00	0.58	+6.55%	0.57	0.58	0.58	-0.02	-3.57%	16.85%	22,488	11.088	09/09/19

And another interesting point: MDT had to issue a report AFTER the exercise date of these options. Therefore, those who bought the October calls did not play on the reports. There was probably some other catalyst we don't know about.

These call options had a low delta and high time erosion. Having shown some patience, you can wait for the opportunity to buy them much cheaper if the stock decreases a little.

A great feature of trading based on unusual option activity is that you do not need to generate your own ideas. It is enough just to follow those who are considered to be well-informed traders.

You may be a little bit bothered by my use of option-specific terms such as delta, etc. You probably would like to hear simpler explanations. Well, then I will comment on transactions in a language that is understandable to everyone, even people who do not know much about the options.

A MAJOR PLAYER BUYS OPTIONS BASED ON INSIDER INFORMATION

Unusual option activity often occurs on the eve of some kind of catalyst that leads to a rise or fall in the stock price. It's important to be on the right side of the trade.

I noticed the beginning of some bullish option activity at Fox Corp. (FOXA)- someone bought about 2000 calls of $33 for 25 cents. A lot of call options are always sold for this stock, but my attention was attracted by the exercise date of those contracts: It was very close, and it seemed suspicious to me. Someone bet $50K that the price of FOXA would exceed $33 before the exercise date (and there was about a week left before it).

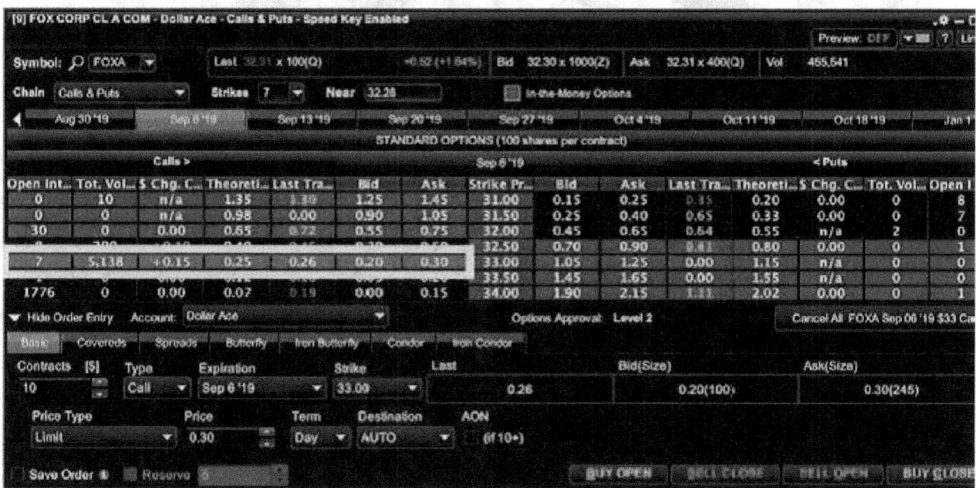

Please note that the total volume (second column) on that day was 5,138 with an open interest (first column) of only 7. This indicated that traders were opening new positions on FOXA, and that a sharp movement could be expected soon.

When I noticed the mentioned large bid, the stock was trading at $32.31. Considering how actively options with a strike price of $33 were being bought up, I had no doubt that FOXA would rise above $33.

In addition to the fact that someone invested a lot of money in options on FOXA, an interesting formation was observed on the price chart.

The stock dropped quite a bit, finding support just below $32 (blue horizontal line). In addition, FOXA was moving out of the oversold zone, which increased my chances of success.

So I bought 100 contracts on FOXA, deciding to follow in the wake of the giants from Wall Street. This allowed me to control 10,000 shares by investing only $2,500.

To buy 10,000 shares of FOXA directly, I would have to spend a lot of money - $323 100 (when buying at the current price of $32.31 at the time when I noticed the option activity).

Remember what we said about unusual activity? It is often followed by a catalyst.
Did I know what kind of catalyst it would be?

I did not. I don't use illegal information, but I'm not naive either. I know that some traders have access to non-public information and use it for trading.

What do you think happened the next day? A catalyst appeared. The price rose above $33 very quickly.

Trading Dollar Options

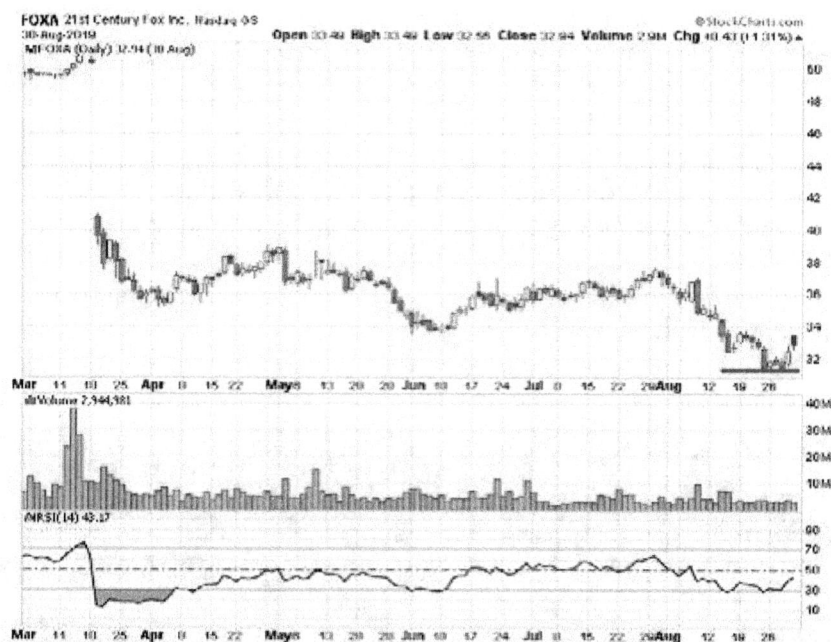

Do you want to know what was the profitability of my option position? Incredible 120% in just one night!

As you remember, I bought 100 contracts for $2500, and the next morning I received $3000 profit.

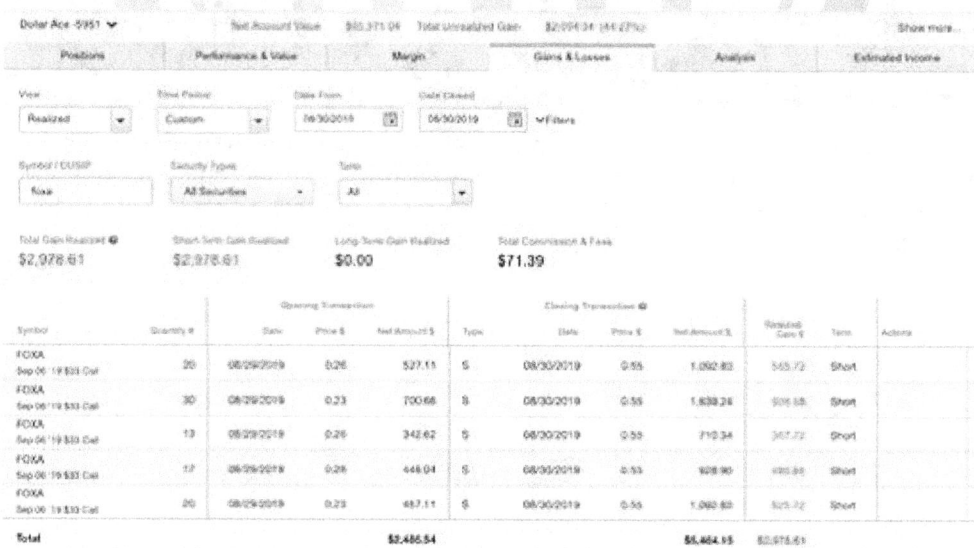

The Smell Of The Cash

Imagine that you invest $1,000 in a trade and make a profit of $1,200. And if you had invested $5,000, then your wallet would have added $5,000 in live money. Now do you understand why I like options priced under one dollar so much?

If you don't, here are some more examples.

SUCCESSFUL PERFORMANCE OF THE NAZARIAN BROTHERS ON CNBC

I had a trade on PDD. Let's look at how the situation developed and how much I managed to earn with the help of cheap options.

In PDD, I noticed an unusual call purchase - several thousand contracts with a strike price of $34 for about 70 cents were quickly bought out.

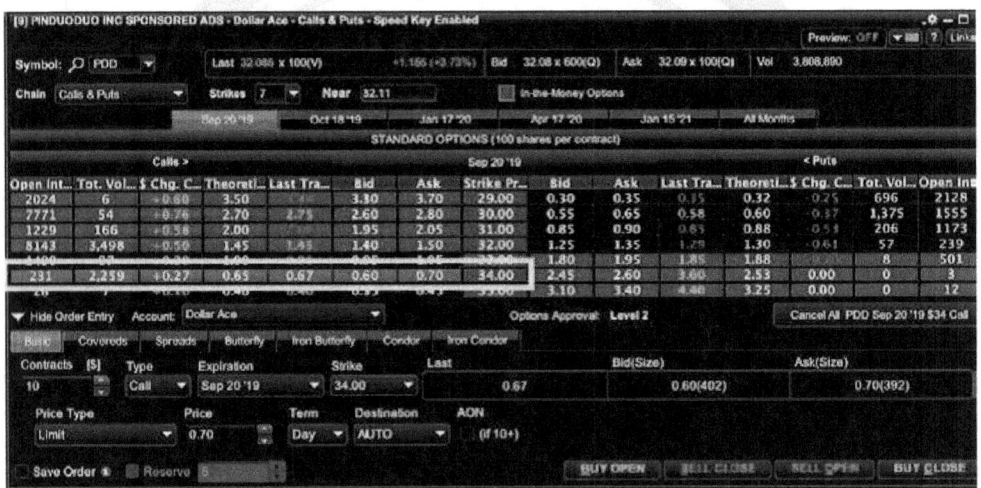

At that time, the stock was trading at 32 cents, and the strike price was $34, which is about 6% more. Looking into the Level 2 window (buy and sell order book), I saw that these were very liquid contracts, so it was not difficult to build a position.

Trading Dollar Options

What do you think happened after I bought these calls? They told about the stock on CNBC.

Did I know that the Nazarian brothers were going to appear on television? Of course, I did not! I only followed the option activity and the price chart. The PDD stock was near its historical high, which is an important resistance level. In such zones, traders usually bet against the stock.

But with emergence of a good catalyst, PDD could break through this level and fly into the skies.

Option activity and, to some extent, the CNBC footage led to an increase in demand for the stock and helped it break through the key level, reaching $33.88 (almost to the price of the strike options I bought).

Just a few hours after opening a trade, I was able to take 80% of the profit, which amounted to about $2,600!

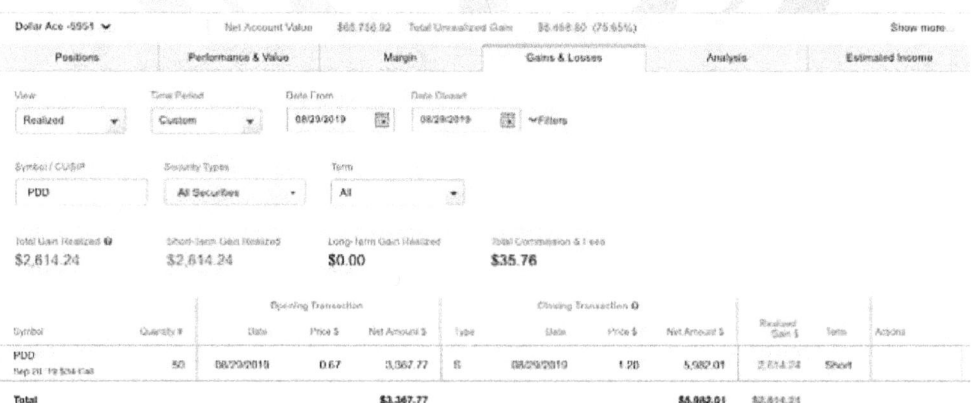

Would you be able to participate in such a movement too? Undoubtedly, because those who bought these options with me also made a decent profit.

Unusual option activity often appears on the eve of the release of banks' comments. In many cases, such option buyers have the opportunity to familiarize themselves with the content of the comment in advance.

Major banks, such as P Morgan Chase, Goldman Sachs, Bank or America Merrill Lynch, Opennheimer, Barclays, Citi, Wells Fargo, and others regularly express their opinion on a particular stock. In fact, they assign it a rating – "buy", "hold" or "sell", predict whether the stock will behave stronger or weaker than the market and its sector. And they outline the target price levels. When an analyst speaks publicly about a particular stock, it can definitely lead to a move in it.

Let's consider one such transaction. No, I didn't have the information beforehand. I just noticed that 20,000 $46 call option contracts changed hands that day (marked by a yellow rectangle in the figure below).

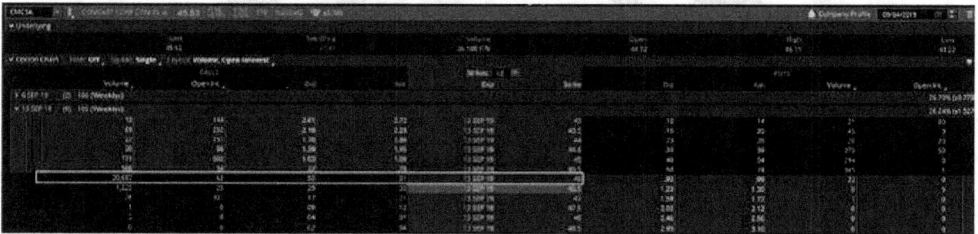

Call options on Comcast Corp. (CMCSA) were actively bought, while the stock chart looked very interesting.

CMCSA formed a "flag" pattern, but most importantly, there was no resistance above, except for the psychological level of $50.

The stock was being traded in a range around the $45 price level. If it is broken, momentum-trading buyers may come in and the stock will move toward $50. I don't know how this can be explained from the point of view of psychology, but people like round numbers, so they often act like a magnet.

As for this particular trade, I bought 100 $46 call contracts at a cheap price – only 38 cents!

I repeat, I did not know in advance what the catalyst would be. But then an analyst came out with his comment and launched a bullish movement on CMCSA.

The very next day I sold my position with a profit of 145% (about $5000). And I wasn't the only one who made money on these options using my system.

LOOK FOR OPTIONS PRICED UP TO $1, READY TO MOVE

Why do some traders manage to earn steadily on the stock market, while others do not? It would seem that we all look at the same charts and listen to the same news... But no, not all of us.

Do you believe that everyone works in the same conditions? Hedge funds, banks, company insiders, and prop trading firms? I don't believe it either.

But instead of complaining and discussing the "conspiracy theory", I have developed a simple strategy that allows me to earn together with "smart money." You have seen the full power of my specially designed options scanner, which allows me to detect the actions of the most astute minds on Wall Street. You can also make a huge profit by trading options with a price of up to $ 1!

BASIC OPTION STRATEGIES.

1. Straddle

The straddle strategy involves the simultaneous buy/sell of a call and put option with the same expiration date and strike price. The strike is selected in such a way that both options are on-the-money or their deltas are about 50% in absolute terms.

Straddle is the most common instrument for investors who expect significant fluctuations in the price of the underlying asset, regardless of the direction. Options traders begin to pay attention to the straddle price (and not to the imputed volatility) about a week before the expiration of options. As the expiration date approaches, traders shift their attention from vega (volatility) to gamma (straddle prices), as vega decreases over time, and the gamma of at-the-money options increases.

2. Strangle

A strangle is formed by buying/selling call and put options with different strike prices but the same expiration dates. As a rule, both options are out-of-the-money. If the call and put options were bought, then the investor has a long strangle position. If the options have been sold, then such a position is called a short strangle.

The strangle strategy has many similarities with the straddle, since call and put options are either bought or sold together. However, the value of the strangle is lower due to the fact that out-of-money (OTM) options are used, but the profit and loss potential is also lower than that of the straddle. The motives for buying a strangle are similar to the buy of a straddle – the expectation of an increase in imputed volatility and/or the likelihood of large fluctuations in the asset price. The only difference is that the buyer expects more significant movements in the spot price of the asset.

3. Butterfly strategy

The strategy is formed by combining options with 3 strikes. A long butterfly position implies the buy of one option with a relatively low strike K1 and one with a high strike K3, and the simultaneous sale of two options with a strike K2. Note that K2 is usually half way between K1 and K3. In practice, traders select strike prices in such a way that the average strike is equal to the forward price of the underlying asset, i.e. that options with a K2 strike are on-the-money, and thus have the highest gamma and vega.

A long position brings profit if the price of the underlying asset does not show major fluctuations and remains near the average strike until the expiration. This strategy will lead to small losses with a significantly volatile behavior of the asset price, since the sale of options with average strikes close to the forward price of the underlying asset implies a short gamma position.

The butterfly strategy can be built with both put options and call options. Therefore, the butterfly value of put options should be equivalent to the butterfly value of call options. In the opposite case, there is a possibility of arbitration in the market.

4. Calendar spread

The calendar spread (horizontal spread) is formed by buying an option with one expiration date T1 and simultaneously selling an option with another - T2. When buying a long-term option (futures) and selling a short-term option (futures), a trader has a long position of the calendar spread. This strategy us also called time spread and horizontal spread.

A trader can build a calendar spread by selling a straddle on the S&P 500 index with expiration in August 2015 and buying a straddle with expiration in December 2015. If the term structure of volatility has a normal form, then the calendar spread will have a negative gamma and a positive vega.

The calendar spread is used by traders in several cases:
1) trading with a term volatility structure;
2) gamma trading with short-term options and vega hedging through the buy/sale of long-term options.

6. In simple words, **CALL option** is the same as a long position on stocks or Forex. This option gives the holder the right (namely the right, not the obligation!) to buy a certain asset at a pre-agreed price at a certain point in the future, which is also called the expiration of the option. Of course, it will be beneficial for the holder of such an option if the asset price goes up, because then it will be possible to either buy the asset at a price below the market price or sell the option for good money and make a profit from it. Therefore, at the time of the buy, the buyer of the call option should be sure that the price will rise.

As a hedging instrument, the call option is used as insurance against an excessive rise in price. For example, if a person has opened a short position on some underlying asset, say gold, then it will be unprofitable for them if the price rises. However, if the same person also owns the call option for gold, then their losses from the upward movement of the underlying asset will be counterbalanced by the profit from the upward movement of the option price.

7. PUT Option

Put option works exactly in the opposite way, that is, it is very similar to short positions on, say, stocks. A put option gives its holder the right to sell a specified asset at a specified price at a certain point in the future. The holder of such an option benefits if the asset price goes down in order to sell the asset above the market price in the future.

The put option is used to minimize losses from a decrease in the price of the underlying asset.

An option (Latin optio - choice, desire, discretion) is a contract under which the buyer of an option (a potential buyer or potential seller of the underlying asset — a commodity, a security) receives the right, but not the obligation, to buy or sell this asset at a pre-agreed price at a time specified in the contract in the future or within a certain period of time. Thus, the option seller is obliged to sell the asset accordingly or buy it from the option buyer in accordance with its terms.

An option is one of the derivative financial instruments. There are options for sale (put option), for buy (call option) and two-sided options (double option). In many respect, options and futures are similar financial instruments, but they have some fundamental differences. In a futures transaction, the buyer is obliged to buy (or sell) an asset upon expiration of the contract, whereas with an option, they can refuse it.

EXAMPLE OF BUYING OPTIONS

Let's look at the example to make it clearer. Suppose you have purchased shares for a certain period of time. But at the same time, there is a possibility that the value of these shares can begin to decline. You choose the classic path and set protective orders to limit the losses. But here there is another big "BUT" - the probability that your protective orders will work and the value of the shares you bought will grow in the future is not high. As a result, you may lose your deposit.

But you can go the other way to limit your losses - buy options. Let's say you buy shares at a price of 100 RUB/pce. And after that, you buy options that allow you to sell these shares at the acquisition price, at any time convenient for you. Let's assume that the option price (it is also called a premium) per share will be 4 rubles.

This price is determined by factors such as volatility, strike price, value of the underlying asset, time value and others – all of them affect the value of option contracts.

In the event of an increase in the prices of the shares you bought, say up to 120 RUB/pce, your profit will be 16 rubles, that is, 120-100-4 = 16.

And in the case of a reduction in the price of shares down to zero, you will lose only 4 rubles (the amount of the premium). During the price decline, you can simply exercise the option and then sell the share at the acquisition price, that is, 100 rubles. In this case, the price at which the contract will be executed is called the "strike" price. As you can see, protecting your positions with options is obvious.

Here we have examined the use of the right to sell shares at fixed prices. Please note that by buying an option, you buy the RIGHT, not the obligation, to buy and sell shares. If we talk about futures, then you would acquire an obligation to buy an asset.

Why is options trading a pre-limited risk?

According to investors, buying options is an investment with a known, limited risk in advance. This risk, or rather the fee for avoiding it, is the price of the option for buyers. In other words, investors pay the price of options and thereby transfer all risks to their sellers. Thus, depending on the intentions of the buyer, options are divided into types. Let's take a closer look.

Call and Put options, terms of their execution and types

So, what types of options exist and how to work with them? Options are differentiated by actions, that is, by the intentions of their buyers and are divided into Call options and Put options.

Also, for a Call option, there is such a thing as "in-the-money" asset - when the value of our underlying asset is above the strike price, as well as an "out-of-the-money" option, when the value of the underlying assets is below the strike price.

Put options can also be "out-of-the-money options" when the asset price is below the exercise cost and in-the-money - when the opposite situation is observed – the prices of the underlying assets are above the exercise cost.

Also, there is a term called "at-the-money" option. In such cases, the value of the underlying assets are close to the cost of execution. The intrinsic value of options is the amount in which options are still in the money.

Among other things, Call and Put options are differentiated by the terms of their execution:

European type of options aka European options. This type of options makes it possible to make transactions exclusively on the last day on which the option is still valid;

American type of options aka American options. This type of options allows you to both buy and sell options at any time of the contract.

By the asset type, Call and Put options are divided into:
- **Stock options. The buyer of these options either sells or buys shares;**
- **Currency options. This type allows you to sell or buy foreign currencies;**
- **Commodity options. These options give the right to purchase sell and buy a certain amount of commodity assets (precious metals, energy carriers, etc.).**

TYPE OF OPTION

There are two most common types of options: American and European.

The American option can be exercised on any day before the expiration of the option. That is, for such an option, a period is set during which the buyer can exercise this option.

The European option can be exercised only on the specified date (expiration date, exercise date, maturity date).

Option premium

The option premium is the amount of money paid by the option buyer to the seller at conclusion of the option contract. In economic terms, a premium is a payment for the right to make a transaction in the future.

Often, when we say "option price" we mean the option premium. The stock option premium is a quote on it. The amount of the premium is usually set as a result of the alignment of supply and demand in the market between option buyers and sellers. In addition, there are mathematical models that allow calculating the premium based on the current value of the underlying asset and its stochastic properties (volatility, profitability, etc.). The premium calculated in this way is called the theoretical option price. As a rule, it is calculated by the organizer of trades or by a broker and is available along with the quotation information during the trades.

Automatic option exercise

In most countries, the legislation in exchange trading does not regulate the procedure for exercising the options, therefore, automatic exercise of options in the form of cash settlements has been introduced on some exchanges. This procedure eliminates the risks associated with late submission of an application for the exercise of options. For example, automatic exercise of options was introduced on the Moscow Stock Exchange in 2015.

What is the difference between the option and the futures?
Option and futures are quite similar instruments of exchange trading. But each of them has its own characteristics. **Futures is considered a simpler instrument.** So, when concluding a futures contract on the exchange, the bidder takes into account only one amount – the price of buying the futures at trading. This figure, when divided by the lot of a futures contract, will make it possible to determine the immediate value of the asset itself. The amount of the guarantee is fixed in the document and remains unchanged.

The situation with options is much more interesting. The buyer and seller agree in advance on the price of the option contract exercise, that is, how much the asset is expected to cost. This amount is called strike price. If a trader wants to make a profit, then the value of the underlying asset option should be greater than the strike value if it is a call option. And, on the contrary, for the trader to make a profit, the price should be lower than the strike, if it is a put option. But the strike is not the amount that the seller will receive in the case of the transaction. The exercise price often does not correspond to what the underlying asset is really worth at the time of the transaction.

The exchange provides the trader with a choice from a wide range of numbers during the transaction. The actual option price is the premium paid for the right to buy or sell an asset and is the main subject of exchange trading. Its price is determined by the market, not the exchange. Therefore, traders can negotiate and specify the amount of the premium they want to earn on the transaction.

BULL CALL SPREAD OPTION STRATEGY

This strategy is a little more complicated than the others, because it involves simultaneous execution of a transaction with two Call options on different strikes. In this case, the trader sells one of them and buys the second one. Based on this, we can say that the strategy uses such a tool as hedging.

What the Bull Call Spread strategy is
The trader applies two options, both of which are Call options.

- *The trader BUYS the first Call option.*
- *The second Call option is SOLD by the trader.*

Thus, the price (option premium) of the sold option is always lower than that of the bought option, while the Strike Price of the sold option is higher.

The expiration moment is the same for both options.

What does this give to the trader?

If the price of the asset at the time of expiration goes above the Strike Price of the bought option, then the trader makes a profit, and it is the higher the greater the distance.

Since the Strike Price of the sold option is higher than the Strike Price of the bought one, when the price is between these marks, the trader to whom the Call option was sold will not want to exercise their right, because the market price is still lower than the Strike Price.

If the market price exceeds the Strike Price of the sold option, the trader who sold it suffers losses. However, they are compensated by the fact that the bought call option brought a significant profit.

If the price reverses and goes down, the bought option will lose. However, this is compensated (partially or completely) by the option premium on the sold option.

Advantages of the Bull Call Spread Strategy

Its main advantage is that you can insure yourself in case the price goes the wrong way.

Other advantages:

- *It is convenient when the market is not very volatile. A price increase is needed, although it should be insignificant*
- *Losses are limited.*

Disadvantages of the Bull Call Spread Strategy

- **The disadvantages are that there may still be losses, but this is true for absolutely any format of exchange trading.**
- **Profit when using Bull Call Spread is also limited, which makes this format less profitable than the standard one (buying one option).**

The Bull Call Spread strategy is suitable for cautious traders, large time scales, and situations where there is no reason to assume sharp price jumps. It is advantageous to use it for underlying assets with low volatility.

BEAR CALL SPREAD OPTION STRATEGY

The Bear Call Spread strategy involves simultaneous buying and selling the call options. It is called bearish because the trader using it expects that the price will decrease in comparison with the current levels or at least will not change.

What the Bear Call Spread strategy is

Using this strategy, the trader makes two transactions.
- **Buying a Call option.**
- **Selling a Call option.**

Both options belong to the same asset and have the same expiration moment. They only have different Strike Prices. The strike price of the bought option should be higher than that of the sold one.

By trading with these two options, we expect that the price will decrease, but not too much. A moderate decrease in the price (or the fact that it will remain almost unchanged) allows us to get our option premium as a seller of a Call option, while not fulfilling our obligations to its buyer (it will be unprofitable for them to demand the fulfillment of these obligations).

- ***The maximum income for such a strategy is exactly the difference between the two option premiums.***
- ***The trader gets the maximum loss on such a strategy if the price goes up.***

In this case, both options are executed, but the trader gets a negative result due to the fact that they have to fulfill their obligations as a seller of the Call option.

Advantages of the Bear Call Spread strategy

The advantage of such a strategy is that it limits the potential losses of the trader and therefore does not involve such a risk as direct buy and especially sale of options, and especially the assets themselves

Another advantage is that in order to achieve the desired result, that is, making a profit, you do not need much market mobility. While simple option trading involves a significant change in the price of an asset to generate a large income.

Disadvantages of the Bear Call Spread strategy

The downside is that the profit on such a strategy is limited, while a strong price movement in both directions turns out to be unprofitable for the trader. When using this strategy, it is important to have reasons to expect that the price will not go out of a specific small range.

An additional disadvantage is that not all brokers allow transactions on one asset in both directions at the same time, as well as the fact that the broker may require additional conditions to be met by the option sellers.

SHORT CALL OPTION STRATEGY

Although from a technical point of view, this strategy is one of the simplest, but it is also one of the riskiest, basically, like most option strategies that use an uncovered sale. Therefore, it is necessary to use such strategies with extreme caution, having some experience in option trading.

What the Short Call strategy is

If a trader is a buyer of an option, then they get the right (but not the obligation) to buy/sell an asset at a set time and at a set price. Thus, the seller is obliged to deliver this asset to them or buy it at an agreed price, regardless of whether it is beneficial for the seller or not.

If a trader chooses a Short Call strategy, then they become a seller. In the case of a Call option, it is beneficial to their buyer that the asset price increases. Hence, it is not profitable for the seller.

You should act as a Call option seller only if you are firmly convinced that the price of the asset will NOT go up.

In some cases, in order to be a Call option seller, a trader should have the required amount of assets available (under the option agreement): stocks, futures, commodities. Therefore, the broker may force them to purchase this asset before granting them the right to become a Call option seller.

Advantages of the Short Call strategy

The main and almost the only advantage of this strategy is the fixed profit that the option seller receives immediately, at the moment when this option is bought from them. This profit is called the option price, or option premium.

An additional advantage can be considered the opportunity to earn a lot by actively selling Call options in a falling or stationary market. However, this is offset by the risk of huge losses if the market goes up.

Disadvantages of the Short Call strategy

The main disadvantage is the unlimited losses, because if the price of an asset grows significantly, you will first have to buy it at very high price and then sell it much cheaper to the option buyer. And this is extremely unprofitable.

For the Call option seller, it is useful to immediately buy the right amount of the asset, so as not to do it later at a loss in the event of a price increase.

In order for a transaction with such an option to be breakeven for its seller, the price of the asset may even rise slightly, but the loss from the rise should not exceed the option premium.

It is worth selling Call options only if you have good reason to believe that the price will NOT rise in the time before the expiration.

Unlike the option buyer, the seller may need to fulfill additional conditions of the broker before they are allowed to make such transactions, which you should also be prepared for.

LONG PUT OPTION STRATEGY

Long Put is one of the simplest strategies when trading options on the FORTS market. Thus, it can be profitable if you use it correctly and open a position at the moments when the probability of increased volatility in the market increases and there are also prerequisites for a corrective movement after a prolonged growth of the asset.

What the Long Put strategy is

The essence of this strategy is buying a Put option, which allows you to SELL a specific asset, for example shares, at a specific price at a certain, pre-agreed moment (expiration moment).

The price at which option will be sold is called Strike Price and does not depend on the price of the asset in the market at the time of expiration. This is what gives the trader who bought the option a profit.

In order for a trader to profit from a Put option, the market price at the time of expiration must be LOWER than the strike price. In this case, the holder of the option "imposes" its seller to buy the asset at a price that is unprofitable for the seller and is higher than the market price.

Advantages of the Long Put strategy

The main difference between buying an option and actually trading the underlying asset is that the potential profit of a trader can be infinite, with fixed risks. In reality, profits are usually limited by global support and resistance levels and historical lows/highs for this asset. But with a significant price movement, the trader will get a big profit.

Thus, the trader cannot incur a loss exceeding the option premium ("option price"), which is paid to the seller at the time of buying the option. So the trader knows what he is risking in advance.

Another advantage of the Long Put strategy is that it can be used for hedging.

Hedging in exchange trading means making a transaction in the opposite direction compared to a previously made transaction. In this case, wherever the price goes, one of the transactions will end successfully, and the second will not. This allows neutralizing losses or even exceeding them.

However, the Long Put strategy can also be used as an independent one if the trader is sure that the asset price will decrease.

Disadvantages of the Long Put strategy

The main disadvantages of this strategy include the following:

- ***The trader will incur losses if the price exceeds the Strike Price.***
- ***Even a short-term excess of this mark by the price at the time of expiration leads to losses.***

Before buying an option of this type, it is useful for a trader to carefully analyze the market and get serious confirmation that the price should fall below the initial mark by the time of expiration.

Thus, buying a Long Put option implies that the price decrease from the Strike Price should be such as to at least compensate for the option premium; otherwise, the trader loses funds, even if the option is closed "in the money".

LONG CALL OPTION STRATEGY

If a trader is just starting to trade options on the FORTS market, they usually tend to use the simplest strategies. Long Call is one of such strategies.

What the Long Call strategy is

Its essence is that a trader buys a Call option, that is, an option that makes it possible to BUY a specific asset at a pre-agreed time at the price set by the option agreement (strike price).

In order for a trader to profit from buying such an option, the market price of the said asset should be HIGHER than the price set in the option agreement at the time of expiration.

In this case, the trader has the opportunity to buy an asset at a price that is lower than the market price. And this is a benefit.

If the difference between the strike price and the market price at the time of expiration is equal to the option premium, then the trader receives nothing and loses nothing. In this case, the option is considered "zero".

Advantages of the Long Call strategy

The main advantage of this strategy is a potentially unlimited profit with fixed possible losses.

Let's explain it. Since the price can theoretically move up indefinitely, the entire difference between the acquisition price of the option and the market price of the asset at the time of expiration becomes the real profit of the trader (the holder of the option).

When buying assets directly, there is always a risk that they will depreciate greatly; in the case of stocks, there is a possibility of a fall in value to almost zero. In this case, the trader incurs huge losses.

However, the Long Call strategy allows neutralizing this risk, since in the event of a fall in the exchange rate, the trader will not have to make unprofitable transactions and will not lose anything, except for the option premium, which is paid to the option seller at the time of the transaction.

Consequently, a trader who follows a Long Call strategy risks a small amount of money (an option premium) and has the opportunity to get significant profit in case of favorable development of events.

Disadvantages of the Long Call strategy

The main disadvantage of the Long Call strategy is that at the time of expiration, the option expires anyway. If it is "out of the money" (in the case of the Call option, this means that the market price is less than the Strike Price), then the trader incurs losses, even if shortly before the expiration the price was in the winning zone and will return there in a while.

A sharp short-term jump in price, which would not be a tragedy for a trader who actually has asset in his hands, ends in losses for the option holder.

The Long Call strategy is generally recommended if there are serious reasons to think that the asset price will rise, and the trader is so confident in this that they are ready to risk the amount of the option premium.

ADDITIONAL INFORMATION DIRECTLY RELATED TO THE OPERATION OF THE SYSTEM.

In this section, I plan to talk about several useful services that are not directly related to the trading strategy, but can significantly strengthen it.
I use them on a regular basis.

DataRoma.

This is a unique service that allows you to monitor all changes in the portfolios of institutions.

You should understand that our role is to skillfully sit on the tail of a major player.

And this service allows you to do it masterfully.

There are several tables on its main page.

Let's look at them:

Here you can see the latest changes that have occurred in recent days.

Superinvestor Portfolio Updates RSS Feed

- Meridian Contrarian Fund   Updated 26 Nov 2021
- Christopher Davis - Clipper Fund   Updated 26 Nov 2021
- Bill Nygren - Oakmark Select Fund   Updated 23 Nov 2021
- Mason Hawkins - Longleaf Partners   Updated 22 Nov 2021
- Torray Fund   Updated 19 Nov 2021
- Ruane, Cunniff & Goldfarb - Sequoia Fund   Updated 18 Nov 2021
- Prem Watsa - Fairfax Financial Holdings   Updated 18 Nov 2021
- Howard Marks - Oaktree Capital Management   Updated 18 Nov 2021
- Harry Burn - Sound Shore   Updated 17 Nov 2021
- David Katz - Matrix Advisors Value   Updated 17 Nov 2021
- Lee Ainslie - Maverick Capital   Updated 15 Nov 2021
- Alex Roepers - Atlantic Investment Management   Updated 15 Nov 202
- Bill & Melinda Gates Foundation Trust   Updated 15 Nov 2021
- Bill Ackman - Pershing Square Capital Management   Updated 15 Nov
- Daniel Loeb - Third Point   Updated 15 Nov 2021
- David Einhorn - Greenlight Capital   Updated 15 Nov 2021
- Glenn Greenberg - Brave Warrior Advisors   Updated 15 Nov 2021
- Bruce Berkowitz - Fairholme Capital   Updated 15 Nov 2021
- Li Lu - Himalaya Capital Management   Updated 15 Nov 2021
- ValueAct Capital   Updated 15 Nov 2021
- Eddie Lampert - RBS Partners   Updated 15 Nov 2021
- Christopher Bloomstran - Semper Augustus   Updated 15 Nov 2021
- Norbert Lou - Punch Card Management   Updated 15 Nov 2021
- Valley Forge Capital Management   Updated 15 Nov 2021
- Warren Buffett - Berkshire Hathaway   Updated 15 Nov 2021
- Carl Icahn - Icahn Capital Management   Updated 15 Nov 2021
- David Tepper - Appaloosa Management   Updated 15 Nov 2021
- Stephen Mandel - Lone Pine Capital   Updated 15 Nov 2021
- Viking Global Investors   Updated 15 Nov 2021
- Bill Miller - Miller Value Partners   Updated 15 Nov 2021
- Glenn Welling - Engaged Capital   Updated 15 Nov 2021
- Chase Coleman - Tiger Global Management   Updated 15 Nov 2021
- Francis Chou - Chou Associates   Updated 15 Nov 2021
- Leon Cooperman   Updated 15 Nov 2021
- Michael Price - MFP Investors   Updated 15 Nov 2021
- Michael Burry - Scion Asset Management   Updated 15 Nov 2021
- Thomas Russo - Gardner Russo & Quinn   Updated 15 Nov 2021
- Jefferies Financial Group   Updated 15 Nov 2021
- Pat Dorsey - Dorsey Asset Management   Updated 15 Nov 2021
- Chris Hohn - TCI Fund Management   Updated 15 Nov 2021
- Greg Alexander - Conifer Management   Updated 15 Nov 2021
- Nelson Peltz - Trian Fund Management   Updated 12 Nov 2021
- Seth Klarman - Baupost Group   Updated 12 Nov 2021
- Robert Olstein - Olstein Capital Management   Updated 12 Nov 2021
- David Abrams - Abrams Capital Management   Updated 12 Nov 2021
- David Rolfe - Wedgewood Partners   Updated 12 Nov 2021
- Chuck Akre - Akre Capital Management   Updated 12 Nov 2021
- Third Avenue Management   Updated 12 Nov 2021
- Jensen Investment Management   Updated 12 Nov 2021

Lets talk about useful services for traders

And this is an equally important column.

Top left - TOP10 most owned stocks.

TOP 10 most most bought stocks across all portfolios. We can conclude that these are the strongest stocks.

Top 10 Stocksby% is the percentage of the strongest stocks in the portfolios.

Top big bets are the stocks on which large funds bet the most.

Top 10 buys last quarter - the 10 most bought stocks in the last quarter.

Top 10 buys last quarter by % - the same, but as a percentage.

Top 10 buys last 2 quarter - TOP 10 most bought stocks in the last two quarters.

Top 10 buys last quarter by % - the same, but as a percentage.

Superinvestor Portfolio Stats

Top 10 most owned stocks
- FB - Meta Platforms Inc.
- GOOGL - Alphabet Inc.
- GOOG - Alphabet Inc. CL C
- MSFT - Microsoft Corp.
- WFC - Wells Fargo
- V - Visa Inc.
- AMZN - Amazon.com Inc.
- BRK.B - Berkshire Hathaway CL B
- CMCSA - Comcast Corp.
- UNH - United Health Group Inc.

Top 10 stocks by %
- GOOG - Alphabet Inc. CL C
- FB - Meta Platforms Inc.
- BRK.B - Berkshire Hathaway CL B
- BAC - Bank of America Corp.
- MU - Micron Technology Inc.
- BRK.A - Berkshire Hathaway CL A
- MSFT - Microsoft Corp.
- GOOGL - Alphabet Inc.
- JOE - St. Joe Co.
- WFC - Wells Fargo

Top "big bets"

	Max % of portfolio	Ownership count
MU - Micron Technology Inc.	58.76%	10
ATCO - Atlas Corp.	49.53%	2
BRK.B - Berkshire Hathaway CL B	45.53%	18
ALLY - Ally Financial Inc.	43.55%	4
BAC - Bank of America Corp.	43.35%	15
AAPL - Apple Inc.	42.78%	10
CVS - CVS Health Corp.	40.68%	7
BRK.A - Berkshire Hathaway CL A	37.23%	13
SRG - Seritage Growth Properties	36.79%	3
WFC - Wells Fargo	32.80%	22

Top 10 buys last qtr (Q3 2021)
- BABA - Alibaba Group Holdings
- AMZN - Amazon.com Inc.
- V - Visa Inc.
- BKNG - Booking Holdings Inc.
- FDX - FedEx Corp.
- GOOGL - Alphabet Inc.
- PVH - PVH Corp.
- ATVI - Activision Blizzard Inc.
- WFC - Wells Fargo
- RH - RH

Top 10 buys last qtr by %
- HLMN - Hillman Solutions Corp
- LMT - Lockheed Martin Corp.
- BABA - Alibaba Group Holdings
- BRK.B - Berkshire Hathaway CL B
- GT - Goodyear Tire & Rubber
- DNA - Ginkgo Bioworks Holdings Inc.
- AMZN - Amazon.com Inc.
- FISV - Fiserv Inc.
- ACN - Accenture
- CNI - Canadian Natl Railway Co.

Top 10 buys last 2 qtrs
- BABA - Alibaba Group Holdings
- AMZN - Amazon.com Inc.
- FB - Meta Platforms Inc.
- V - Visa Inc.
- BKNG - Booking Holdings Inc.
- FISV - Fiserv Inc.
- GE - General Electric
- VIAC - ViacomCBS Inc.
- CHTR - Charter Communications
- NFLX - Netflix Inc.

Top 10 buys last 2 qtrs by %
- HLMN - Hillman Solutions Corp
- BABA - Alibaba Group Holdings
- AMZN - Amazon.com Inc.
- LMT - Lockheed Martin Corp.
- DISCK - Discovery Communications Inc. CL C
- BRK.B - Berkshire Hathaway CL B
- FISV - Fiserv Inc.
- VIAC - ViacomCBS Inc.
- OVV - Ovintiv Inc.
- FNF - Fidelity National Financial Inc.

Lets talk about useful services for traders

Superinvestor stocks with most insider buys in the last 3 months

Stock	Count	Total Amount $
TPL - Texas Pacific Land Corp	196	1,242,800
GDRX - GoodRx Holdings Inc	32	46,025,411
ED - CONSOLIDATED EDISON INC	29	64,930
ASAN - Asana Inc	20	161,317,174
ASPU - ASPEN GROUP Inc	18	394,410
OSCR - Oscar Health Inc	18	59,373,358
RNR - RENAISSANCERE HOLDINGS LTD	18	4,359,714
CANO - Cano Health Inc	15	16,024,893
MGI - MONEYGRAM INTERNATIONAL INC	14	2,342,214
LOV - Spark Networks SE	14	4,622,243
INTC - INTEL CORP	13	4,745,774
TCBI - TEXAS CAPITAL BANCSHARES INC	13	6,183,950
ETWO - E2open Parent Holdings Inc	12	27,711,187
FYBR - Frontier Communications Parent Inc	12	11,428,768
GH - Guardant Health Inc	12	17,692,277
SPG - SIMON PROPERTY GROUP INC	10	279,228
CARE - Carter Bankshares Inc	10	33,843
VOXX - VOXX International Corp	10	1,407,124
MED - MEDIFAST INC	10	973,912
BCBP - BCB BANCORP INC	10	147,618
SUP - SUPERIOR INDUSTRIES INTERNATIONAL INC	9	1,082,062
EBAY - EBAY INC	8	62,446
COMM - CommScope Holding Company Inc	8	1,373,435
PTON - PELOTON INTERACTIVE Inc	8	99,999,998
CME - CME GROUP Inc	7	441,143
BBBY - BED BATH & BEYOND INC	7	982,100
CLR - CONTINENTAL RESOURCES INC	7	16,735,452
VICI - VICI PROPERTIES Inc	6	703,367
ATEC - Alphatec Holdings Inc	6	2,662,401
FPI - Farmland Partners Inc	6	133,852
WMPN - William Penn Bancorp	6	124,910
ZIOP - ZIOPHARM ONCOLOGY INC	6	625,085
AUD - AUDACY Inc	6	863,044
DBI - Designer Brands Inc	6	24,093,378
PYPL - PayPal Holdings Inc	6	2,287,697

And here is an equally interesting column. Here you can see a **list of stocks that insiders have bought over the past 3 months**.

Lets talk about useful services for traders

The next tab is **Superinvestors**

Portfolio Manager - Firm	Portfolio value	No. of stocks	Top 10 holdings (left to right)									
AKO Capital	$9.65 B	25	LIN	BKNG	ACN	TMO	GOOG	EBAY	ALC	ZTS	OTIS	EFX
Alex Roepers - Atlantic Investment Management	$298 M	11	HUN	UNVR	WRK	GT	LEA	AVT	BERY	EMN	OI	BLDR
Bill & Melinda Gates Foundation Trust	$23.2 B	22	BRK.B	WM	CAT	CNI	WMT	ECL	MSFT	CCI	KSU	UPS
Bill Ackman - Pershing Square Capital Management	$9.46 B	6	LOW	CMG	HLT	QSR	HHC	DPZ				
Bill Miller - Miller Value Partners	$2.94 B	98	AMZN	DXC	SPLK	GOOGL	FB	ADT	NCLH	TEVA	FANG	BABA
Bill Nygren - Oakmark Select Fund	$4.98 B	23	GOOGL	CBRE	ALLY	NFLX	CHTR	C	fb	BAC	COF	AIG
Bruce Berkowitz - Fairholme Capital	$1.24 B	15	JOE	EPD	CMC	INTC	KMI	ENB	ET	BRK.B	WMB	WES
Carl Icahn - Icahn Capital Management	$22.5 B	17	IEP	LNG	OXY	CVI	NWL	BHC	CLDR	HRI	FE	XRX
Charles Bobrinskoy - Ariel Focus	$61 M	29	MOS	APA	GS	BOKF	BWA	SJM	LAZ	WBA	SNA	NLSN
Charlie Munger - Daily Journal Corp.	$225 M	5	BAC	WFC	BABA	USB	PKX					
Chase Coleman - Tiger Global Management	$52.1 B	161	MSFT	JD	SE	DASH	DOCU	AMZN	CVNA	CRWD	FB	SNOW
Chris Hohn - TCI Fund Management	$41.6 B	13	GOOG	CHTR	MSFT	V	CNI	CP	MCO	SPGI	GOOGL	BXP
Christopher Bloomstran - Semper Augustus	$309 M	38	BRK.B	BRK.A	OLN	VIAC	NEM	KGC	XOM	HFC	SBUX	VLO
Christopher Davis - Clipper Fund	$1.12 B	29	COF	BRK.A	WFC	GOOGL	BK	USB	FB	MKL	AMZN	CI
Chuck Akre - Akre Capital Management	$16.2 B	23	MA	MCO	AMT	V	ORLY	KMX	KKR	ADBE	CSGP	CRM
ClearBridge Value Trust	$2.03 B	65	WFC	AIG	BAC	PXD	GE	EQH	SYF	ORCL	DXC	GS
Daniel Loeb - Third Point	$18.3 B	112	UPST	S	DHR	PCG	DIS	AMZN	INTU	GOOGL	CSGP	INTC
David Abrams - Abrams Capital Management	$4.59 B	18	LAD	ABG	FB	GOOGL	UHAL	CHNG	TDG	WLTW	TEVA	ET
David Einhorn - Greenlight Capital	$1.49 B	58	GRBK	BHF	AAWW	TECK	CHNG	CC	CEIX	CNXC	ODP	DNMR
David Katz - Matrix Advisors Value	$67 M	32	MSFT	GOOG	JPM	GS	fb	CVS	AAPL	MS	VIAC	USB
David Rolfe - Wedgewood Partners	$709 M	40	EW	AAPL	GOOGL	FB	MSI	TSCO	PYPL	MSFT	CDW	V
David Tepper - Appaloosa Management	$4.2 B	51	GOOG	FB	TMUS	AMZN	OXY	MU	M	PCG	XLE	DHI
Dodge & Cox	$90.2 B	70	WFC	COF	SCHW	GOOG	SNY	CMCSA	MET	CHTR	DELL	JCI
Eddie Lampert - RBS Partners	$155 M	2	AN	LE								
First Eagle Investment Management	$39 B	310	ORCL	CMCSA	XOM	FB	WLTW	NTR	TSM	PM	NEM	CHRW
FPA Queens Road Small Cap Value Fund	$400 M	53	SYNA	SFBS	AEL	IDCC	HMN	FN	MTZ	CNO	RLI	SWM
Francis Chou - Chou Associates	$159 M	15	BHC	BRK.A	RFP	WFC	MBI	JPM	C	BB	GS	MGA
Glenn Greenberg - Brave Warrior Advisors	$2.86 B	24	ANTM	FNF	PRI	JPM	VVV	RJF	PGR	BRK.B	APO	HCA
Glenn Welling - Engaged Capital	$1.39 B	9	HAIN	EVH	RCII	NEWR	STKL	NCR	GIL	QUOT	IWM	

You can see a **list of 10 stocks for each of the funds**. It's just a unique tool.

Next, on the **activity** tab:

Portfolio Manager - Firm	Period	Top 10 Buys/Sells									
AKO Capital	Q3 2021	ACN	BKNG	CHTR	V	LYFT	ABEV	LIN	ICE	TMO	NKE
Alex Roepers - Atlantic Investment Management	Q3 2021	GT	EPC	BERY	WRK	BLDR	HUN	NOMD	LEA	AVT	UNVR
Bill & Melinda Gates Foundation Trust	Q3 2021	BRK.B	MSFT	KSU	DE	CNI	WMT	UPS	CAT	CCI	MSGS
Bill Ackman - Pershing Square Capital Management	Q3 2021	A	CMG	DPZ	LOW	HLT	QSR	HHC			
Bill Miller - Miller Value Partners	Q3 2021	HLF	MTTR	TUP	DM	BA	DXC	AYI	OMF	FANG	COIN
Bill Nygren - Oakmark Select Fund	Q3 2021	ALSN	GOOGL	HUM	EOG	BAC	GE	CBRE	COF	HCA	REGN
Bruce Berkowitz - Fairholme Capital	Q3 2021	EPD	JOE	CMC	INTC	VST	KMI	ET	WES	ORI	ENB
Carl Icahn - Icahn Capital Management	Q3 2021	NAV	IEP	OXY	SWX	DAN	OXY.WS				
Charles Bobrinskoy - Ariel Focus	Q3 2021	ORCL	MSGS	LH	APA	GS	NTRS	BOKF	SNA	NLSN	MOS
Charlie Munger - Daily Journal Corp.	Q3 2021	BABA									
Chase Coleman - Tiger Global Management	Q3 2021	WRBY	RBLX	HOOD	APO	SNOW	BLND	VTEX	PTON	MTTR	ZM
Chris Hohn - TCI Fund Management	Q3 2021	V	MSFT	CNI	INFO	SPGI	BXP	ARE	CHTR	KRC	
Christopher Bloomstran - Semper Augustus	Q3 2021	DLTR	VIAC	BRK.B	ALK	KGC	NEM	SBUX	VLO	HFC	COST
Christopher Davis - Clipper Fund	Q3 2021	GOOG	BABA	EDU	JD	CI	PNGAY	AMZN	COF	FB	AXP
Chuck Akre - Akre Capital Management	Q3 2021	MKL	MA	AMT	ORLY	MCO	ROP	KMX	BAM	DLTR	KKR
ClearBridge Value Trust	Q3 2021	MU	DIS	CCL	FDX	CI	COTY	CNHI	SPR	NXPI	NEM
Daniel Loeb - Third Point	Q3 2021	SOFI	UBER	UPST	INTC	JD	ALIT	ATVI	AMZN	PTON	S
David Abrams - Abrams Capital Management	Q3 2021	PCG	TPX	CPNG	CHNG	USCB					
David Einhorn - Greenlight Capital	Q3 2021	SLV	CNXC	SPY	ODP	JOBY	BHF	SNX	TECK	OPAD	LIVN
David Katz - Matrix Advisors Value	Q3 2021	FISV	BDX	QCOM	FDX	ZBH	USB	VIAC	WFC	TFC	EBAY

We can see **what exactly the funds bought and sold over the last quarter.**

Grand Portfolio tab:

Symbol	Stock	% ▼	Ownership count	Hold Price*	Max %	Current Price	52 Week Low	% Above 52 Week Low	52 Week High
GOOG	Alphabet Inc. CL C	1.956	27	$2665.30	18.90	$2861.58	$1699.00	68.43	$3037.00
FB	Meta Platforms Inc.	1.840	33	$339.60	17.05	$333.30	$244.61	36.26	$384.33
BRK.B	Berkshire Hathaway CL B	1.779	18	$272.94	45.53	$283.09	$221.26	27.94	$295.65
BAC	Bank of America Corp.	1.689	15	$42.45	43.35	$45.76	$27.53	66.22	$48.69
MU	Micron Technology Inc.	1.656	10	$70.98	58.76	$83.47	$63.42	31.61	$96.82
BRK.A	Berkshire Hathaway CL A	1.577	13	$411379.04	37.23	$427832.75	$333150.00	28.42	$445000.00
MSFT	Microsoft Corp.	1.414	24	$281.63	11.29	$330.16	$207.37	59.21	$349.67
GOOGL	Alphabet Inc.	1.331	28	$2665.19	10.46	$2848.39	$1694.00	68.15	$3019.33
JOE	St. Joe Co	1.172	1		85.54	$49.73	$31.91	55.84	$57.16
WFC	Wells Fargo	1.145	22	$46.36	32.80	$48.43	$26.91	79.97	$52.36
AMZN	Amazon.com Inc.	0.993	20	$3292.91	10.56	$3508.16	$2881.00	21.77	$3773.08
V	Visa Inc.	0.957	22	$222.75	10.67	$197.65	$191.63	3.14	$251.88
AN	AutoNation Inc.	0.949	1		69.30	$127.19	$60.45	110.41	$133.48
MA	Mastercard Inc.	0.933	15	$347.68	19.08	$324.17	$311.82	4.03	$400.99
AAPL	Apple Inc.	0.919	10	$141.50	42.78	$157.43	$115.51	36.29	$165.70
BABA	Alibaba Group Holdings	0.823	15	$140.74	19.86	$133.35	$131.22	1.62	$278.92
CMCSA	Comcast Corp.	0.765	18	$55.93	13.90	$51.12	$47.72	7.12	$61.53
ALLY	Ally Financial Inc.	0.765	4	$51.05	43.55	$48.38	$29.00	66.83	$56.05
IEP	Icahn Enterprises	0.751	1		54.81	$50.55	$42.91	17.80	$59.91
CVS	CVS Health Corp.	0.696	7	$84.77	40.68	$91.52	$65.40	39.94	$96.57
ATCO	Atlas Corp.	0.680	2	$15.19	49.53	$13.80	$9.41	46.65	$16.35
HAIN	Hain Celestial Group	0.673	1		49.16	$41.61	$35.57	16.98	$48.88
MCO	Moody's Corp.	0.662	11	$355.11	16.31	$384.09	$259.45	48.04	$407.29
DIS	Walt Disney Co.	0.651	11	$169.17	12.83	$148.11	$145.85	1.55	$203.02

It shows a list of stocks that are most often found in the portfolios of major players.

Real Time tab:

Transaction Date	Filing	Reporting Name	Activity	Security	Shares	Price	Total
23 Nov 2021	26 Nov 20:22	LOEB DANIEL S	Sell	Upstart Holdings Inc	9.227	$190.31	$1,756,014
23 Nov 2021	26 Nov 20:22	LOEB DANIEL S	Sell	Upstart Holdings Inc	7.254	$191.41	$1,388,506
23 Nov 2021	26 Nov 20:22	LOEB DANIEL S	Sell	Upstart Holdings Inc	12.516	$192.60	$2,410,527
23 Nov 2021	26 Nov 20:22	LOEB DANIEL S	Sell	Upstart Holdings Inc	18.233	$193.58	$3,529,562
23 Nov 2021	26 Nov 20:22	LOEB DANIEL S	Sell	Upstart Holdings Inc	22.005	$194.39	$4,277,446
23 Nov 2021	26 Nov 20:22	LOEB DANIEL S	Sell	Upstart Holdings Inc	30.765	$195.47	$6,013,595
23 Nov 2021	26 Nov 20:22	LOEB DANIEL S	Sell	Upstart Holdings Inc	18.513	$200.43	$3,710,570
23 Nov 2021	26 Nov 20:22	LOEB DANIEL S	Sell	Upstart Holdings Inc	20.544	$201.35	$4,136,584
23 Nov 2021	26 Nov 20:22	LOEB DANIEL S	Sell	Upstart Holdings Inc	25.277	$202.54	$5,119,679
23 Nov 2021	26 Nov 20:22	LOEB DANIEL S	Sell	Upstart Holdings Inc	15.591	$203.61	$3,174,437
23 Nov 2021	26 Nov 20:22	LOEB DANIEL S	Sell	Upstart Holdings Inc	14.993	$204.59	$3,067,413
23 Nov 2021	26 Nov 20:22	LOEB DANIEL S	Sell	Upstart Holdings Inc	5.082	$205.38	$1,043,757
19 Nov 2021	23 Nov 17:10	LOEB DANIEL S	Sell	Upstart Holdings Inc	48.181	$205.99	$9,924,669
19 Nov 2021	23 Nov 17:10	LOEB DANIEL S	Sell	Upstart Holdings Inc	150.232	$206.91	$31,084,789

Monitors all changes in real time.

Lets talk about useful services for traders

Real Time Insider Data tab:

Filing	Symbol	Security	Reporting Name	Relationship	Trans. Date	Purchase/Sale	Shares	Price $	Amount $
26 Nov 2021 21:52	ATEC	Alphatec Holdings Inc	SEGAL PAUL	10%	23 Nov 2021	Purchase	67,496	10.98	741,106
26 Nov 2021 21:51	ADMQ	ADM ENDEAVORS Inc	JOHNSON MARC	CEO	24 Nov 2021	Purchase	51,000	0.0756	3,856
26 Nov 2021 21:51	ADMQ	ADM ENDEAVORS Inc	JOHNSON MARC	CEO	24 Nov 2021	Purchase	500	0.0773	39
26 Nov 2021 21:51	ADMQ	ADM ENDEAVORS Inc	JOHNSON MARC	CEO	24 Nov 2021	Purchase	43,000	0.078	3,354
26 Nov 2021 21:51	ADMQ	ADM ENDEAVORS Inc	JOHNSON MARC	CEO	24 Nov 2021	Purchase	19,475	0.0782	1,523
26 Nov 2021 21:51	ADMQ	ADM ENDEAVORS Inc	JOHNSON MARC	CEO	24 Nov 2021	Purchase	99,000	0.079	7,821
26 Nov 2021 21:51	ADMQ	ADM ENDEAVORS Inc	JOHNSON MARC	CEO	24 Nov 2021	Purchase	20,000	0.0791	1,582
26 Nov 2021 21:51	ADMQ	ADM ENDEAVORS Inc	JOHNSON MARC	CEO	24 Nov 2021	Purchase	10,000	0.0799	799
26 Nov 2021 21:51	ADMQ	ADM ENDEAVORS Inc	JOHNSON MARC	CEO	24 Nov 2021	Purchase	72,000	0.08	5,760
26 Nov 2021 21:51	ADMQ	ADM ENDEAVORS Inc	JOHNSON MARC	CEO	24 Nov 2021	Purchase	5,000	0.0803	402
26 Nov 2021 21:51	ADMQ	ADM ENDEAVORS Inc	JOHNSON MARC	CEO	24 Nov 2021	Purchase	1,200	0.0815	98

It is very interesting tab allowing you to track buys and sales for a certain period of time and by a certain percentage.

Conclusion.

I strongly recommend you to explore this service. Play with it and it will definitely bear fruit.

Captain Solutions.

What is Captain?

FinTwit (aka Financial Twitter aka Stock Market Twitter) has become a powerful trading community where market insights, ideas, and opinions are shared and discussed. The downside? As a free, open-access platform, it's easy to get lost in the clutter or overwhelmed by the firehose of information. Or worse, blindly trust the information you find without doing research of your own.

We're fixing that. Our FinTwit Toolkit, Real-Time Alerts and daily Email Alerts are designed to save you time and give you an advantage. Using powerful A.I., Captain monitors conversation across FinTwit, but not all of FinTwit. We look specifically at more than 100 top traders who have earned the respect of thousands with their proven track record. We analyze their ideas and opinions, turning them into digestible, actionable trends. The result? FinTwit insights that are built to support your trade decisions and investment research.

Why Captain vs. Twitter directly?

Consider Captain as your personal dream team of analysts. In a matter of seconds, we provide market information that would require hours of scrolling through Twitter. In just a few clicks, you can identify which stocks are trending in conversation and why top traders are talking about them.

FOR THOSE THAT ALREADY USE FINTWIT AS A TRADING RESOURCE, CAPTAIN IS A NO-BRAINER.

FOR THOSE THAT DON'T, THIS IS THE TOOL THAT YOUR ARSENAL IS MISSING.

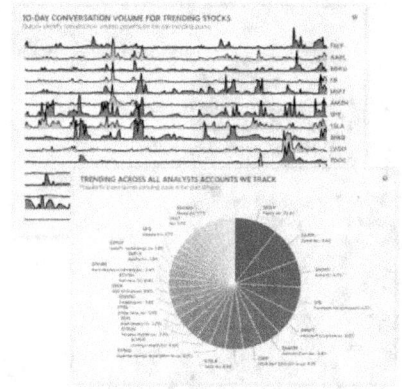

Lets talk about useful services for traders

If you haven't bought my secret list of Twitter accounts on my website yet, then this service may suit you well.

Its operation consists in monitoring the Twitter accounts of advanced traders.

That is, in fact, it does all the dirty work for you. Now trading on Twitter is becoming much more enjoyable.

Its features:

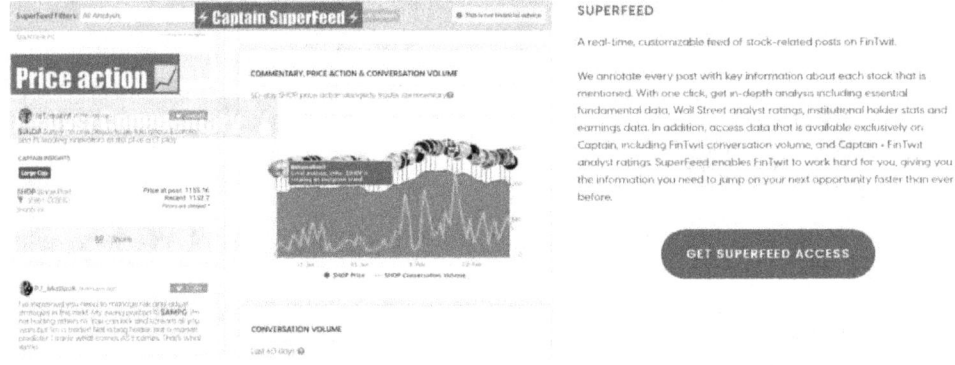

Superfeed - all tweets of the followed traders are received here in real time.

SUMMARY DASHBOARD

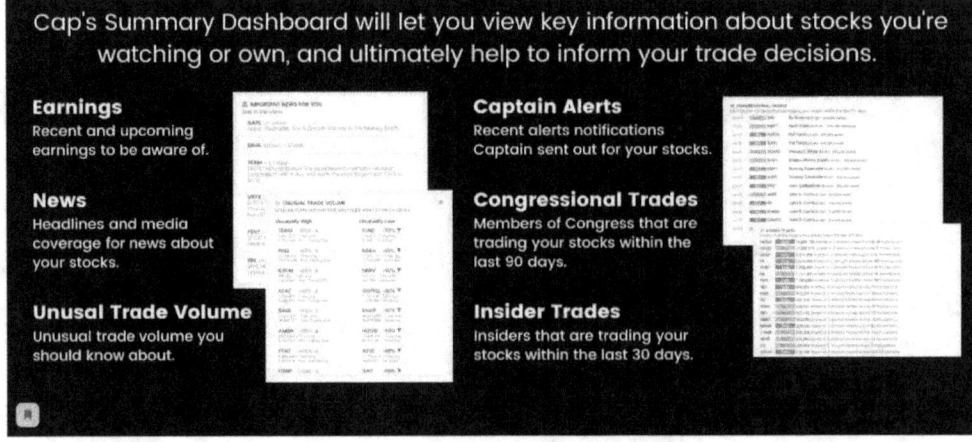

It is a kind of service that allows you to monitor stocks from your portfolio. It offers detailed statistics. Including:

Lets talk about useful services for traders

- **Reports,**
- **News,**
- **Unusual volume,**
- **Alerts,**
- **Congressmen's trades,**
- **Insider trades.**

CAPTAIN GADGETS

As a trader, your screen real estate is valuable and there's little to no room for noise when you're in the zone. Captain Gadgets are a suite of small, hyper-focused social media trading tools that help you stay-in-the-know while staying-out-of-your-way.

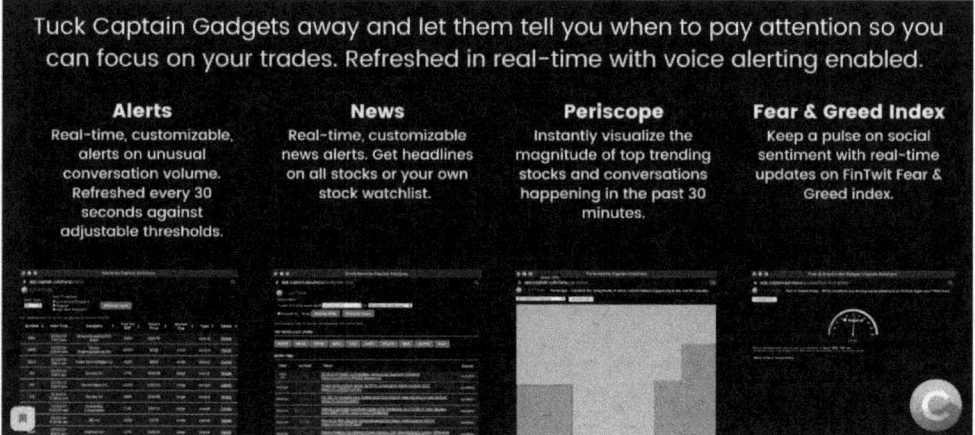

Well, it's just a smash. A set of unique tools:

- **real-time alert window,**
- **Realtime news window,**
- **Periscope,**
- **Fear and greed index.**

Be sure to try each of them! I just don't turn them off.

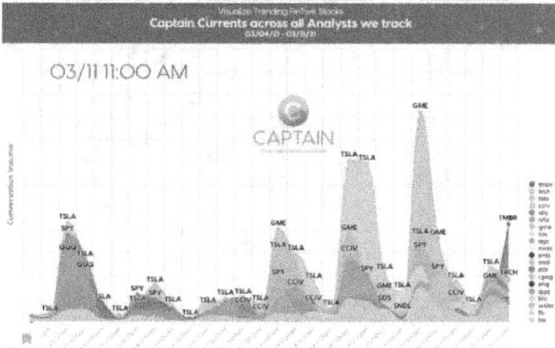

Lets talk about useful services for traders

Thanks to this tool, you can monitor the current trends in the market.

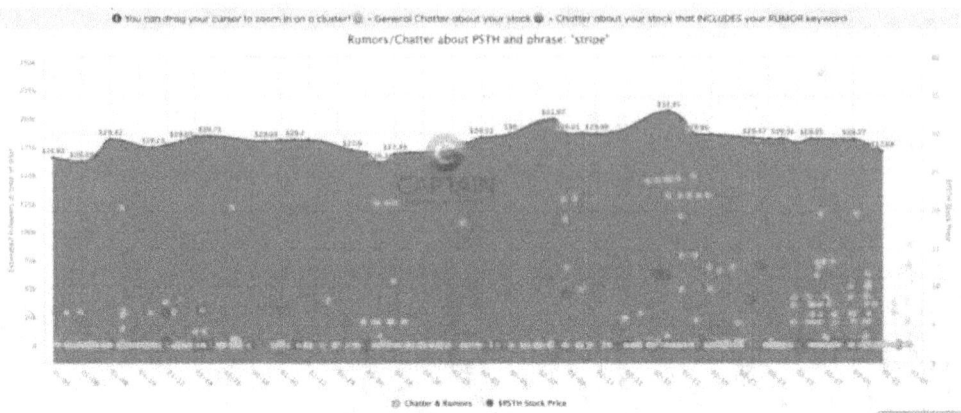

An interesting tool. You can use it to track the impact of rumors on the market.

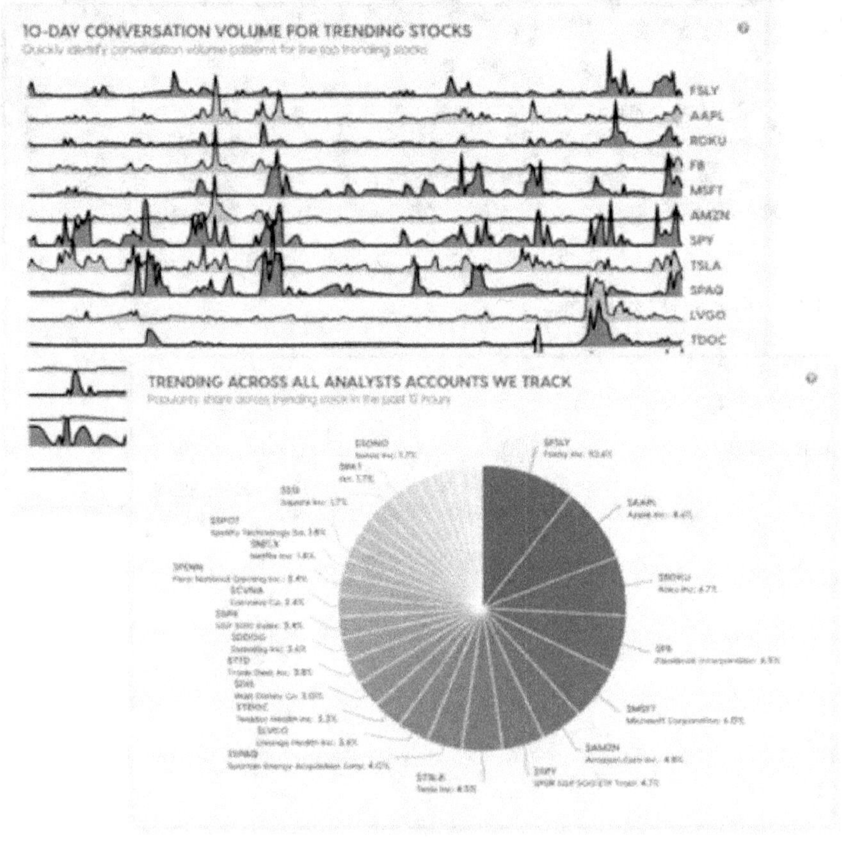

TRENDS.

Tracking the development of local trends over the past 12 hours.

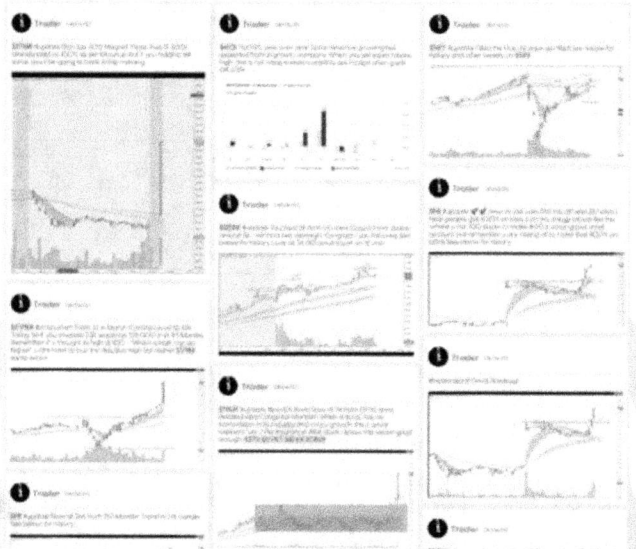

Charts. All charts of the followed traders are concentrated here.

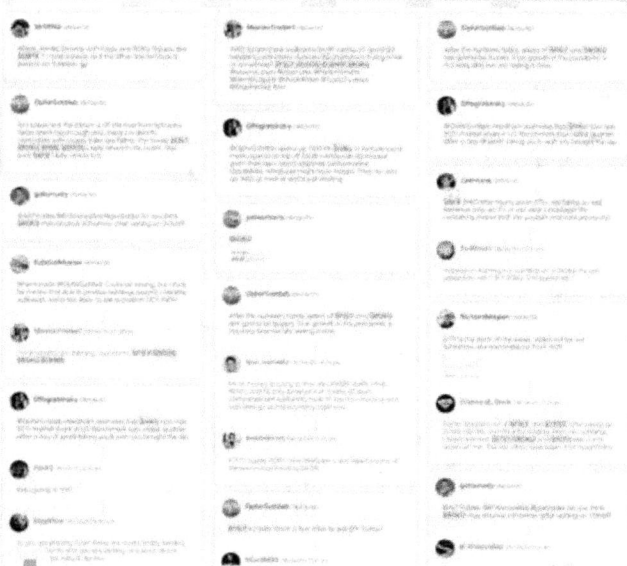

Thread explorer. All the tweets of our favorite traders in one place.

The Smell Of The Cash

Lets talk about useful services for traders

Email Alerts

CAPTAIN ALERTS WILL TELL YOU WHAT STOCKS TOP TRADERS ARE TALKING ABOUT, WHILE IT STILL MATTERS.

Each alert allows you to quickly view which stocks have moved up or down in rankings, identify new stocks that traders have fresh focus on, and pinpoint which stocks are creating buzz. Alerts are sent out 3X daily: Pre-market (8:15 am ET), Midday (2:05 pm ET), After-Hours (8:05 pm ET), Sunday Market Prep (8:05 pm ET).

In addition to our Global Alerts, Pro Members can turn alerts on/off based on personal stock and/or trader watchlists.

Included within each alert:

TRENDING STOCK RANKINGS	NEW STOCKS ENTERING CONVERSATION	HOT STOCKS OWNING CONVERSATION
Quickly view which stocks have moved up or down in rankings based on conversation volume.	Identify which stocks top traders have a new focus on compared to previous alerts.	Pinpoint which stocks are generating widespread buzz across top traders.

There is also a possibility to subscribe to the mailing list. That's what I did. And I receive 3 emails from the company during the day. The first comes before the start of the session, the second - in the middle of it, and the third - after the session. It's very convenient.

Tiblio.

When I first started using this service, it was just a screener for finding good spreads.

Currently, this is already a full-fledged platform for successful trading.

Two developers are successfully promoting and developing this project.

I am sincerely glad to use their works.

Maximize trading outcomes.

A complete stock & crypto trading system to help you find the best trading opportunities and make smart decisions.

START TRIAL >

Try Tiblio for 7 days for just $1!

Better invest today with pro level tools, the fastest market news, and real-time alerts.

The Smell Of The Cash

Lets talk about useful services for traders

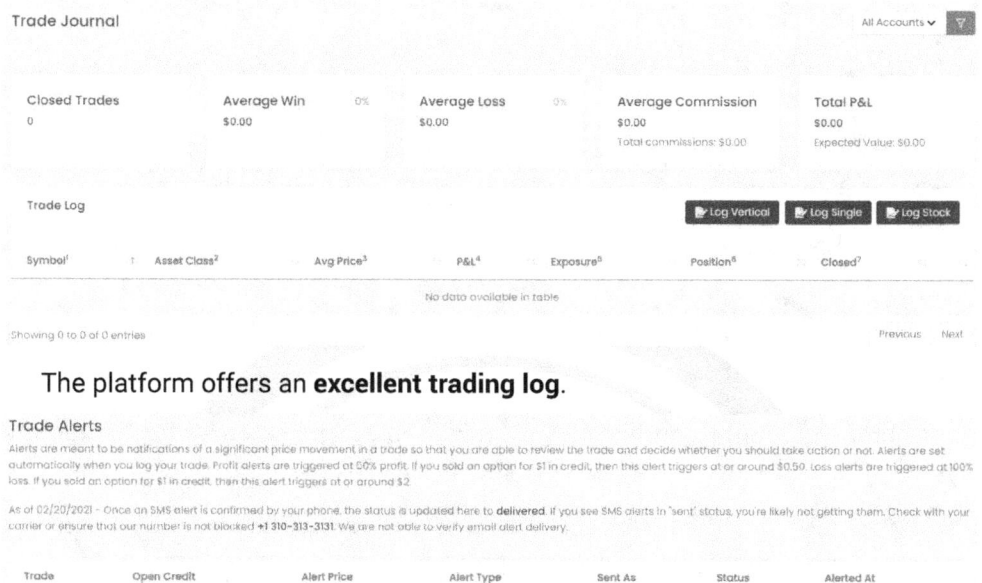

The platform offers an **excellent trading log**.

It is very convenient that there is a **trade log with a handy alert system**. When a certain percentage of profit is reached, it prompt you to close the trade.

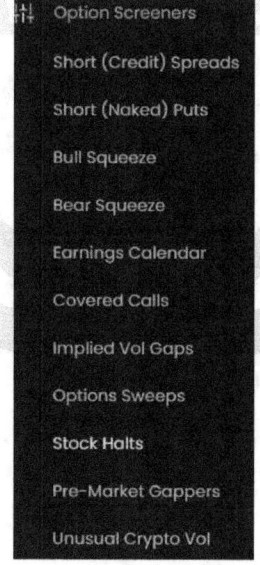

As you can see, the number of screeners is very impressive. And this list is constantly growing.

Lets talk about useful services for traders

Pre-Market Gappers

Stocks rising 8% or more in current session from prior day close.

Symbol	Market Cap	Price	Change	Change %	
SLHG	$314,749,064,260	1.78	0.46	35%	Related News
TOHW	$9,957,499,650	1.05	0.25	31%	Related News
BLBX	$32,993,993,040	3.98	0.92	30%	Related News
TOMZ	$37,041,838,730	2.21	0.48	28%	Related News
JCS	$34,485,757,500	3.7	0.66	22%	Related News
TOI	$182,390,000	7.93	1.44	22%	Related News

It's premarket time, and that's why I'm interested in a **screener for finding the gaps**.

Unusual Crypto Volume

Crypto coins that have an increase in their volume and a price change, can indicate bullish or bearish activity
Exchanges: Coinbase, Bitfinex, Bitstamp, and Kraken
Results as of Dec. 1, 2021, 7:25 a.m. EST

Symbol	Today's Volume (12h)	Average Volume (20d)	Volume Multiple	Price	Todays Change %
QSH	181,367	40,234	4.61	$0.079649	-2.36%
NEXO	1,075,768	268,639	4.00	$2.8123	5.05%
WAX	235,251	93,566	2.51	$0.66313	-3.19%
BTC	11,230	6,134	1.83	$57257.62	0.57%
ETH	140,884	92,152	1.53	$4702.71	1.54%
REQ	189,923,265	128,195,702	1.48	$0.68227	53.30%
LUNA	840,084	612,610	1.37	$57.326	-3.92%
ANT	9,763	7,467	1.31	$5.8836	2.19%

It's a very interesting tool for finding cryptocurrency coins with the greatest potential for a surge in volume. As you can see, the platform counts how many times the volume has increased today.

Let's say the NexoUSDT coin has a 4-fold increase in volume today. Let's examine it by applying our trading system.

Lets talk about useful services for traders

As you can see, the situation is very favourable for buys. We have a multi-day cumulative flat, which was terminated in buys. Horizontal volumes are already support. Our Tiblio tells us that the volumes have increased 4 times. This means you can either buy now, or you can buy after the Sellers' Accumulation Zone which is higher in the 3.4 area is traded, which is the safer option.

I'll risk buying now.

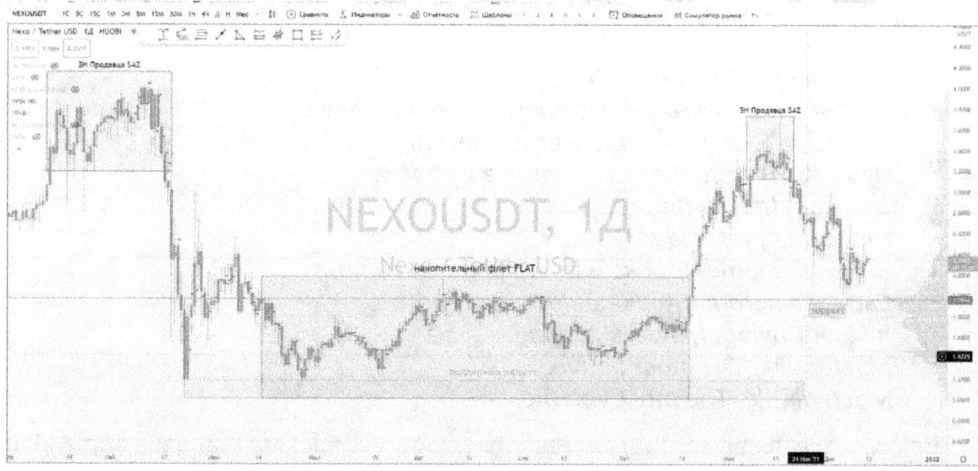

Look, despite the fact that I was knocked out of position, because the Bitcoin exchange rate collapsed sharply, the price has fallen to a powerful support, from which I will re-open the deal.

FinViz.

In trading circles, this service is widely known and very popular.
I start my trading day with it.

In its columns, you can find a list of stocks:

- **TopGainers.** The most active stocks for today.
- **TopLoosers.** The most declining stocks for today.
- **NewHigh.** Stocks that have made new high.
- **NewLow.** Stocks that have made a new low.
- **Overbought.** Overbought stocks.
- **Oversold.** Oversold stocks..
- **Unusualvolume.** Stocks with an unusual volume.
- **Earnings before.** Stocks before the report.
- **Insider Buying.** Insiders' buying.
- **Mostactive.** The most active.
- **Mostvolatile.** The most volatile.

Below, you can see another interesting window with tickers that gave some kind of signal. For example, break in the resistance or channel guide.

Below, there is a window with the latest news.

Even lower, there is a window with insider buying.

Lets talk about useful services for traders

And at the bottom - changes with futures.
In the right side, there is a heat map. But we'll talk about it a bit later.
Below you can see a window with tickers on which the news had the greatest impact.
Then - a list of tickers with upcoming reports and a window with the most bought insider stocks.

The News tab.
This tab gives us a broad view of the news in the market. And from different sources.
As you know, trading on the news is a great opportunity to make money.

The Screener tab.
In my opinion, it is one of the most important tabs.
It allows sorting and finding the most important tickers by the specified criteria.
Here, in this book, I want to share my most popular settings with you.

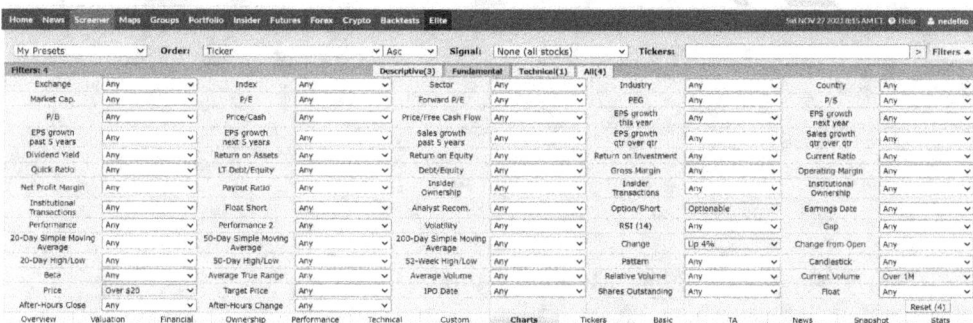

Here is an example of a scanner that enables finding the stocks with a 4% price change.

And here is a screener for finding the most declining stocks to search for sales.

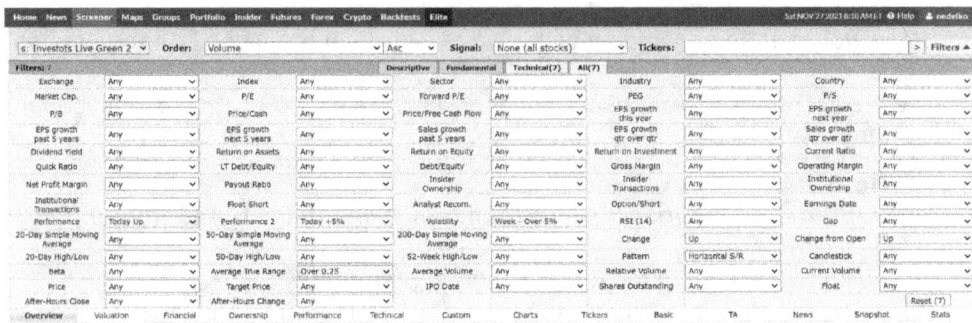

With this, on the contrary, we can find good buys.

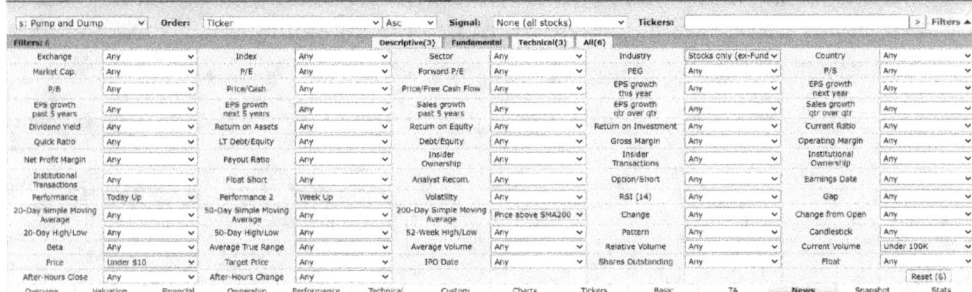

Using it, we are looking for PumpandDump.

And this is Gap and Go

The most active stocks during the day.

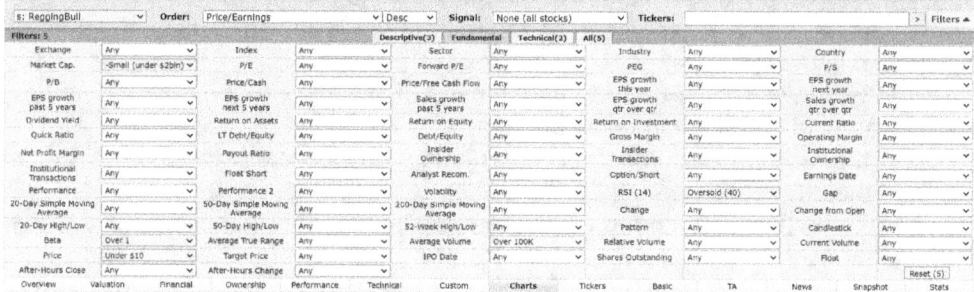

We look for penny stock.

And this one is my favorite for finding the strongest stocks in the market. With the help of such a screener, you can find excellent options for swing trading.

We move to the Heat Map tab.

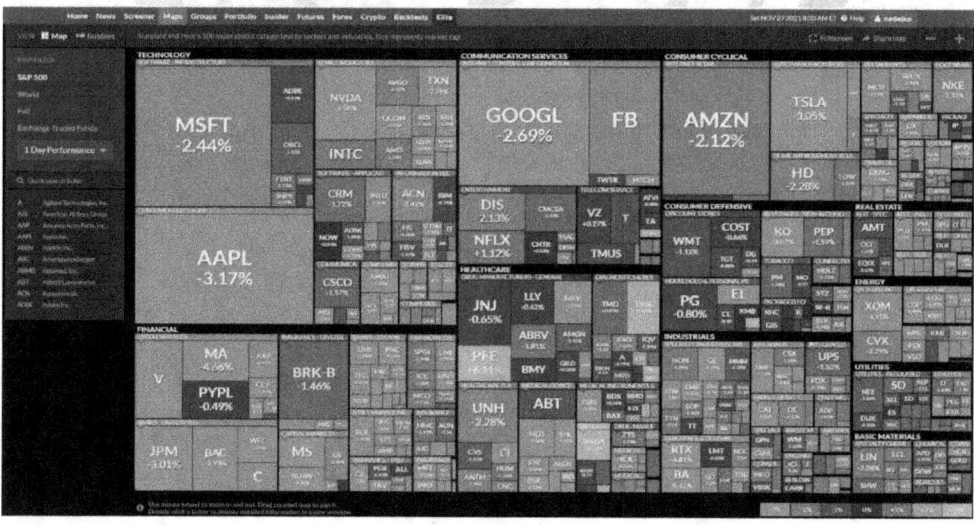

Lets talk about useful services for traders

It is a unique tool that even a beginner can understand.

Here you can observe changes in the market in real time.

As you can see from the screenshot, the market is falling, because almost all tickers are in the red zone.

What is convenient is that by the intensity of the color you can judge on how much a particular stock has fallen or risen.

Well, therefore, it becomes very interesting why several stocks have turned green at the moment?

There must have been good news there, which means we should take a closer look at them.

There is a great menu on the left where you can change the observation interval. And change it from daytime to any other.

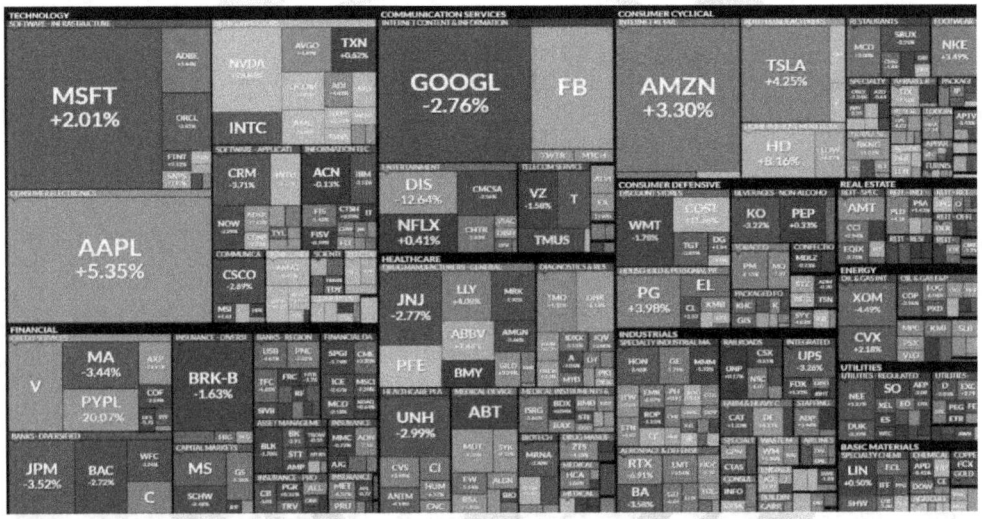

Here, see how our map on a month scale looks like.

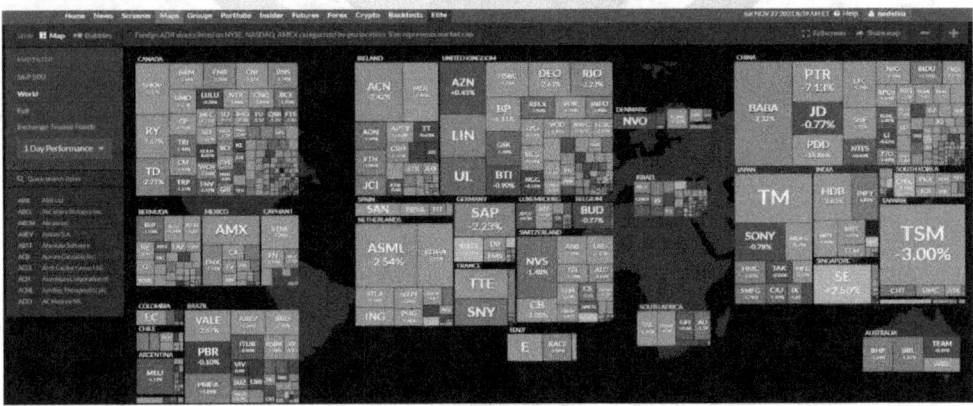

The Smell Of The Cash

And here is a heat map of the world. Well, isn't it beautiful?

The Groups tab.

It allows you to monitor changes in a particular sector of the economy over the past few days, weeks, months, or more.

It is a very useful tool, because you can find a suitable positive sector in recent days or weeks and use it during screening, thereby significantly increasing your chances of success.

Moreover, while positive activity within the day and week is suitable for day trading, for swing trading, you need to look at green activity for a month or more.

This tool is a kind of filter.

Use it widely!

The Portfolio tab.

It provides an opportunity to monitor the stocks included in your portfolio. And, by creating several, you can observe them.

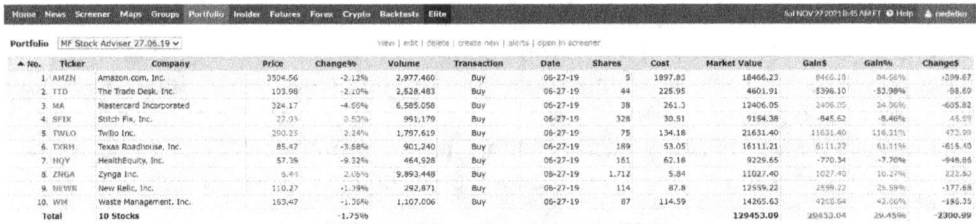

The Insider tab.

With its help, you can monitor the latest changes in insider trades. Both during the day and the whole week.

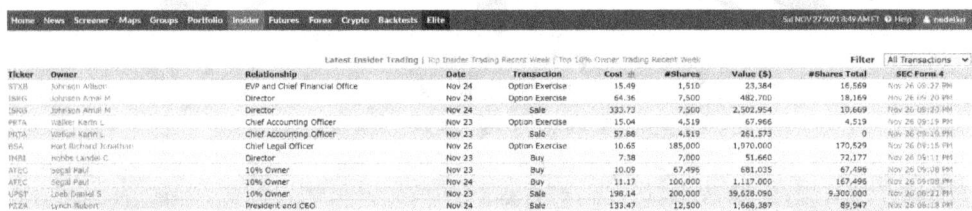

The Futures tab.

We follow the changes in the futures market.

The Smell Of The Cash

The Forex tab.

We follow the changes in the Forex market.

The Crypto tab.

The same - with crypto assets.

Lets talk about useful services for traders

The Elite tab.

By going Elite, you will gain access to these features:

Real-time and Extended Hours
Real-time stock quotes, premarket, and aftermarket data in all stock features

Advanced Charts
Technical studies & Interactivity

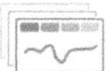
Backtests
Profitability research on technical indicators

Correlations
Performance tracking of correlated stocks

Advanced Screener
Statistics, Data Export and Custom filters

Alerts & Notifications
E-mail notifications about important events

You can also use the free version of the platform. Especially at first. But for the more experienced public, there is a paid version with advanced functions.

Scanz.

Find it. Trade it. Profit

Scanz is the "all in one" market scanning platform for day traders and swing traders.

We go beyond real-time to deliver **'extreme real-time'** data & news. If your goal is to be a laser-focused trading sniper, then Scanz is the only platform that matters.

Start Your Free Trial | **See Scanz in Action**

This is really one of my favorite screeners. And, perhaps, it is one of the most powerful platforms for searching for stocks online.

Let's look at its capabilities:

- **ProScanner.**

The most powerful feature of the platform for finding just the right stocks. Really great possibilities for fine-tuning the necessary criteria.

Lets talk about useful services for traders

- **EasyScanner.**

A simplified version of the scanner. For less demanding traders.

- **NewsScanner.**

News scanner. It allows tracking only the news that is important to you. It's a very cool thing!

- **BreakoutScanner.**

Searches for stocks that have made a breakout or a breakdown for you.

- **52 WeekHighLowScanner.**

Searches for stocks that are on 52 high or low.

And many more useful things for every day.

It is worth noting that I have not seen such a number of settings anywhere else!

But a quick support and a lot of instructional videos on the site will save you from getting confused.

An intuitive interface and the ability to integrate with the largest brokers is undoubtedly a big advantage for the developers.

SectorSPDR.

One of my favorite online services that allows me to significantly strengthen my trades.

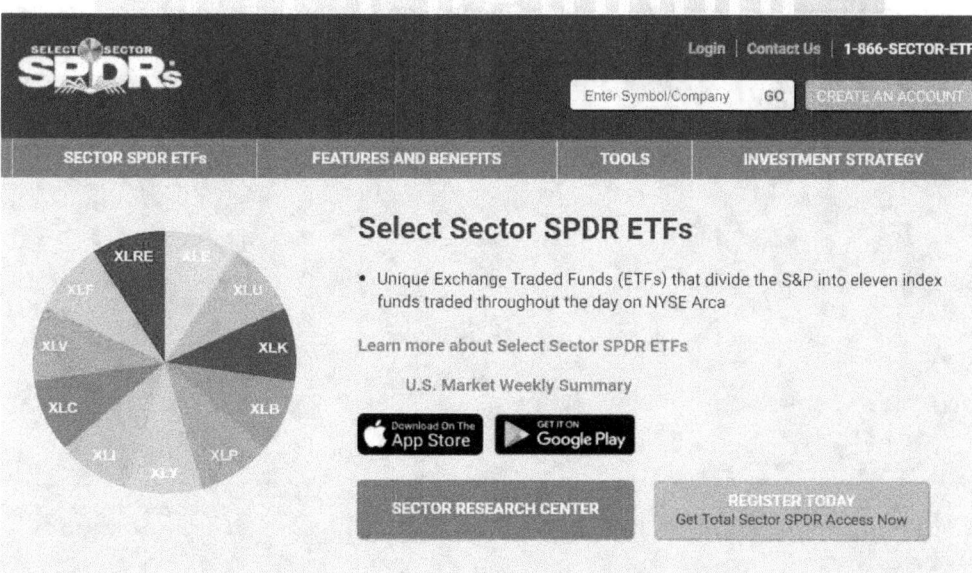

The idea of the site is that it allows you to find the right stock based on the sectoral situation in the market.

Lets talk about useful services for traders

That is, it enables monitoring changes in the entire sector inside the SPY index. This means that we, having such information on a specific sector, can use it in screening.

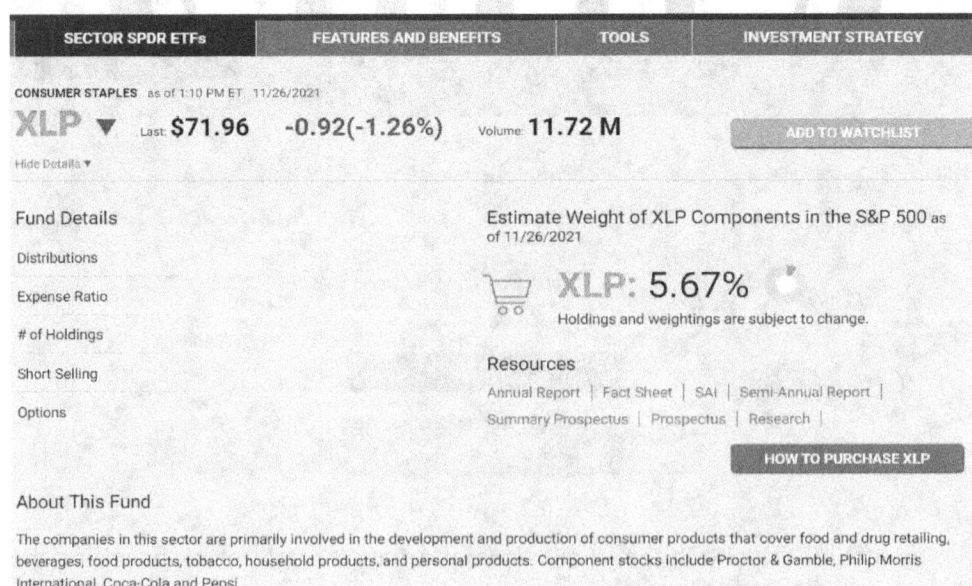

In this table, we can see how the dynamics within the index by sector has changed over the past day.

Lets talk about useful services for traders

There is also an opportunity to observe a separate sector.

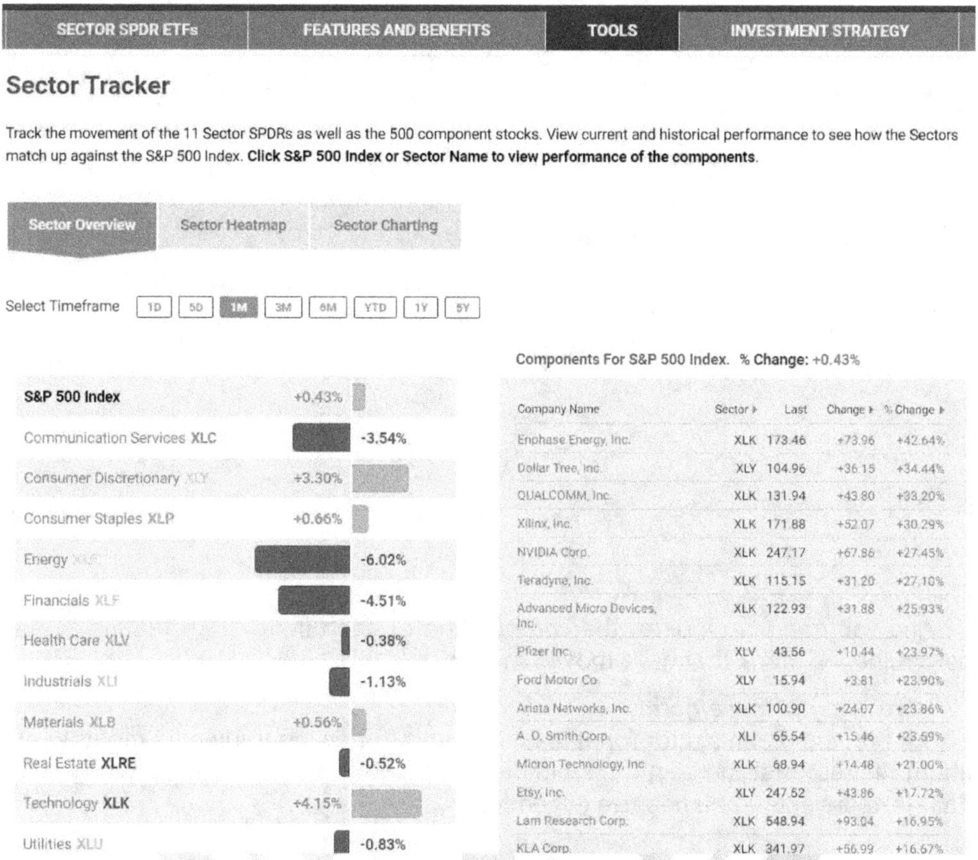

Sector Tracker

Track the movement of the 11 Sector SPDRs as well as the 500 component stocks. View current and historical performance to see how the Sectors match up against the S&P 500 Index. **Click S&P 500 Index or Sector Name to view performance of the components.**

But the coolest thing is the ability to observe the behavior of all sectors over a different period of time and see the percentage change in price for each of the stocks.

Lets talk about useful services for traders

And you can also look at the composition of each index from the inside and determine the stock that have moved the most.

Here is my usage algorithm:

1. I find the green sector for at least a month (for swing trading - 3 months). It's about the fact that the sector should be green on a monthly, 5-day and daily slice. That is, there should be positive dynamics.

Here, look. What sectors were the greenest in six months?
You're right - XLY, XLK, XLRE:

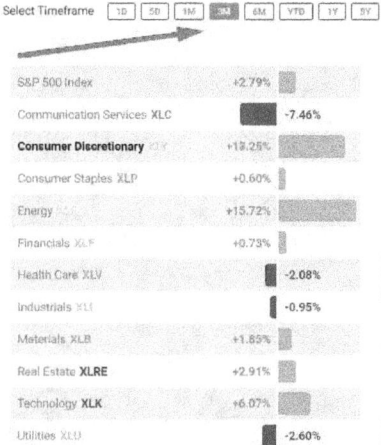

On a three-month slice, we see that these are XLE, XLY:

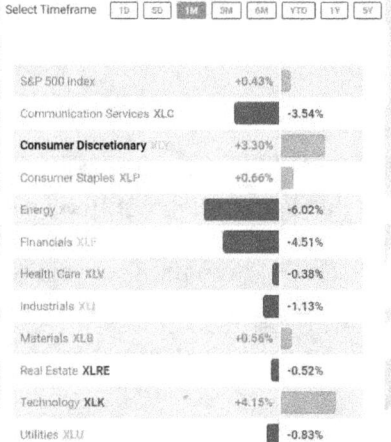

On a month slice - XLK and XLY. The energy industry has been severely depressed. This means that we will no longer take their shares into account!

After analyzing it, we came to the conclusion that we are interested in stocks only from the Technology and Consumer Discretionary sectors.

2. On the right side of the window, we have a list of all the stocks in these sectors.

Components For Technology. % Change: +4.15%

Company Name	Index Weight ▶	Last	Change ▶	% Change ▶	Company Name	Index Weight ▶	Last	Change ▶	% Change ▶
Dollar Tree Inc	0.74%	104.96	+36.15	+34.44%	Enphase Energy Inc	0.30%	173.46	+73.96	+42.64%
Ford Motor Co	1.74%	15.94	+3.81	+23.90%	QUALCOMM Inc	1.77%	131.94	+43.80	+33.20%
Etsy, Inc.	0.83%	247.52	+43.86	+17.72%	Xilinx Inc	0.50%	171.88	+52.07	+30.29%
Dominos Pizza Inc	0.44%	465.78	+64.10	+13.76%	Nvidia Corp	7.02%	247.17	+67.86	+27.45%
Horton D.R. Inc	0.72%	88.70	+10.05	+11.33%	Teradyne Inc	0.22%	115.15	+31.20	+27.10%
Under Armour Inc A	0.10%	21.55	+2.43	+11.28%	Advanced Micro Devices	1.68%	122.93	+31.88	+25.93%
Under Armour Inc-C	0.10%	18.56	+2.07	+11.15%	Arista Networks Inc	0.25%	100.90	+24.07	+23.86%
Pool Corp	0.50%	503.62	+55.57	+11.03%	Micron Technology Inc	0.84%	68.94	+14.48	+21.00%
Tractor Supply Co.	0.59%	206.82	+21.54	+10.41%	Lam Research Corp	0.82%	548.94	+93.04	+16.95%
Whirlpool Corp	0.32%	206.00	+20.00	+9.71%	KLA Corporation	0.54%	341.97	+56.99	+16.67%
Ulta Beauty, Inc	0.49%	366.06	+33.47	+9.14%	HP Inc	0.37%	30.14	+4.44	+14.73%
Home Depot Inc	9.50%	369.20	+33.50	+9.07%	Juniper Networks Inc	0.09%	27.49	+3.96	+14.41%
NVR Inc	0.40%	4870.98	+420.12	+8.62%	Zebra Technologies Corp	0.28%	525.41	+65.31	+12.43%
Hasbro Inc	0.29%	91.36	+7.39	+8.09%	Seagate Technology	0.18%	88.07	+10.55	+11.98%
Lowe's Cos Inc	3.94%	231.07	+16.62	+7.19%	VeriSign Inc	0.21%	215.71	+25.31	+11.73%
Tapestry, Inc	0.26%	39.11	+2.69	+6.88%	F5, Inc.	0.12%	203.90	+22.35	+10.96%
Lennar Corp A	0.66%	100.45	+6.59	+6.56%	Intuit Inc	1.63%	608.61	+58.30	+9.58%
Tesla, Inc	19.48%	1018.43	+63.49	+6.23%	Applied Materials Inc	1.17%	132.00	+11.29	+8.55%
TJX Cos Inc	1.88%	65.33	+4.03	+6.17%	Microchip Technology Inc	0.39%	73.79	+6.28	+8.51%
Carmax Inc	0.53%	137.44	+8.31	+6.05%	NXP Semiconductor NV	0.50%	196.15	+16.30	+8.31%

And all we have to do is to choose the 10 strongest of them!

3. And then we just run this list through our trading system and look for good points to buy.

Let's take the well-known QCOM from the Technology sector:

We see that the stock is really very strong and shot a powerful upward impulse. Therefore, we need to wait for a pullback and look for a point on a smaller timeframe to open a trade.

On the 130-minute chart, I have found two areas from which we can look for further purchases.

Now let's take a stock from the XLY sector. Let it be FordMotors, also known to everyone.

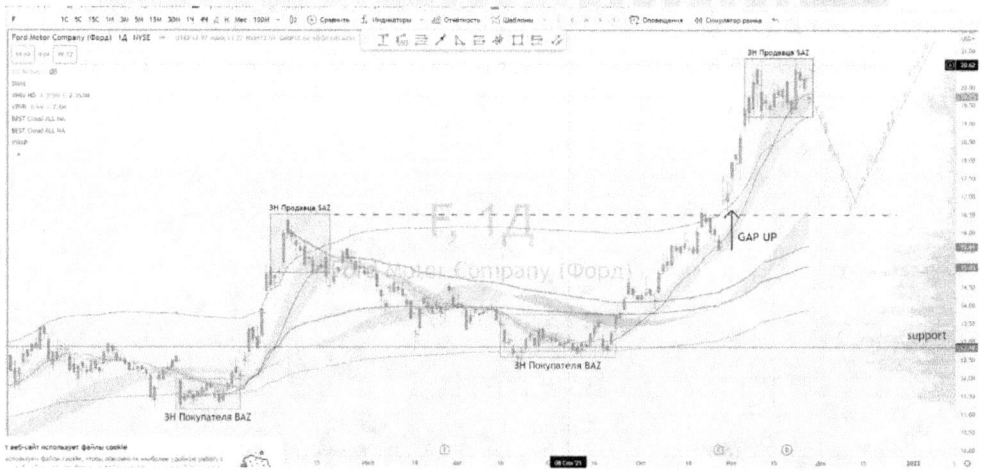

On the daily chart, we also see a strong impulse movement. At the moment, it seems that the seller's AZ is being formed and it is worth waiting for a correction and, most likely, buying on the support test that was resistance.

But there is another way to use the information from this source!

You can simply insert the necessary green sectors into a screener like a finviz.

Lets talk about useful services for traders

And the screener will offer us a list of stocks from this progressive green sector, but with the specified criteria! What's even cooler than just picking the top 10 from each sector.

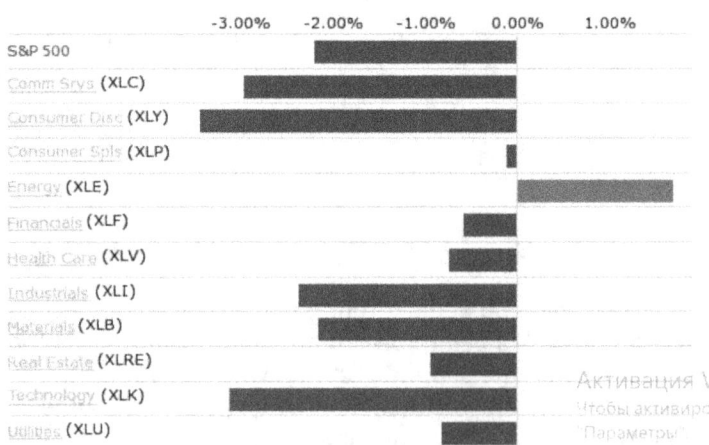

At the moment, these are only two stocks.
And this service also sends you its reports weekly to make it more convenient for you.

Lets talk about useful services for traders

BioFarmCatalyst.

Simply the best service for working with biotech stocks.
Offers excellent data on upcoming clinical trials.

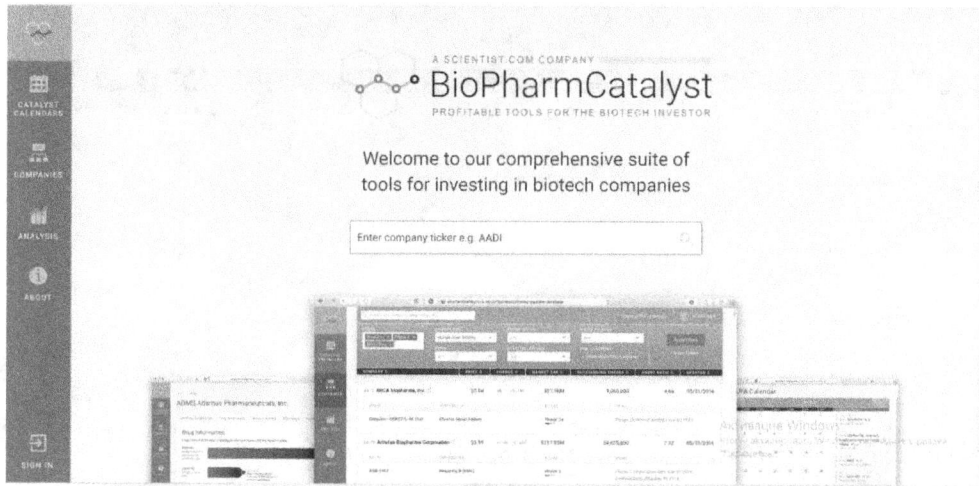

There is an excellent screener here that shows what is to come:

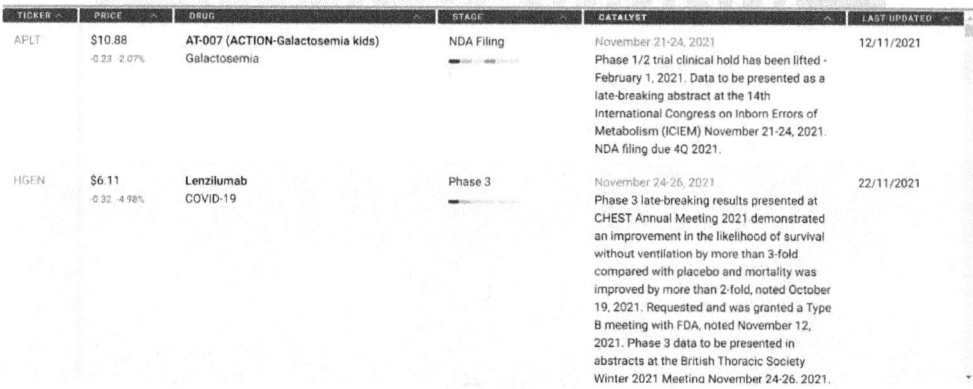

The Smell Of The Cash

Lets talk about useful services for traders

Upcoming IPOs or their history:

TICKER	COMPANY	COMPANY LEAD MANAGERS	SHARES	ESTIMATED VOLUME	EXPECTED TRADE DATE
NVCT	Nuvectis Pharma, Inc.	ThinkEquity	2.3 Million	29.9 Million	12/01/2021

Historical IPO Database

Last 342 IPO's

TICKER	COMPANY	IPO PRICE	PRICE AFTER FIRST DAY	CURRENT PRICE	RETURN	OFFER DATE
NVCT	Nuvectis Pharma, Inc.	N/A	N/A	N/A	0.00%	12/01/2021
DERM	Journey Medical Corp.	$10.00	N/A	$8.25	-17.50%	11/12/2021
VAXX	Vaxxinity, Inc.	$13.00	$16.55	$17.35	33.46%	11/11/2021
BEAT	HeartBeam, Inc.	$6.00	$4.69	$4.14	-31.00%	11/11/2021
TIVC	TIVIC HEALTH SYSTEMS, INC.	$5.00	$5.19	$3.67	-26.60%	11/11/2021
BJDX	Bluejay Diagnostics, Inc.	$10.00	$5.32	$3.24	-67.60%	11/10/2021
MYNZ	MAINZ BIOMED B.V.	$5.00	$9.99	$10.15	103.00%	11/05/2021
IOBT	IO Biotech, Inc.	$14.00	$15.65	$7.30	-47.86%	11/05/2021
EVO	Evotec SE	$21.75	$22.00	$23.33	7.26%	11/04/2021

It is an excellent screener only for biotechs:

COMPANY	PRICE	CHANGE	COMPANY	PRICE	CHANGE
PTN Palatin Technologies Inc.	$0.79	+0.2324 +41.68%	NAVB Navidea Biopharmaceuticals Inc.	$1.15	-0.15 -11.54%
STSA Satsuma Pharmaceuticals Inc.	$5.96	+0.71 +13.52%	IKT Inhibikase Therapeutics Inc.	$1.91	-0.15 -7.28%
BYSI BeyondSpring Inc.	$16.25	+1.9 +13.24%	PSTI Pluristem Therapeutics Inc.	$2.52	-0.17 -6.32%
ACHL Achilles Therapeutics plc	$5.39	+0.55 +11.36%	BPTS Biophytis SA	$5.40	-0.36 -6.25%
OGEN Oragenics Inc.	$0.60	+0.0488 +8.87%	APVO Aptevo Therapeutics Inc.	$12.26	-0.81 -6.20%

Advancers

COMPANY	PRICE	CHANGE
BFRI Biofrontera Inc.	$7.90	+2.68 +51.34%
NRXP NRX Pharmaceuticals Inc.	$6.75	+2.25 +50.00%
ADGI Adagio Therapeutics Inc.	$25.12	+6.39 +34.12%

Decliners

COMPANY	PRICE	CHANGE
LGVN Longeveron Inc.	$30.67	-11.63 -27.49%
AMTI Applied Molecular Transport Inc.	$16.33	-2.66 -14.01%
NEXI NexImmune Inc.	$7.94	-1.06 -11.78%
IGMS IGM Biosciences	$49.63	-6.56 -11.71%

Unusual Volume

COMPANY	PRICE	REL VOL
COCP Cocrystal Pharma Inc.	$0.97	5.84
DRNA Dicerna Pharmaceuticals Inc.	$37.99	5.82
ADGI Adagio Therapeutics Inc.	$25.12	4.99
BCLI		

In general, I highly recommend it!

The Smell Of The Cash

TraderSync.

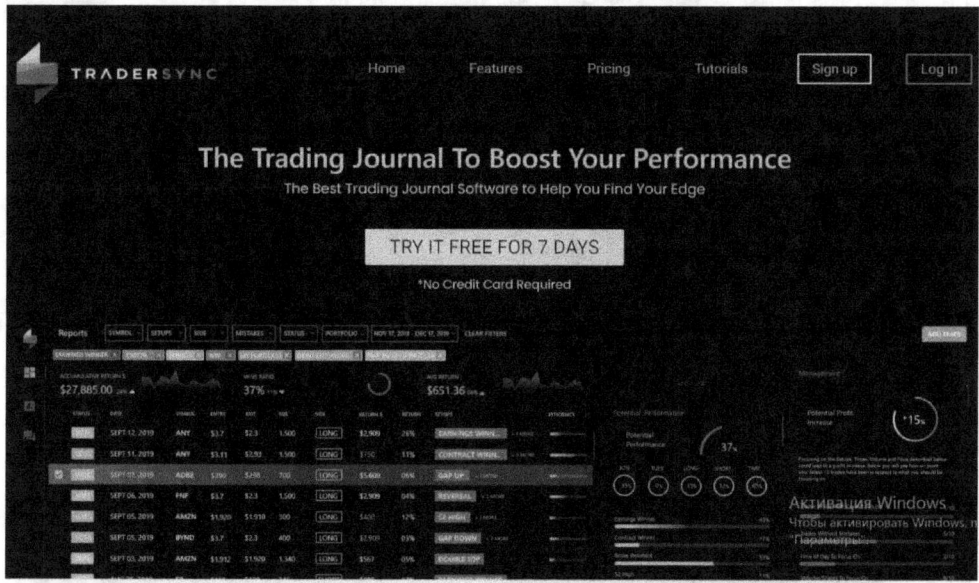

I've been long searching for a log for recording my trades and have tried many of them, but when I saw this masterpiece I immediately realized that it was simply the best.

You can't find such an abundance of statistics anywhere else. This software service can satisfy any of your whims.

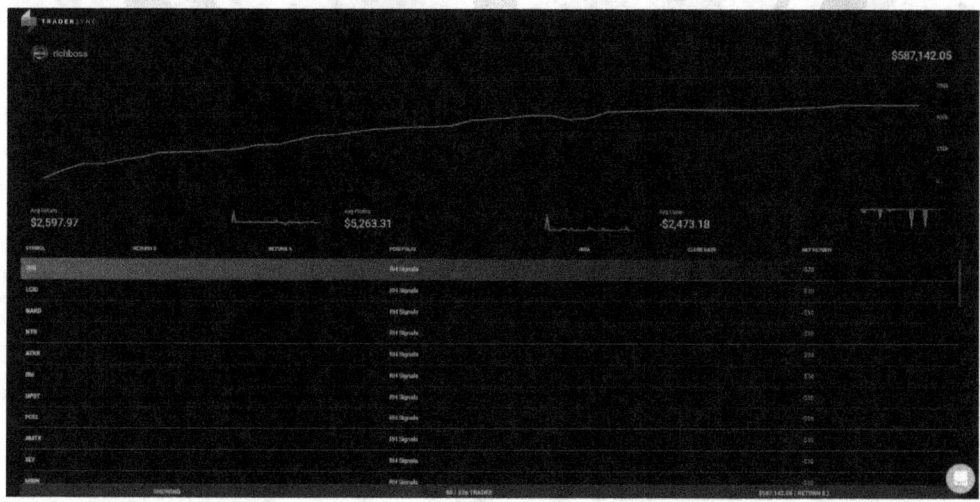

This is what my statistics look like. And you can always see it on my website.

Lets talk about useful services for traders

And here are the possible options for sorting your statistics.

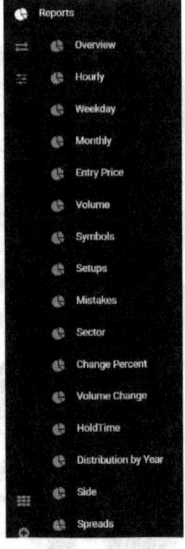

As you know, all my signals in a Private Chat are divided into rooms. And with this service, it is also possible to monitor only them.

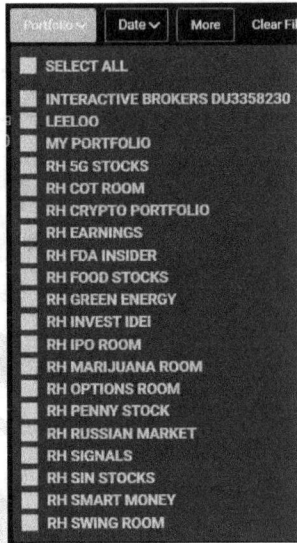

You can sort by date, errors, setup, etc.

There is a possibility of connecting a real brokerage account, and then the system will do everything completely automatically.

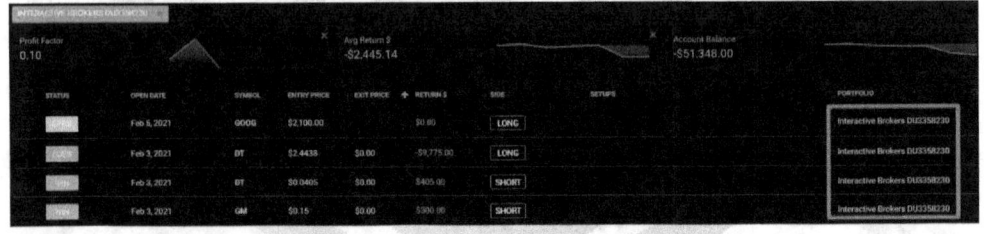

Lets talk about useful services for traders

Trades can also be added manually.

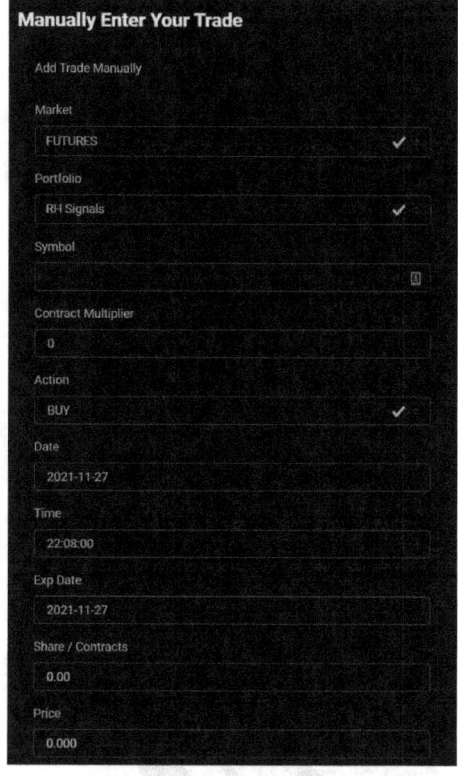

As you can see, my current success rate is about 72%.

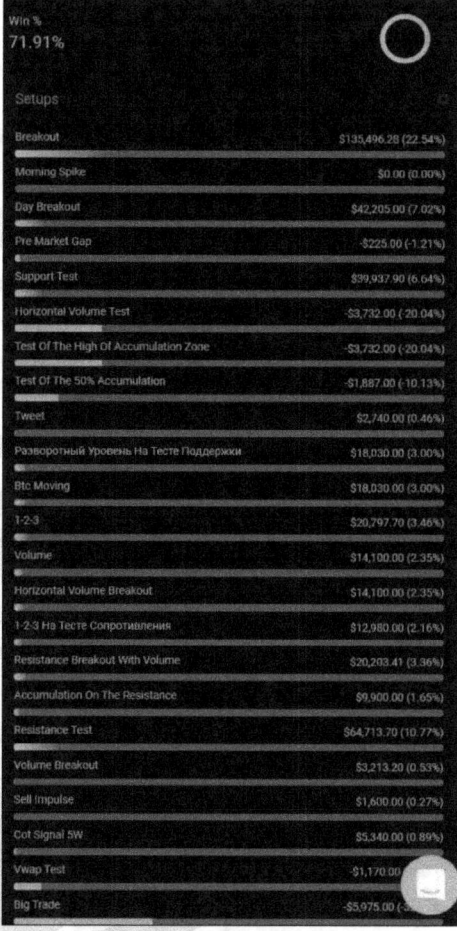

And this window gives detailed statistics on the triggered setups.

In general, it is worth mentioning that it is thanks to the internal analysis generated by the platform that it is possible to draw appropriate conclusions about the methods that work and do not work well.

Again, if you look at the very top, you can see that the breakouts brought me the greatest profit and I incurred the greatest losses on the horizontal volume level test.

Just don't forget to fill in all the fields completely when opening and closing a deal. It's even better to add a screenshot.

All in all, be sure to try it and I promise you won't be disappointed!
It is really the best solution!

UNUSUAL OPTIONS ACTIVITY (UOA)

This topic is very important and extremely relevant. The options market is very transparent. It is impossible to hide in it.

And big players - insiders - work here.

And they usually have the correct information. And they won't risk their millions for no reason. Surely they have information that we don't know yet.

But the problem is that very often buying options can act as a stop loss, and not as a driver of growth or decline.

So I use the following tactics:

At the moment, UOA can be tracked in a lot of places. We'll talk more about it below.

But I use the free version of one of my favorite sites more often:

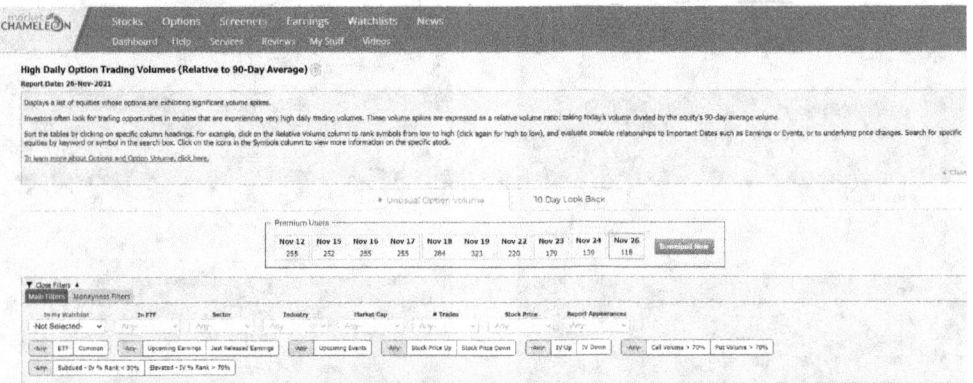

The point is to sort only stocks with a Relative Volume of more than 20.

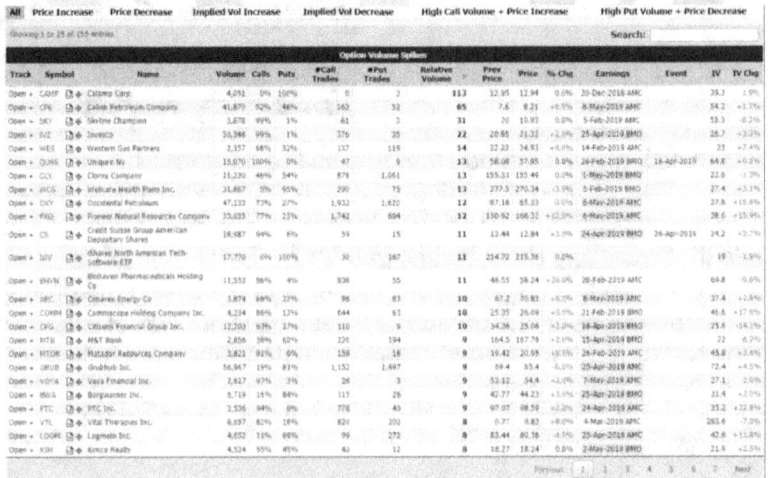

Then I choose the stocks where the Put&Call ratio is more than 95%.
In our case, this is CAMP, SKY, IVZ.
We do not take CPE into account, because there is no sharp advantage in one of the sides. There is no imbalance. Apparently, the crowd is just selling.

So, we chose stocks. But we need to dig deeper.

We go to CAMP, click on the ticker and select 'Trades' from the left navigation links to see the trades.

Let's sort the list by '$Nat'l' in descending order, that is, by the cumulative premium paid by the player for the trade.

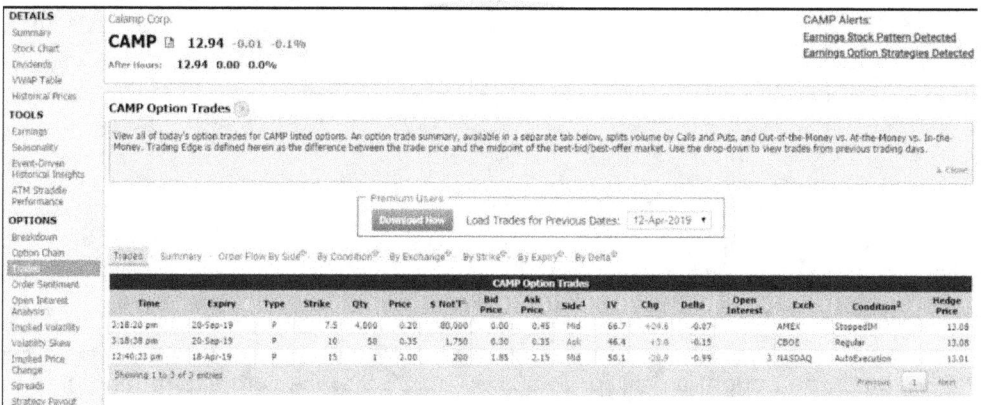

Here we see that the player bought Puts, 4000 contracts for $ 80,000 ... eh, this turned out to be a small fish, so we go further down the list.

And then we have SKY:

Lets talk about useful services for traders

Here we see two interesting trades of $152250 and $109620 with one strike of 22.5, on different expiration dates, but made at the same second. I'm sure these two trades were made by the same person. Although the amount of $250,000 is not that big, but let's look at the chart:

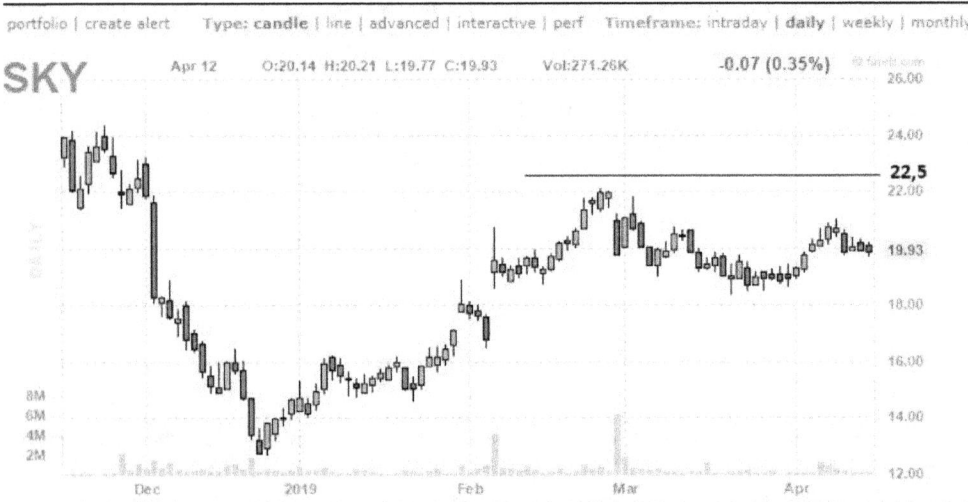

So, a person bought a Call for $250,000 on 22.5 strike with expiration dates in May and August, quite close. The amount is small and the buys were made where stops are usually placed. So I think the guy sold stocks for about 2 million or more and put a stop loss at 22.5. Here you can buy a Put, if we want to follow. I won't do it because of the small amount of the player.

Let's look at the last paper, IVZ.

There is one interesting trade for $3187500, the buy of Call options for strike 25 with an expiration date in January 2021. We look at the chart:

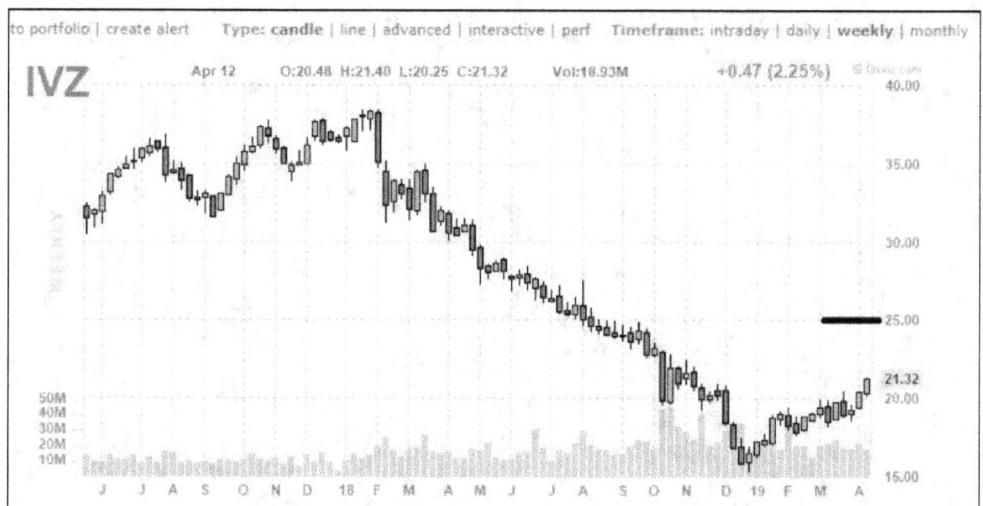

It looks like a bet on growth. I will refrain. Firstly, in addition to our 3 million, there are a lot of trades with amounts of $40,000, $20,000, $10,000. I prefer one, two, or three large buys and the rest should be small, about $1,000 or less, or a little more. Secondly, in my opinion, the strike is far away and I prefer those that have a strike at the money or in the money.

So, we don't have a candidate today.

But you understood the system, did not you?

There are already ready-made platforms for searching for option activity.

FlowAlgo.

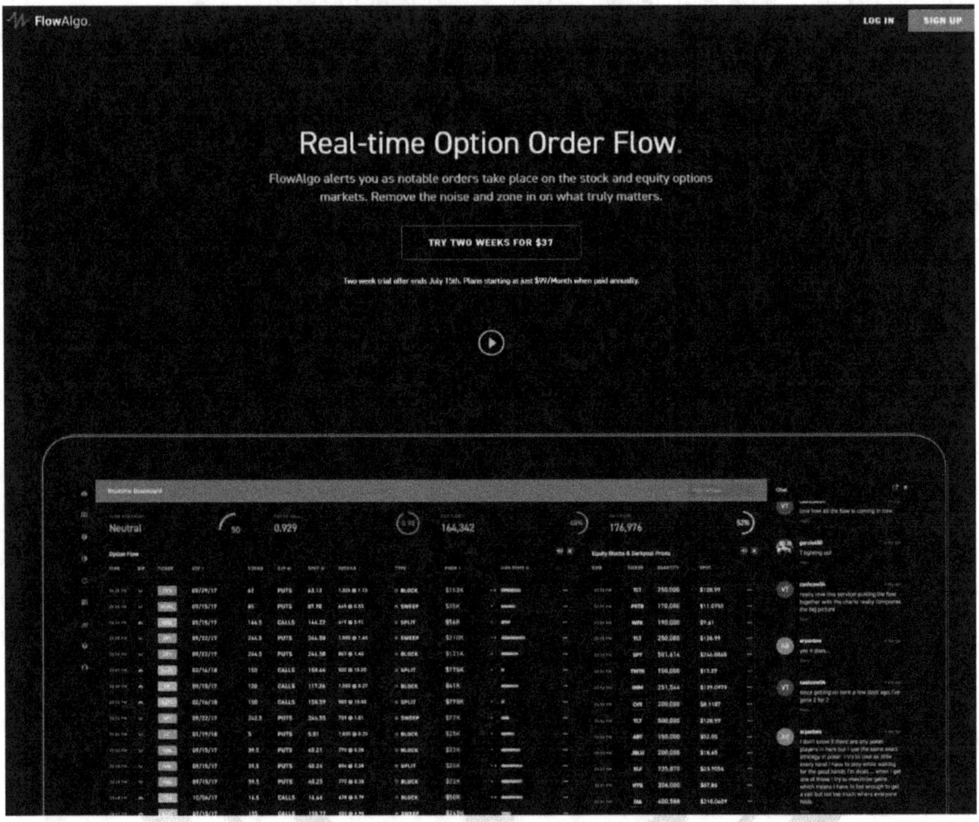

I've tried many similar platforms, but this one is the best of its kind. Yes, it is the most expensive of them, but it has unique inherent functions:

- Equity Block & Dark Pool Order Data,
- Alpha Ai Signal,
- Dark Pool Insight,
- Flow Algo Levels,
- Top Open Interest Changes.

Lets talk about useful services for traders

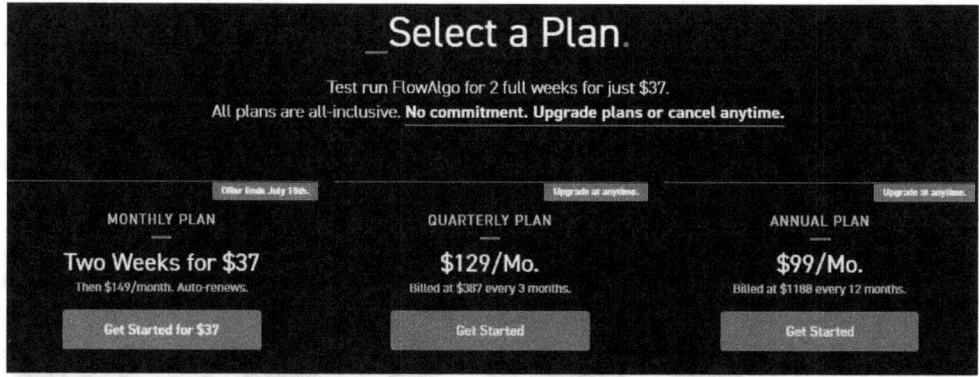

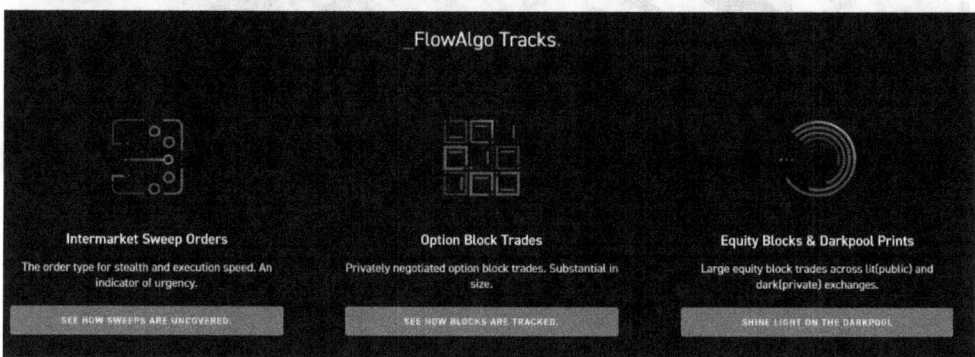

I have tried many similar platforms. Now we see a huge surge in such solutions. But none of them offers such functionality.
I especially liked the opportunity to see important levels formed by big deals. Such levels almost always work!
In general, be sure to study it.

ATAS

It is one of my most favorite platforms. And it is really the most powerful one, as the author assures.

But its capabilities and support are simply impressive.

I plan to write a dedicated course on working with it.

And within the framework of this book, I will only mention its main functions:

- Cluster charts,
- Unique order book,
- SmartTape,
- Unique templates.

By the way, I have developed my own unique templates for each instrument. They are very informative. It took me several years to develop them.

My students and I use only them in a Private Chat to understand each other without a word.

They can be found here: https://richharbour.ru/obuchayushchie-materialy.html

Lets talk about useful services for traders

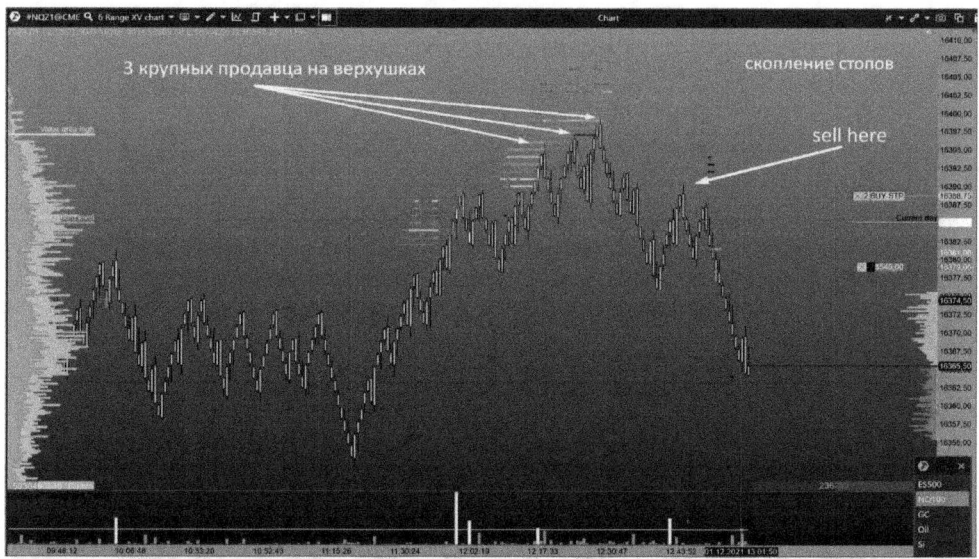

Look, a special indicator shows the accumulation of stops. Another indicator shows the arrival of 3 large sellers on highs.

Therefore, it was possible to wait for the formation of the accumulation zone here and sell on its test.

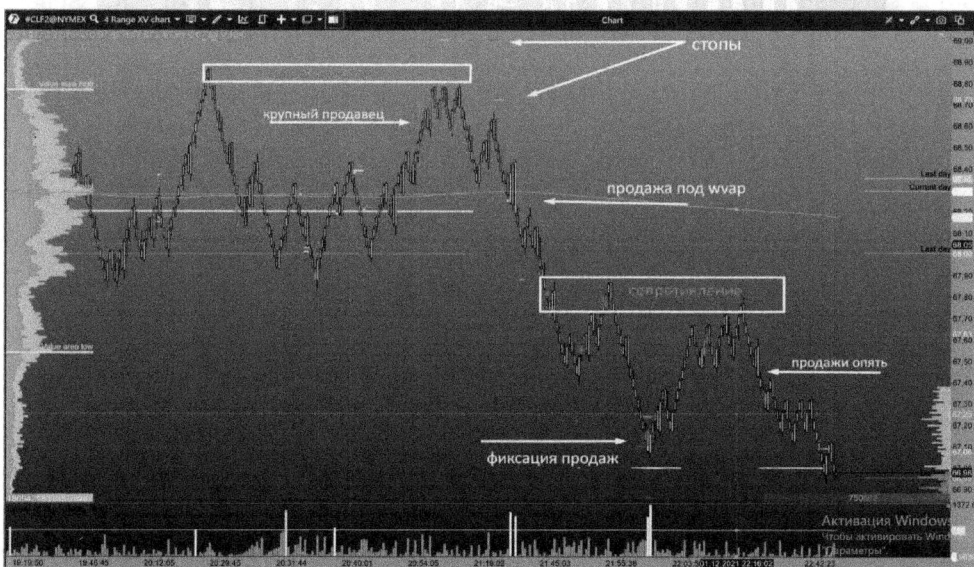

Here is an example of oil trading. Again, a big seller came at the resistance test. This acted as a signal for selling. And it was necessary to close the position when this seller was closing it. All this can be seen on the chart thanks to ATAS.

And none of the other platforms can give such a detailed representation.

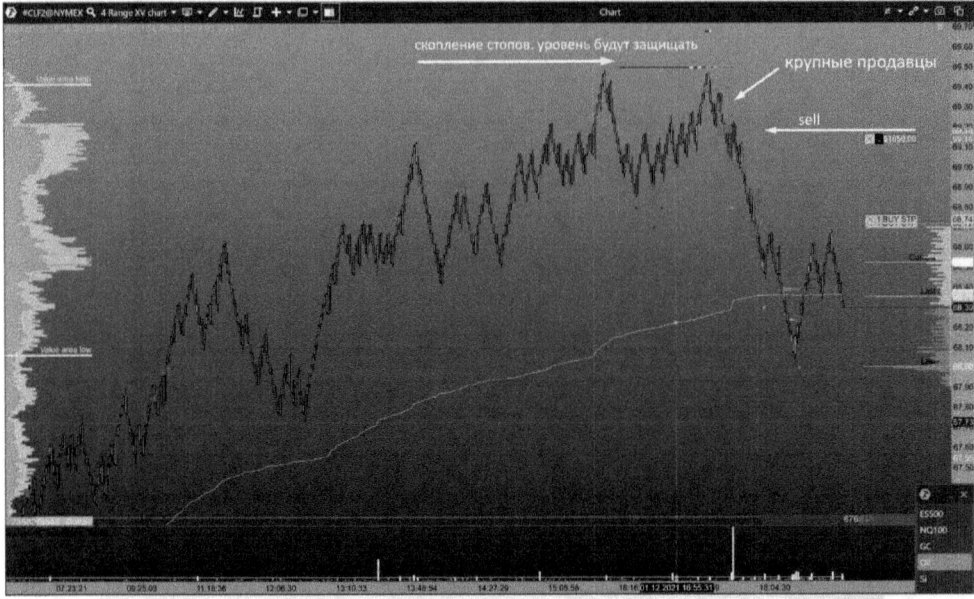

And here is another example of oil futures trade. Look - the accumulation of stops suggested that the level will be protected. And the arrival of large sellers confirmed the game plan. The result is a good, and most importantly, predictable profit.

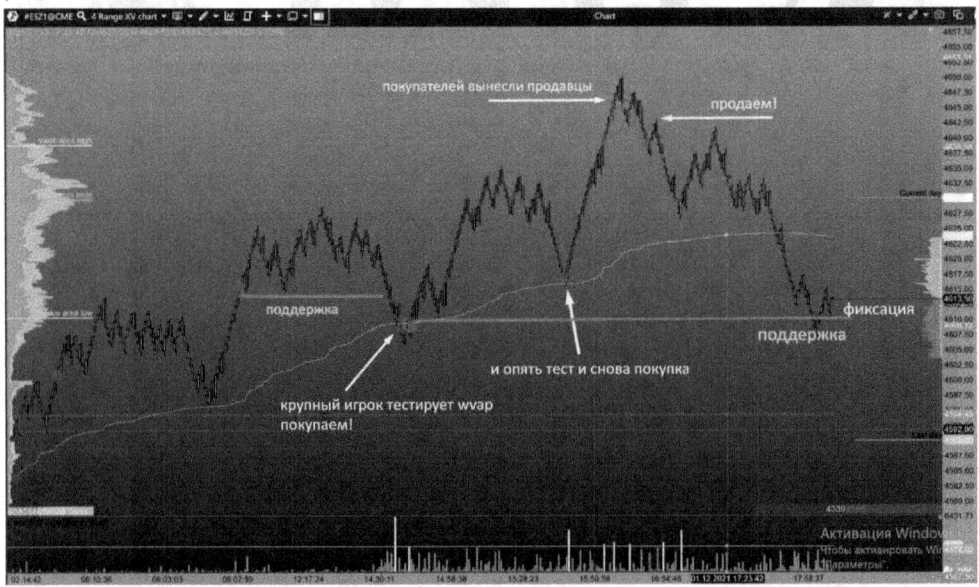

Lets talk about useful services for traders

ATAS is an X-ray apparatus for the market. I don't trade without it in today's market conditions.

I have ATAS on one monitor and everything else on the other!!!

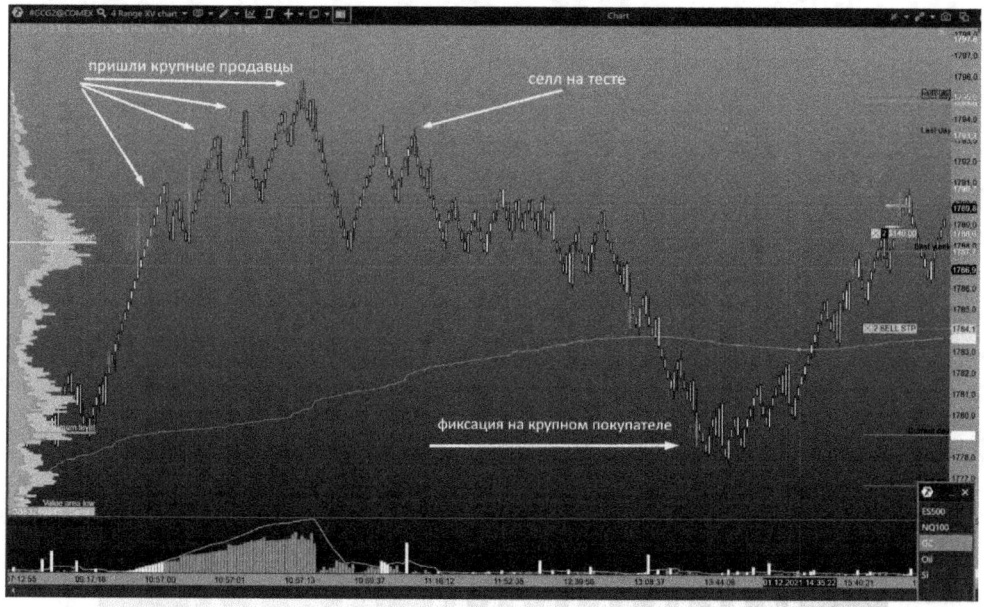

The Smell Of The Cash

FxCash

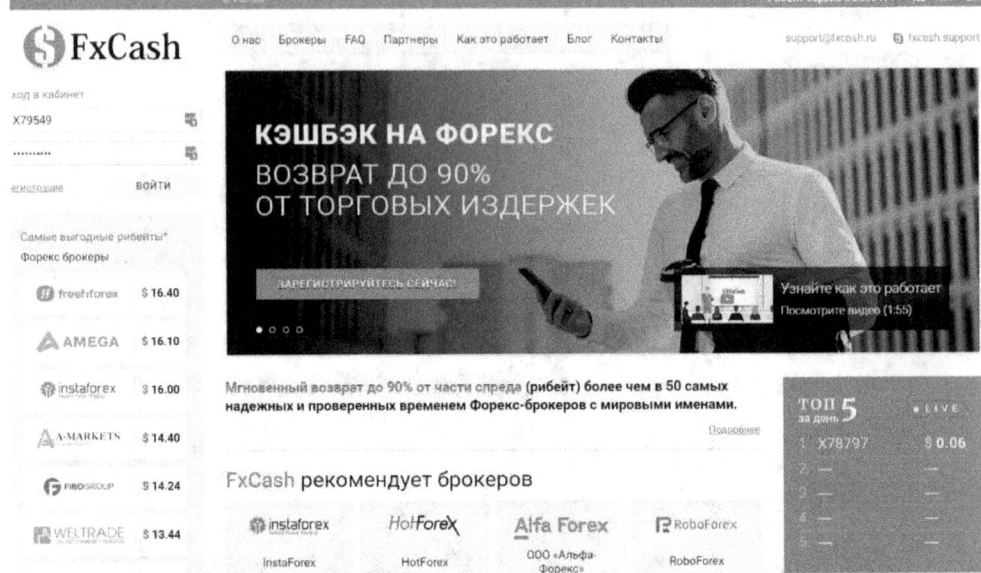

I won't go into details here. This is just a convenient service for returning the spread from Forex.
Registration is intuitive.
The point is to return part of the difference in the spread.
I use it and I like it.

Choosing a Broker.

Well, everything is simple here. I trust the largest and most trusted brokers. And there is no need to be concerned about the fact that they are registered in Cyprus. I have not encountered any problems. Everything works like clockwork.
But you should not keep all the eggs in one basket. Be sure to distribute your money between several brokers in different countries.
If you want to sleep well, then you should contact only licensed brokers.
So that you can always file a complaint or go to court.
I trust:

- *Alpari*
- Exante
- IB
- Fins
- Opening

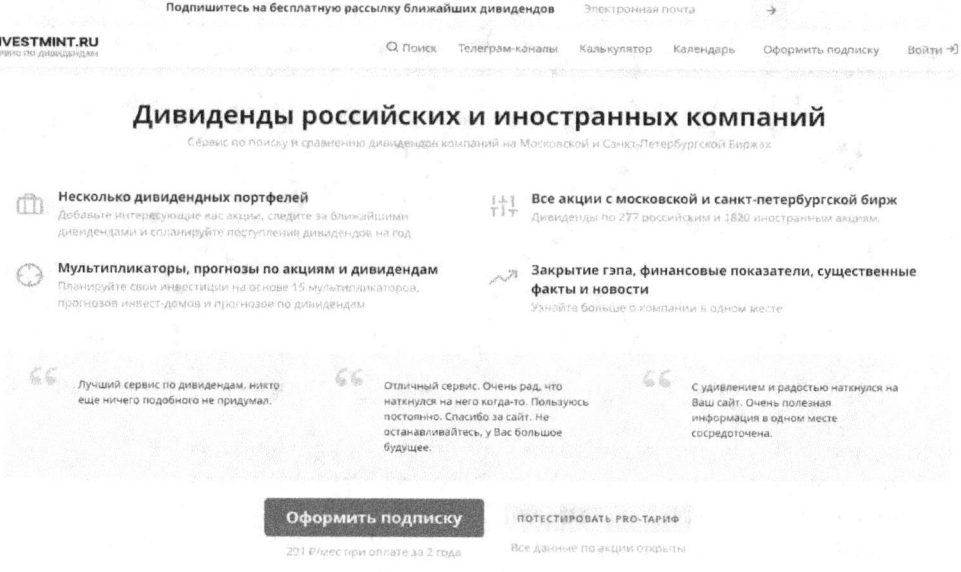

If you are passionate about collecting a portfolio of dividend stocks, then this service will help you perfectly.

The dividend calendar and telegram channels will help you.

Benzinga

I am sure that in the modern world of trading, few people are not familiar with this unique platform.

Its functionality is impressive. The support is at a very high level.

And the price is reasonable for the quality and features offered.

In fact, this is an all-in-one platform.

Perhaps its main feature is the presence of a powerful news block, with which you can easily scan the market and find goodies.

To be honest, you can just drown on this site for several weeks in a row.

I won't even describe all its functions to you, because it will take a lot of time.

I suggest you study it yourself.

Calendars	Trade Ideas
Earnings Calendar	Insider Trades
IPO Calendar	Trade Idea Feed
Guidance Calendar	Analyst Ratings
FDA Calendar	Unusual Options Activity
Dividend Calendar	
Stock Split Calendar	
Conference Call Calendar	
Economic Calendar	

Intelinvest

Here, the story of finding the best logbook to record the trades repeats.
This service allows us to monitor our investment portfolios.
It provides complete statistics on your portfolios.

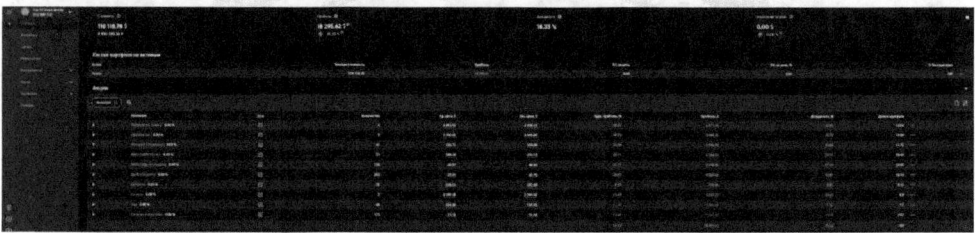

It enables monitoring portfolios of other clients. And there are many prominent persons among them.

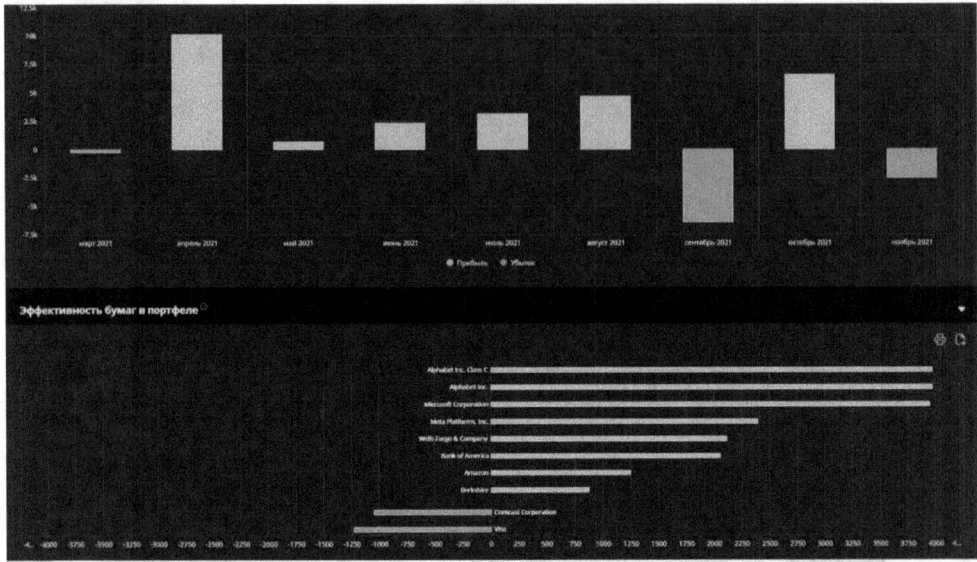

And it provides detailed analytics.

TradeIdeas.

This screener has been recognized as the best by many reputable portals multiple times.

There are a lot of settings and the result is really impressive.

I'm not a fan of his graphic design. This presentation of information hurts my eyes.

But if you are a beginner and are looking for a powerful scanner, then you definitely should try it.

New & Noteworthy

Recent Awards and Recognition

Inc. magazine today revealed that Trade Ideas is No. 2946 on its annual Inc. 5000 list, the most prestigious ranking of the nation's fastest-growing private companies...Read full article

The individual investors in the market today are at odds. They need real-time decision support and risk management to make informed decisions while trading equity... Read full article

The company is proud of developing artificial intelligence that helps traders choose the stocks.

And indeed, these are not empty words. I've tried it in practice. The signals passed through the artificial intelligence are different from the usual ones from the scanner.

The company has been working in the market since 2003 and has flawless support and reputation.

This is, of course, one of the most powerful software packages for stock search.

Finandy.

If you think that Binance terminal is not suitable for you, then pay your attention to Finandy.
I have not seen a more convenient platform for crypto trading.
The developers managed to combine the convenience of trading view charts with the Binance functionality and added many more tricks.

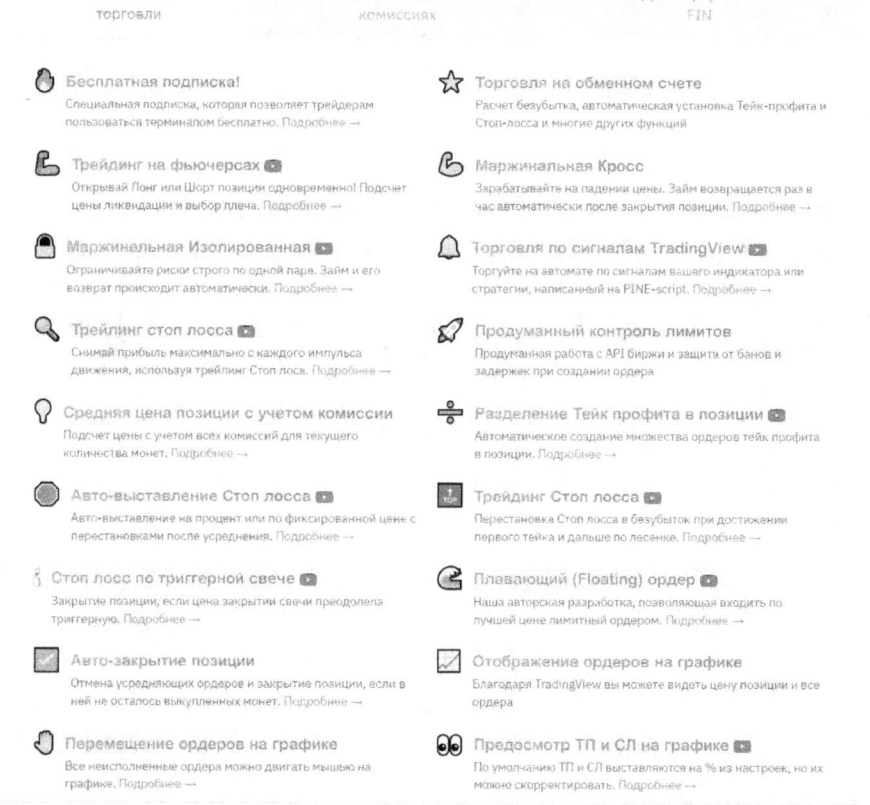

Click here to enter a date.
For me, the most important function that I did not find in the Binance terminal was the ability to pull up orders on the chart.
But, as you can see, this is not the only feature of the platform.
The floating order alone is worth something.
In general, I will not describe every trick, because this information can be found on the developer website.

Tickr.

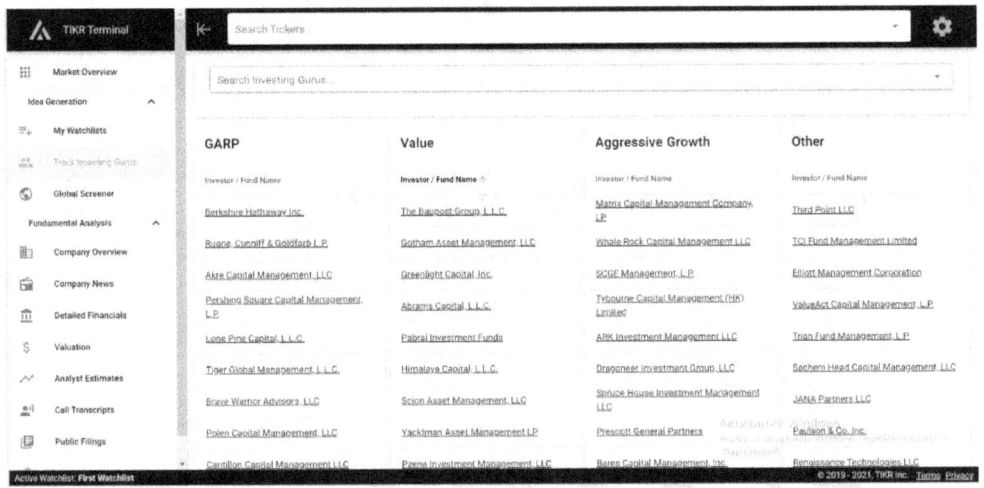

This is another powerful tool for monitoring the actions of institutions.
In its functionality, it resembles a DataRoma and offers a lot of useful information about past major trades, on the basis of which you can build your strategy.
Be sure to play with it and choose the option that is convenient for you.

TipRanks.

Perhaps my favorite foreign service for portfolio monitoring, which allows finding the most promising stocks of the most worthy traders.
Its unique system of evaluation and selection of shares is constantly being improved and deserves close attention.

⑩ Top Smart Score Stocks

Top Smart Score Stocks displays the best stocks according to the TipRanks Smart Score. This unique score measures stocks on their potential to outperform the market, based on 8 key factors. These include how the best performing analysts are rating stocks, whether hedge funds are buying or selling, as well as fundamental and technical factors.

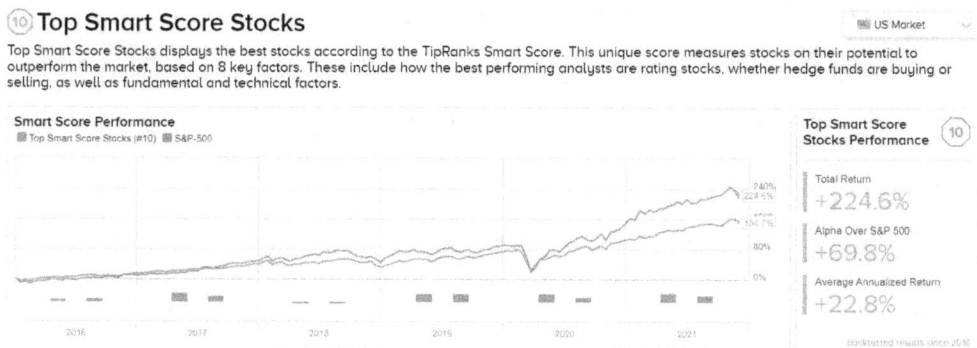

The principle of stock selection is based on 8 key factors, which allow us to outperform the main indexes by 70% in the annual quantities.
This is an excellent result!

Analysts' Top Stocks

Stocks with a 'Strong Buy' or 'Strong Sell' rating consensus, according to the best performing analysts.

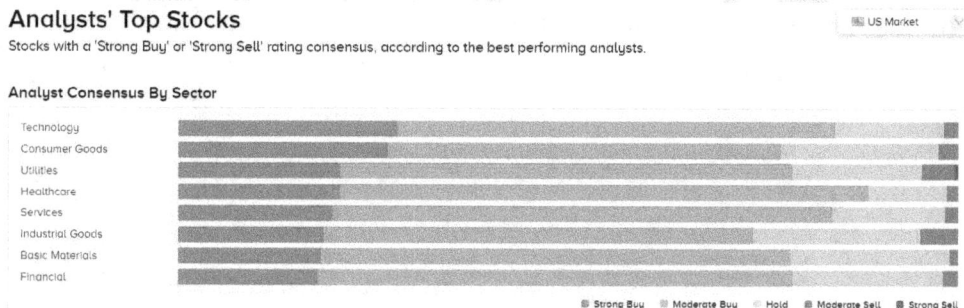

An equally important opportunity is to see the list of stocks selected by the world's leading analysts.

That is, the service offers the ability to follow the ideas of analysts and sort them by the number of stars, so that it is easier for us to navigate.

I conducted an experiment. I formed a portfolio of the top 3 stocks of 10 leading analysts from TipRanks. And it showed a great result:

And this is in the falling market.

Lets talk about useful services for traders

The next tool is the ability to track insiders' trades:

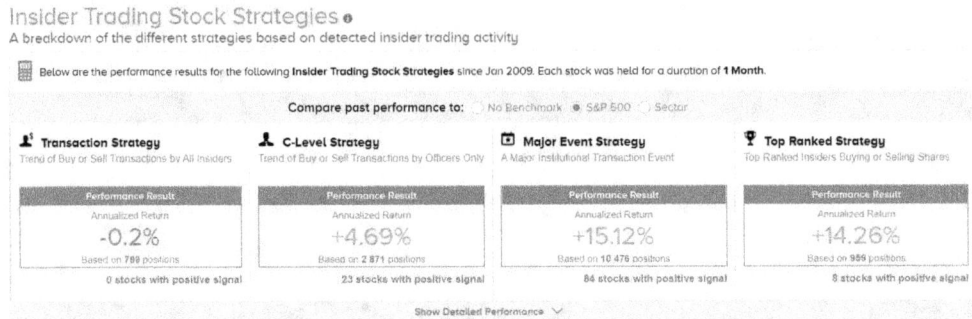

As you can see, even here the profit is 15% higher than the SPY index in annual comparison.

And here you can see the stocks that have been in trend for the last few days. And you can sort them by capitalization and sector.

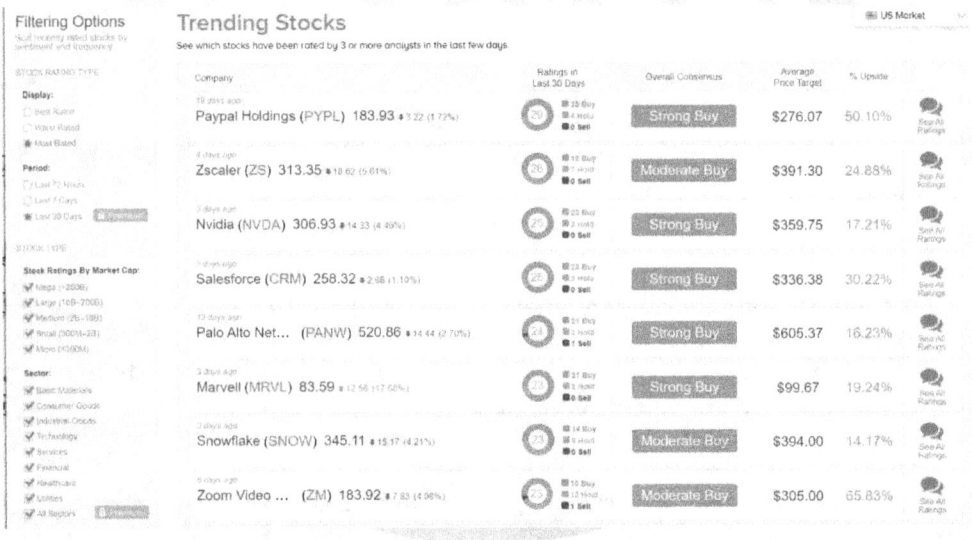

New features. The service now offers the ability to monitor penny stocks:

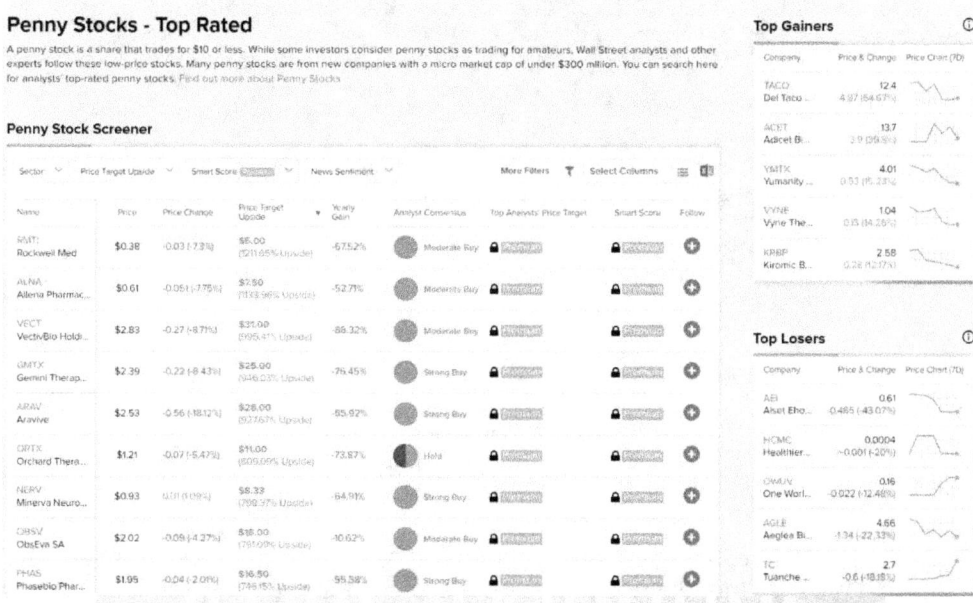

There is also a dividend calculator for finding the stocks with a good dividend profitability:

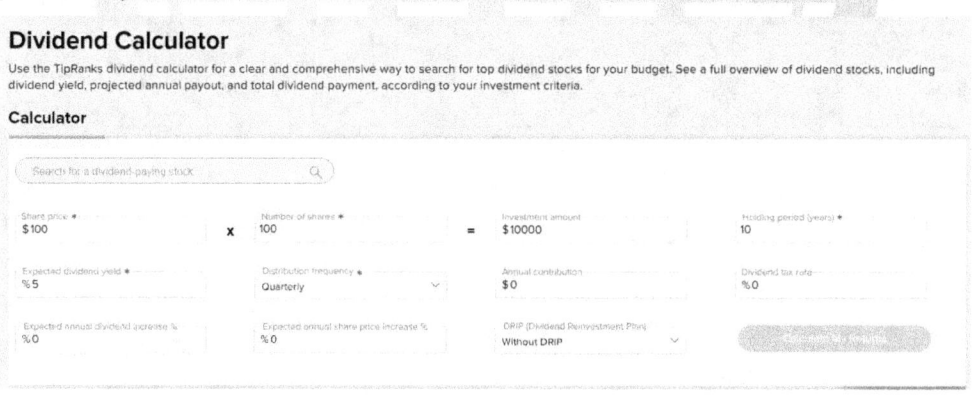

A great novelty! The ability to track the most visited sites with trading content.

Lets talk about useful services for traders

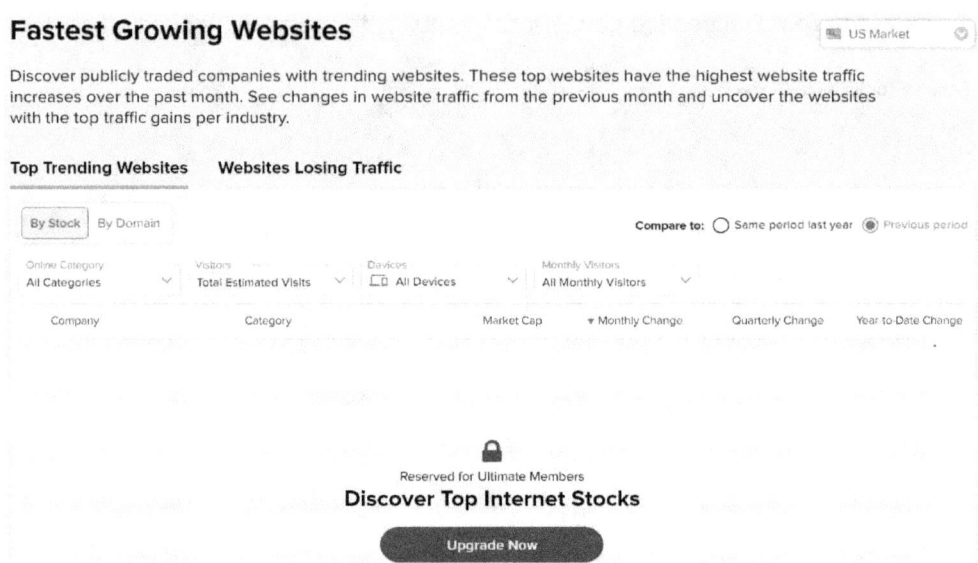

An excellent screener enables finding what is really worthy of your attention. It's a pity that most of the features are only available in the premium version. But this is America with its developed capitalism.

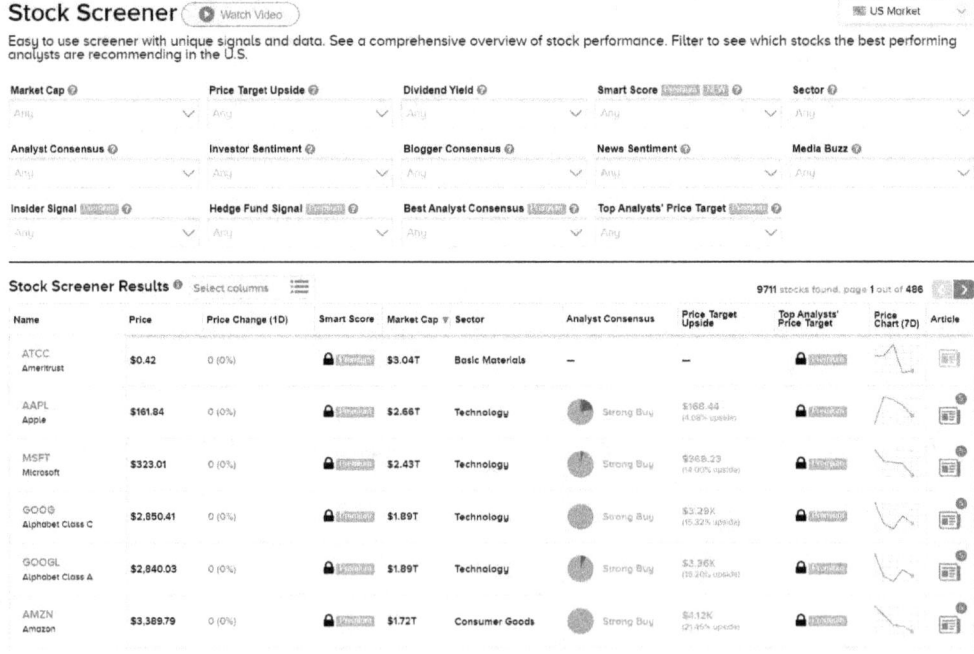

The portfolio tracking service deserves special mention. This is so-called Smart Portfolio.

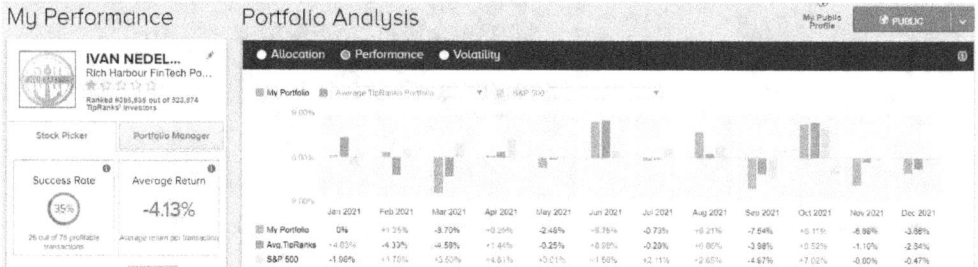

It is unlikely that you will find a service with greater features and statistics offered.

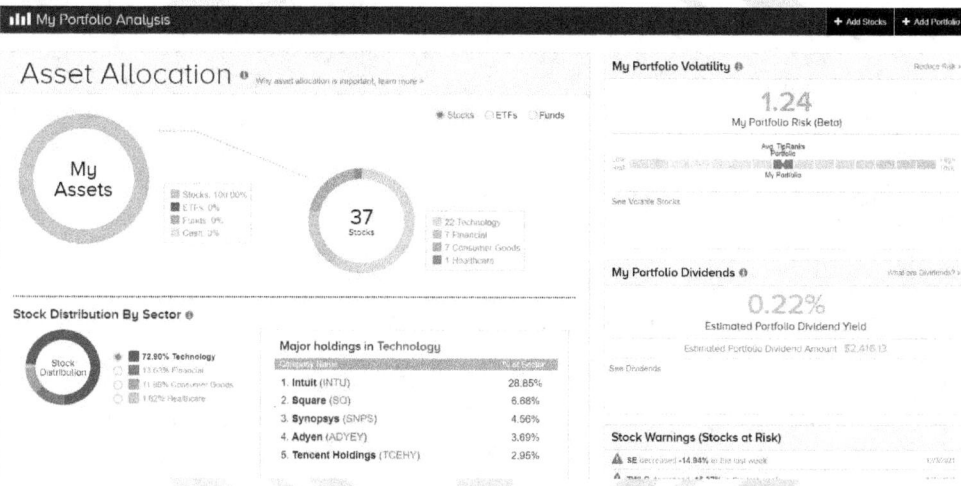

As you can see, the service offers a huge amount of customizable statistics.
It is also possible to make your portfolio public.
In general, this is a unique set for the most demanding user.

Lets talk about useful services for traders

	100% No-Risk Guarantee If you are not fully satisfied, place a request to cancel within 30 days of your purchase and receive a full refund.	 ULTIMATE 49^{95}/Month Billed annually **Start Now**	 PREMIUM 29^{95}/Month Billed annually **Start Now**	 BASIC $0/Month ⊙ Current Plan
Stock Analysis		Full Access	Advanced	Limited
Investment Ideas		Full Access	Advanced	None
Smart Portfolio		Full Access	Advanced	Limited
Research Tools		Full Access	Full Access	Limited
Daily Insights		Full Access	Advanced	Limited
Top Experts		Full Access	Advanced	Limited
Email Alerts		Unlimited	Up to 30 Stocks	Up to 5 Stocks
Export Data		PDF + CSV	PDF Only	None
Support		Top Priority	Priority	Upon Availability

And the prices are quite affordable!

EPILOGUE:

Dear readers, I am proud and happy to announce that we have come to the end of this wonderful book.

I tried to impart you all the best practices that the market has taught me over the years.

With proper understanding and subsequent regular training, this book will certainly bring you financial success and independence.

I sincerely wish you success in the financial markets.

And I will be glad to see you every day in my Private Chat, where I publish my trades and comment on yours.

This is the only format that will ensure your success. This has already been proven by years of practice.

At the moment, I have invested a large amount of money to develop a stock and options scanner that works according to my trading system. You can find numerous similar products in the market, and I have tried many of them. As a result, I came to the conclusion that the average person does not need a huge number of settings and does not want to spend their time on studying, and then risk their money. The average person wants to get the product as easy to use as possible. And with a simple interface.

> *This is exactly the kind of scanner with a bunch of indicator settings that I am introducing to the Russian market.*

I will take only the most useful functions from each of the services listed above and create one universal platform adapted to the Russian client.

The price should correspond to the realities of life in Russia.

Everything will be simple - clicking on the button - getting a list of stocks for the selected strategy. Performing a brief analysis and making the right decision.

Clicking again and seeing all important levels of traded options and dark pools on the screen.

I created my trading school alone, without attracting capital from outside. But dozens of specialists worked on it. When I started, I didn't even think it was so difficult to create a high quality product.

At the moment, I am looking for traders-coaches who will teach trading on the basis of a Private Chat according to my trading system.

I have developed an exam for them that includes about 300 questions. I am sure that not everyone will manage to pass it! But the one who can do it will get an unconditional victory and the opportunity to become one of us. The winner will receive the coveted certificate confirming their high qualification and place in the sun.

So if you feel that you are ready to take a risk and have a desire to become part of a strong team - just contact me. We'll discuss everything.

The exam is available not only for future coaches, but also for people who want to test their knowledge of my system.

For this purpose, a special site with a training and examination module is developed.

In general, I try my best to promote trading.

But that's not all! I'm launching a franchise for the Rich Harbor project. Now everyone who wants and is determined to achieve results can start this ready-made business in their city and promote the idea of financial independence under my flag and with my support. You can conduct online training and trading. You can earn and help others.

But hurry up, because no more than 1 school can be opened in one city!

Teaching trading for pushing the boundaries!

Ivan Nedelko.

www.ingramcontent.com/pod-product-compliance
Lightning Source LLC
Chambersburg PA
CBHW052344220526
45465CB00003BA/941